The Public Library Policy Writer

A Guidebook with Model Policies on CD-ROM

Jeanette C. Larson
and
Herman L. Totten

Neal-Schuman Publishers, Inc.

New York   London

Published by Neal-Schuman Publishers, Inc.
100 William St., Suite 2004
New York, NY 10038

Printed and bound in the United States of America

The paper used in this publication meets the minimum requirements of American National Standard for Information Sciences—Permanence of Paper for Printed Library Materials, ANSI Z 39.48-1992.

Library of Congress Cataloging-in-Publication Data

Larson, Jeanette.
    The public library policy writer : a guidebook with model policies on CD-ROM / Jeanette C. Larson and Herman L. Totten.
        p. cm.
    Includes bibliographical references and index.
    ISBN 978-1-55570-603-6 (alk. paper)
    1. Public libraries—United States—Rules and practice. 2. Public libraries—United States—Administration—Handbooks, manuals, etc. 3. Library rules and regulations—United States—Handbooks, manuals, etc. I. Totten, Herman L. II. Title.

Z704.L37 2008
025.1'974—dc22
                                                        2008017622

Contents

Part I: Policy Development

Part II: Policy Areas and Model Policies

Part III: Essential Professional Resources Needed for Good Policy

Quick Guide to Model Policies

Preface

Every librarian knows a colleague or has heard of a situation in which the lack of a policy or having an obsolete or poorly constructed policy has led to a public relations nightmare. Unfortunately, in today's ever-changing world, we often think of our policy manuals but ask ourselves and our colleagues, "Who has the time anymore to sit down and review policies, much less write new ones?" The question posed should really be, "What manager can afford not to make the time to deal with this critical aspect of library administration?"

Directors, board members, and managers who don't make the time to review, revise, and develop policies will usually discover that not doing so costs more in time, political fallout, and public relations than it would have taken to do the work in the first place. Especially when dealing with hot-button issues like the USA PATRIOT Act, intellectual freedom, and filtering, it is imperative that library directors have a streamlined, ongoing process for reviewing and updating policies and for keeping the library's governing authorities in the loop and up to date on the issues related to the policy being considered.

Staff and boards may feel that they should not "rock the boat" by opening up discussion about how gifts are acquired and disposed of by the library. We may not want to draw attention to how we deal with unattended children or the homeless in the library. And who wants to face the heat from a discussion about which groups can use the library meeting rooms? Yet in today's political, social, and economic climate, having up-to-date, workable guidelines for service are essential. Libraries must accommodate the inevitable evolution of technology and changes in social mores and laws. Unfortunately, law often lags behind technology, creating an environment where regular policy review is more critical than ever. For instance, technologies that emerge to access private electronic records—wiretapping, remote sur-veillance, etc.—are sometimes available long before the laws are passed to govern their use. Library policies that are informed by the ethical founda-tions of our profession provide guidance while lawmakers and the courts sort out the legal issues.

PURPOSE AND AUDIENCE

This book and CD-ROM package, *The Public Library Policy Writer*, pro-vides a systematic, utilitarian way for small and medium sized library direc-tors, along with their staff and board members, to:

- assess the quality and currency of policies that are already estab-lished,
- revise those that need to be updated, and
- develop new policies that may be needed, but are missing, in your organization.

While clearly the terms "small" and "medium" are subjective and open to a variety of interpretations, we wrote *The Public Library Policy Writer* with libraries serving populations of fewer than 100,000 in mind. We also know that the model policies have proven to be useful for libraries around the world, but it is written with an emphasis on issues, laws, and practices in the United States.

The policies included here are intended to serve as *models*. We chose this word because they are based on our own experience managing public libraries, input from our consulting and teaching work, and from reviewing policies that have been approved by libraries of all sizes around the country. They are intended to serve as patterns or examples for you to use in devel-oping your own policies, not as templates or simple "fill-in-the-blank" forms.

We also chose the word "model" because as you will quickly notice, our policies follow a pattern. This model concept can also provide guidance for libraries needing to develop policies not included in this book. Having a utilitarian policy outline to follow may help make additional policy develop-ment less labor-intensive as well as provide a consistent look and feel to the resulting body of policies.

HOW TO USE THIS PACKAGE TO DEVELOP YOUR POLICY MANUAL

Library directors, especially those in smaller public libraries, have expressed concern about their ability to develop policies from scratch. Some have indicated that they feel more comfortable with a model policy from which to construct their local policy. A standard way in which many librarians develop policy is by collecting samples from other libraries and copying or benchmarking the parts that seem to best match the needs of their library. Good librarians know that research, especially quality research, is valuable, and we encourage you to look at policies from other libraries. Fortunately, many are readily available on the Internet. However, while it is useful to examine what other libraries are doing, this cannot be the end of your research!

Beginning with Part I, "Policy Development," this book explores the major issues related to specific policies and raises questions that must be discussed and resolved locally if the developed policies are to be useful and supportable. By avoiding the "cut-and-paste" method, the results will be policies that best suit the needs of your community and the service priorities and abilities of your library. Librarians who do not have immediate access to legal counsel will also find this handbook useful for developing ideas and questions before seeking counsel. The CD-ROM included with this book includes the full text of all the model policies printed in these pages. They are arranged in the same order they appear here for easy location. You can use these as the "foundation" for your library's own policies, customizing them to fit your local needs and priorities.

In many libraries, but especially in those with fewer staff members, policy development and revision is most frequently initiated and carried forward by the library director. Therefore, throughout the book we frequently refer to "you" when discussing issues to be considered, assuming that it is most likely the library director who is reading these words. Although the realities of the workplace may result in a lot of the work being performed by one or two people, good management practices suggest that you involve staff members, volunteers, board members, and others in the process. These are the policies of the library, and they "articulate the library's position on matters of philosophy and operations."[1] As such, input and review by others who are affected by the policies or who must carry them out or support them is crucial. Policies that are misunderstood, ignored, or dismissed may be worse than no policy at all.

In a world where information changes before the print dries, there is the commonly held viewpoint that policies become outdated as soon as they are set on paper. While this often may be true, it is unwise to put off developing policies just because changes may be necessary within a year or so. Time passes quickly, and, indeed, the policy may not be revised as quickly as you anticipated. Additionally, regular review of policies is good practice, so to some degree, you will always be reconsidering what has been written. In fact, as you will see in Chapter 2, policies should be reviewed and revised on a regular schedule, and it becomes a less time-consuming and tedious process if policies are kept up to date. Knowing what issues need to be considered will help you develop policies that do not become quickly outdated and will facilitate updating policies or making minor modifications when necessary. Computers make it easy to revise a few policies and redistribute them every year or so, avoiding the onerous situation of having to revise every policy at the same time. Regular review of policies also ensures that staff and board members are familiar with, and understand the need for, the policies.

WHAT POLICIES ARE INCLUDED?

In Part II, "Policy Areas and Model Policies," we have attempted to include the vast majority of policies needed to manage small and medium sized libraries. These include policies for basic personnel and employment practices, common library services, collection development, copyright, Internet and computer access, intellectual freedom, and library programs. We have also included policies for staff and patron conduct, special collections, reference services, and use of resources.

Not every library will need or want every one of the policies we have included. While there are general policies that every library may want to have immediately, such as a collection development policy, other policies might be able to wait or are not relevant to the library's current situation. For example, why have a policy on staff use of library vehicles if you do not have a library vehicle or if the staff is so small that the use or potential misuse has not created any problems? Furthermore, some libraries may find the need for additional policies not included in this book. The Bibliography offers titles that will provide guidance in developing those additional policies.

Policies covering some specific areas are essential. If no written policies currently exist, the first priority should be to develop policies to comply with the USA PATRIOT Act, address the Americans with Disabilities Act, handle copyright, establish the parameters for reconsideration of materials, and determine appropriate patron behavior. These are critical policies for carrying out library business. If you do not already have a policy in place for these services, you should initiate this work immediately. These policies can be revised and refined as you become more familiar with your library and community or as problems and situations develop, but it is essential that they be in place as soon as possible. They are the policies that will provide some protection to you and the library from possible legal action and from situations that could result in poor public relations.

WHAT INFORMATION IS PROVIDED?

When it comes to library policies, one size cannot fit all! While it might be tempting to copy policies from other libraries, changing only the name of the library and its location, this is not a good course of action. Even within the parameters of small or medium sized public libraries, your library is not exactly the same as any other library, and your patrons' needs may be very different from those of another library. It is also best to avoid the inclination to cut and paste, using policies from several libraries to try to piece together a policy that suits your needs. Obviously, we also do not advocate that anyone circumvent the process of deliberation and decision making outlined in this book and simply copy the model policies we have provided. Chapter 1 discusses the importance of policies and describes how they originate. Part of the origination process includes developing buy-in and support from staff (including, if relevant, volunteer staff in the one-person or very small library) and from the library's governing authority. In fact, the discussion that takes place around the policy issues is probably the most important part of the process. For policies to be legal, to withstand local scrutiny if challenged, and to be supported by local authorities, they must have been carefully thought out when they were developed. All of the issues should have been thoroughly discussed and understood by the people (both the staff and the governing authority) who must implement and support the policies.

Background

We have provided background information for each model policy. This information defines the problem or addresses the situation for which your library may decide a policy is needed. We have explored areas of concern and have indicated the rationale for developing a policy on the topic. Background information should also help the library's governing authority and any advisory boards or support groups understand why a specific policy may be needed. When appropriate, we have also suggested additional readings or resources you might want to consult. In most cases, the background information is succinct, offering a basis on which you can begin discussion of the issues. Please keep in mind that Web sites were accurate as of publication but can change rapidly. We have provided the name of the organization that sponsors the Web site so that you can easily search for an updated uniform resource locator (URL) if needed. Unfortunately, occasionally an organization discontinues a valuable Web site, and while we apologize for the inconvenience, we have no control over those changes.

Issues

A number of issues that must be addressed by the library and its staff, board, and governing body as part of developing a policy have been enumerated for your consideration. We have tried to be broad in listing and discussing the issues, although we make no claim to having included every possible topic or subtopic that might be included in your discussions. We have examined policies from a variety of different libraries, small, medium, and large, to see what issues were included in their policies. We also reviewed books, journal articles, and Web sites to obtain various viewpoints and background on the issues. Publications and Internet sites that were useful or that might provide further background for you are included in the Bibliography. We have pointed out areas where local, state, or federal laws may play a role in the development of your policies. The use of volunteers in the library, for example, may be partially governed by union rules and child labor laws. We have indicated areas where you may need to do further research, either in library literature or within your community. For example, it is difficult to set policies pertaining to library hours without knowing the community's wishes; therefore, local research is essential. Similarly, it is difficult to establish a policy on unattended children in the library without knowing local and state laws or ordinances dealing with the age at which children can be left unsupervised.

We have also indicated issues that may be influenced by the American Library Association (ALA) and its policies, guidelines, or the ALA Code of Ethics. While the policies or dictates of the American Library Association do not bind local public libraries, this body represents more than 65,000 librarians; in many ways, the policies and guidelines of this organization act as the mores and values for our entire profession. As such, while a local library may choose not to endorse a specific ALA policy or parts of an ALA policy, this decision should be made with full knowledge of how local issues are affected by these national values. When the specific concerns of a segment of the local community are at odds with national guidelines or policies, ALA's position on topics of professional concern may strengthen support for policies that further the library's mission and goals. Ultimately, the development of local policies rests with the local governing authority, and not with the American Library Association, state library agencies, or state associations. However, it is useful to know and understand the foundations and philosophies on which many library services and principles are based. As the library director, you are in the best position possible to share these statements and explain your professional ethics and values to board members and your governing authority. Local decisions can then be made from a position of knowledge and understanding after careful thought and consideration of the issues and their effect on local services.

Local Decisions

Because you will be making local decisions about the policies of your library, please be sure to write in this book! Recording decisions made during the deliberation process that precedes proper policy articulation will serve as a record of those decisions. This will assist you and your successors as policies are updated and revised. Library board meetings or meetings of other library governing bodies will, of course, have written minutes that record the final decisions made about policies. Nevertheless, much of the thought process that precedes the presentation of a policy for approval will take place in policy committee meetings, staff meetings, or in solitary contemplation. It is easier to recall why decisions were made if notes have been kept, so keep them in this book.

Model Policies

As a convenience and to provide a starting point for writing, we have provided model policies that help staff in small and medium sized public libraries get going. Although we examined policies from dozens of libraries and looked at numerous books and articles on the topics for which policies are provided, we did not base the model on any individual policy. In some instances, there was a great deal of similarity in the policies of different libraries, while in other cases the policies we examined varied widely.

While a specific model policy may appear to be a close fit to the needs of your library, the models were not written with any specific representative library in mind. The models are included to offer a representation of how the issues might be decided and to indicate our opinion as to the relative length of the particular policy. Even a brief policy on selection of materials will be much longer than a policy on cell phone use in the library. We also felt that having a model to serve as a reference point or guide would make the task of developing policies and updating or revising them seem less onerous. We have tried to make your job more achievable. In a couple of instances, two model policies have been provided because resolution of the issues could lead to two very different policies. For example, some libraries will want a policy that details how fees will be assessed for services that are offered on a cost-recovery basis. Other libraries will establish a brief policy that stipulates that no service will be offered that cannot be paid for through the budget of the library.

Approvals and Signature

No library is totally autonomous. Every public library has some governing authority that controls the purse strings and authorizes the existence and regular workings of the library. It may be an elected or appointed board of trustees, a city council, or county commission, or a library board. The members of the governing authority are also the people who will hear the complaints and concerns from angry, upset, or concerned citizens. While some libraries have advisory boards and Friends of the Library groups that may assist them in setting policy, ultimately the authority to implement and enforce a policy rests with the governing authority.

While it is important to have advisory and support groups involved in the process of developing policy, there can be no policy without the approval and attestation of the governing authority. For that reason we have included a statement at the end of each model policy to remind you that the library's governing body must sign and date the policy. Without the signatures attesting support, the library staff may find itself standing alone when a policy is challenged. The process of obtaining approval and signatures also provides the library director the opportunity to explain the issues and answer questions. It is important that these discussions occur before problems arise. If the policy for selection of materials indicates that the library will purchase materials that may be in conflict with the views of some segments of the community, gain support for that policy when it is being developed, not in the middle of a censorship battle!

Professional Resources and Bibliography

Part III, "Essential Professional Resources Needed for Good Policy," includes documents from the American Library Association and its divisions that relate to or support library policies. Because these documents are important in the development of policies for your library, we wanted to present them together. Even if your policy varies from the recommendations indicated in the ALA policy statements, you will want to consider them as you make local decisions.

When your library endorses a specific ALA document or incorporates it into a local policy, it should be referred to in the policy. To ensure that staff and the public have easy access to any ALA documents or policy statements that are accepted by your library, they should be appended to the policy and included in your policy manual.

Because most policies will be established based on the service priorities selected for your public library, either formally through a planning process or informally through practice, we have also included a summary of the Public Library Association's (PLA) Services Responses. Because it will be referred to frequently and should be used as part of the library's ongoing planning process, we recommend that you purchase the book *The New Planning for Results: A Streamlined Approach*[2] and updated editions, including *2007 Public Library Service Responses*, published in 2007.[3] Although we have included the 2007 service responses in the resources, it is not possible to provide detailed information about the ways in which each service response manifests itself in library staffing, resources, services, and equipment needs, so be sure to familiarize yourself with those ideas if they pertain to your planning process.

Throughout this book we have offered suggestions for those who need additional background on an issue or supporting documentation for a policy that is being developed. These books and journal articles, along with others that offer support for policy writers, are included in the Bibliography.

The Public Library Policy Writer is our second book for small and medium sized public library policy development. The first, *Model Policies for Small and Medium Public Libraries,* appeared ten years ago. While much has changed, the basic mission and philosophy of good public library service has fortunately remained constant. We designed the language, tips, and tools contained within these pages to help library directors and board members articulate the parameters and philosophies that inform open access and equitable service for all.

NOTES

1. Weingand, Darlene E. 1992. *Administration of the Small Public Library.* Chicago: American Library Association, p. 60.
2. Nelson, Sandra. 2001. *The New Planning for Results: A Streamlined Approach.* Chicago: American Library Association.
3. Garcia, June and Sandra Nelson. 2007. *2007 Public Library Service Responses.* Chicago: American Library Association.

Part I

Policy Development

Chapter 1

Policies and Their Importance

WHAT ARE POLICIES?

A policy is a set of guidelines that define managerial actions and decisions. The policy serves as the guiding principle for decisions and actions. Policies are designed to help staff deal with particular issues and problems that have arisen, or are likely to arise, in the course of conducting business. The term may also be used more broadly to include procedures, regulations, and other documents that relate to the policy.

While policies may be implied or oral, current best practice emphasizes having written policies that ensure the effective and efficient running of libraries. Policies are based on the library's priorities, and they guide the thinking behind the actions necessary for libraries to achieve their goals and objectives.

Policies can be broad, addressing basic principles that guide the library, or specific, addressing targeted activities, services, or groups of users. An example of a broad policy would be the materials selection policy that affects materials purchased, received as gifts, or otherwise acquired by the library. "Recruitment of Candidates for Positions" with the library is an example of a specific policy. This policy addresses only the recruitment process but provides very specific guidance and sets the tone for that activity. Policies can also be institution-wide, applicable to all segments of the organization, or department specific, applicable to a smaller part of the organization. Policies cover a wide range of topics, which can generally be divided into two groups: managerial and operational.

Managerial policies deal with functions related to planning, organizing, staffing, directing, and controlling. These policies provide consistent guidance and constraints for management of the library and its staff and provide internal controls. For example, a staff development policy might state that all new staff will rotate through all work areas during their first year in order to gain familiarity with all library functions.

Operational policies deal with functions that support the library's service objectives, such as selection and development of resources, finance, and personnel and public relations. These policies deal with interactions with the public and guide both patrons and staff in the provision of services and the allocation of public resources. For example, an acquisitions policy might state that, whenever possible, library materials should be purchased to present various sides of controversial issues.

Although they support and assist in the implementation of policies, procedures, rules, and regulations differ from and are subordinate to policies. Procedures are step-by-step action guides that standardize the methods by which repetitive tasks are performed, usually by listing the steps in the order of performance. They are flexible, and they change as the routine of work changes. Because of their nature, procedures are usually developed by the staff performing the work and do not require approval by anyone other than the manager of the work unit and, in some cases, the library director. Rules and regulations provide for uniformity of action in specific situations that further define the policy by indicating what actions can be taken if policies are not followed. They can outline staff and patron behavior through positive (should) and negative (should not) limits, and they can provide value (good or bad) constraints. Because rules and regulations are proscriptive, they must be approved by the library director, and, depending on the severity and scope, they may need to be approved by the governing authority. For example, if a library's policy states that nonprofit organizations may reserve the meeting room up to ninety days in advance, a subordinate procedure might outline how staff will schedule meeting room use, and a subordinate rule might state how the library will respond to groups that do not cancel their reservations. Procedures and rules and regulations must comply with policies, and policies should support the implementation and enforcement of the rules and procedures.

Be aware of practices! Practice is the way things are actually done or handled on a daily basis in the library and may or may not be supported by the library's policies. In many cases, practice differs between branch locations or different departments and can create confusion and inconsistencies in the delivery of services. Practices should be monitored regularly to ensure that what is actually happening complies with the policies. If practice is out of synch with policy, then perhaps the policy needs to be updated to incorporate new ideas, best practices, and updated methodologies. Often staff settle into new practices as a means of coping with changes that are occurring, but these changes should be reviewed to ensure that they continue to meet the library's priorities and the patron's needs.

WHY ARE POLICIES AND POLICY MANUALS IMPORTANT?

By providing guidelines for decision making, policies ensure some degree of consistency and continuity in the overall administration and day-to-day operation of the library. By reducing uninformed decision making and promoting clarity, policies serve to:

- support the mission, service roles, goals, and objectives of the library;
- clarify relationships and responsibilities within the organization;
- delegate authority by transferring decision making to lower levels of the organization;
- guide acquisitions of library materials;
- protect the rights of individuals inside and outside the organization; and
- protect the organization and its legal authority in case of litigation.

All libraries have policies, whether they are written or unwritten, sound or unsound, followed or ignored, understood or not understood, complete or incomplete. It is important to remember that policies can provide freedom as well as restrict it. There are as many cases of frustration within organizations about the lack of policies, procedures, rules, and regulations as there are about arbitrarily established ones. In the absence of policies, each problem must be resolved on its own merit, which leads to decisions—often crisis responses—that can be uninformed, inconsistent, and conflicting. In the absence of *written* policies, problems are resolved based on often faulty or incomplete memory. Policies prevent the need to rethink the same situation over and over again, saving staff time and energy, and helping to avoid confusion.

Written policy manuals provide the means for communicating policies to all who are affected by them. Policy manuals are important because they are:

- an invaluable managerial tool for clarifying thinking and guiding decisions by the library board, director, and staff;
- a tangible means of supporting and clarifying the library's objectives and intentions in legal cases;

- a consistent form of internal and external communication, providing direction for day-to-day library operations and service to the community;
- a convenient indoctrination and training tool for new staff members;
- a source of documentation in case of legal actions; and
- a public relations tool, demonstrating the library's basic honesty and integrity, protecting rights and ensuring equal treatment of individuals, and generally inspiring confidence in the library's management.

Without a written policy manual, problems and misunderstandings cannot be resolved by reference to a particular set of words or specific language, legal cases may suffer from lack of a critical source of support, and new employees may be confused by misinformation circulating in the organization.

WHERE AND HOW DO POLICIES ORIGINATE?

Policymaking and decision making are synonymous to many people. However, policymaking is actually part of decision making: policies emerge from ad hoc decisions and become general statements or understandings that guide thinking in future decision making. The policymaking process should involve all levels of the organization, from frontline staff and volunteers to the library board. Governing boards are legally responsible for the operation of the library, and they usually have their duties spelled out in the library's articles of incorporation. Advisory boards are appointed by the political entity of which the library is a department to advise the library director and the local government on various matters. While both types of boards play a direct role in policy development and adoption, as well as in providing a means for citizen participation in policy development, the governing board also has responsibility for enforcing library policies. An advisory board may recommend that the city council or county commission approve the policy and should support library policies, but the governing authority is ultimately responsible for approval and enforcement. Although the American Library Association is an excellent resource for examples and advice regarding library policy, public libraries are generally bound to adhere to their local parent institution's policy.

According to Stueart and Moran[1], policies can be categorized four ways, depending on their source:

- Originated policy includes policies that flow mainly from library objectives and are formally written and reviewed. Although the policies can originate at any organizational level, actual policy statements are usually drafted by staff and receive final approval from the library's governing authority. Originated policy is the main source of policymaking, intended to guide the general operations of the library. An example of this type of policy might be that reference books are for use in the library only.

- Appealed policy covers common law, decisions made in specific situations by taking the decision through a chain of command. Over time these decisions may become "common law." Because appealed policies are often made through snap decisions based on the situation and are rarely given thorough consideration, they may cause tension and confusion. For example, the library director may decide that only certain staff members will receive financial support to attend conferences and workshops, although all staff members need continuing education.

- Implied policy develops from actions that employees see repeatedly occurring and thus assume them to be policy. For example, it may appear that children's services staff is not permitted to take vacation time during the summer because of increased workload while students are out of school. It may even be common practice that staff who work with children avoid taking time off when students are out of school. Common practice is not policy; to avoid misunderstandings, staff should be properly briefed on what is and what is not policy.

- Externally imposed policy comes from sources outside of the organization, such as federal, state, and local laws. Library personnel may have no control over implementing external policies, but they must be aware of and incorporate them in the internal policies of the library. For example, state government may require that public libraries retain interlibrary loan records for a period of two or three years.

WHO DEVELOPS POLICIES?

Policy development often originates with the library director, especially in smaller public libraries that lack departments. A newly appointed director may discover inconsistencies in policies or note that needed policies have never been developed. During a planning process the director or staff may have surveyed the policy manual and noted problems. Staff may be motivated by recurring issues or problems to initiate discussion about the need for a policy. Or, the library board or governing authority may have heard from constituents about unfair, at least in their opinion, treatment or access to services and request that a policy be developed. Regardless of who originates the policy, it is critical that staff affected by the policy have time to review drafts and provide input before the final policy is approved by the library director and taken to the governing authority.

Another important question to ask is, "Who implements policy?" Front-line staff and managers have the primary responsibility for implementing library policies. In smaller libraries volunteers may also be implementing the policies. These are the people who will receive and address most questions about access to service, staff privileges, use of materials, etc. Therefore the policies should be readily accessible to all staff at all times. When new policies are initiated or policies are revised and updated, each staff member and, as appropriate, volunteer should receive a copy. Some libraries post a copy and ask that staff initial that they have read the new policy. It is also helpful to include new and revised policies on staff meeting agendas for review and discussion. In many cases, you will want to print out copies of all policies and place them in a loose-leaf binder at the circulation and reference desks for easy access and review by the staff and public. With the pervasiveness of computers, a copy of the policy manual should be maintained online, on the library's intranet if possible, to accommodate regular review and updating of policies and to provide clean printouts for those who request a copy of a policy. Some libraries also post paper copies of specific policies (patron behavior, unattended children, etc.) in the library or post electronic copies on the library's Web site to ensure that the public can easily view policies that may affect them most closely.

WHAT ARE THE LEGALITIES OF POLICIES?

While government-operated public libraries enjoy some immunity from lawsuits, policies provide legal protection and guidance for both staff and users. Privately funded public libraries must be even more cautious as they have no sovereign immunity.[2] Sovereign immunity precludes suing a governmental organization without its consent and provides some protection for cities and counties that is not accorded to private organizations. Even for publicly funded libraries, extra caution should be exercised in areas related to civil rights or when the suit seeks an injunction.[3]

As Minow and Lipinski point out, "there is generally no immunity when a party files suit for an injunction,"[4] such as requiring a change in policy instead of monetary damages. Plaintiffs have sought injunctions in many instances, including requests of the courts to: force reversal policies limiting the use of meeting rooms to nonreligious organizations,[5] remove site-filtering software,[6] and to install site-filtering software.[7]

Although questions may be raised about the manager's interpretation of the policy, it is the promulgator of the policy (the parent institution) that may be sued for unfair administration of the policy. Libraries wanting more information about legal issues might refer to Minow and Lipinski's book *The Library's Legal Answer Book* or to *Law and Libraries* by Lee Ann Torrans.

Library policies must be written in such a way as to withstand judicial procedures and review. In fact, the policy may be enforceable *only* if it is in writing and has been adopted by the library's governing authority. Each policy should be discussed with the library's governing authority, which may be a governing board, a city council, or commissioner's court and, if necessary, with the library's legal counsel. Advisory boards and Friends of the Library groups may also be consulted in the development of the policy and will be advocates for the library's policies but have no authority to approve or enforce policies.

The governing authority for the library should approve each policy by signing and dating it. The policy is generally considered to be operational and legal from the day it is signed until it is revised or deleted. In rare cases, a policy may be approved and distributed to begin as of a certain date. For example, a revised policy may now limit non-library-related use of the meeting room but not be put into effect until after a reasonable amount of time has passed in order to allow groups to make alternative arrangements.

By having each policy attested to separately, the library has better support for the policy and greater protection if the policy is challenged. It is always easier to get political bodies to endorse policy before there is a problem and it is always more difficult to obtain support when tempers and emotions are high. Policies must be consistently and constantly reevaluated to determine whether they should be revised and retained. New laws or changes in legislation, changes in patron needs, new services, etc., may require adjustments to policies or the development of new policies. It is a monumental task to try to originate or revise all of the needed policies at once. Having policies updated and developed on an ongoing basis, with each policy approved and signed individually, breaks the task into manageable segments. This method also allows the governing body to consider fully what they are approving and have ample opportunity to consider the ramifications of the policy. In case of a complaint about library policy, it is usually better to have the full and informed support of the governing authority. A regularly scheduled plan for reviewing policies also may help you avoid pressure to revise a policy immediately after a conflict or problem has occurred. Additionally, regular review of policies will increase staff awareness of, and compliance with, policies, and may reduce staff resistance to policy changes.

Externally imposed policies dictate an action and enforce compliance. For example, state government may require that public libraries retain interlibrary loan records for a period of two years. All publicly supported institutions must abide by the Constitution of the United States and the Amendments to the Constitution and by the laws of their state and local jurisdictions. It is important for library policymakers to stay within the purview of externally imposed laws and policies when developing policies that apply to their personnel and patrons. For example, a decision to digitize all local government records may conflict with laws related to confidentiality of patron records.

Generally, to provide as much legal protection as possible, library policies should also be in sync with those of the American Library Association (ALA) and other relevant professional associations or organizations. At the very least, library policymakers should examine statements such as the ALA's Library Bill of Rights to determine whether local policies tend to comply with national policy statements. When your policies vary from ALA's recommendations, it is important for you, the library staff and support groups, and others involved in the process to understand how and why they do not agree. The ALA also provides guidelines for policymakers, such as *Guidelines for the Development of Policies and Procedures Regarding User Behavior and Library Usage* and *Suggested Procedures for Implementing Policy on Confidentiality of Library Records*. These documents, and others you may need for developing policy, are included in the Resources at then end of this book. ALA also monitors, and therefore can provide up-to-date information and guidance regarding, issues related to the USA PATRIOT Act and other national laws that relate to library services.

Library policies must be valid and legally enforceable. The State Library of Michigan recommends four validity tests[8] for policies. Those tests, and our examples of issues related to those tests, are:

1. **Legality: Does the policy conform to current law? Changes in the law often precipitate policy review.** For instance, many states have retention laws that dictate a specific number of years that libraries in the state's jurisdiction must retain interlibrary loan records. Rather than changing the library's retention policy each time the state law changes, the library should write into its policy that it will comply with time requirements in current state retention law.

2. **Reasonableness: Is the policy reasonable? Many policies, although legal on the surface, could be successfully challenged if they are unreasonable.** For instance, a library may have a statement in their circulation policy that reads, "Reference materials do not circulate so that they are available for use during all open hours of the library." Patrons could challenge the policy using the logic

that the materials should consequently be available for overnight checkout when the library is closed overnight. The library should write policy in such a way as to allow patrons to reserve reference items in special circumstances during the times the library is ordinarily closed. The library could impose heavy penalties for not returning the book as soon as the library reopens.

3. **Nondiscriminatory application: Can the policy be enforced in a nondiscriminatory manner? Policies must be applied fairly to all patrons.** For instance, if the library charges fines, then it should charge the same fine to its own staff and board members. Regardless of how legal and reasonable a policy is, it can be challenged if it is unfairly or unevenly applied. If the library wishes to accord special rights to a specific group of patrons, this decision should be spelled out in the policy. Additionally, policies should provide for a method of appeal so as to provide an opportunity to ensure that the policy is reasonable and being applied evenly.

4. **Measurability: Is the enforcement of the policy measurable? It is difficult to enforce a policy fairly if the behavior specified or prohibited by the policy is not quantifiable.** For instance, many libraries have dress-code policies for staff that use subjective qualifiers such as "appropriate shirts," "modest shorts," or "tasteful slacks" to describe clothing items that meet the library board's requirements. Rather than using qualifiers, which are subject to interpretation, in the policy, policy writers should use objective quantifying statements such as "no tank tops" or "shorts should be hemmed and no shorter than two inches above the wearer's knee." Neither statement is open to interpretation. Even phrases such as "business casual" require definition. Additionally, courts have found that the use of vague words, such as "etc.," encourage interpretation that may be immeasurable and, therefore, invalid restriction.

While it is impossible to guess what courts might or might not do, and in an especially litigious society anyone may decide to test the legality of library policies, keeping these validity tests in mind while developing your policies will reduce the potential for misunderstanding or subjectivity.

NOTES

1. Stueart, Robert D. and Barbara Moran. 2007. *Library and Information Center Management*. Westport, CT: Libraries Unlimited.
2. Minow, Mary and Tomas A. Lipinski. 2003. *The Library's Legal Answer Book*. Chicago: American Library Association, p. 2.

3. An injunction is a court order, considered to be a fair solution, that requires an action or the refraining from an action. The purpose of an injunction is to "right a wrong" or prevent a future wrongdoing that is not explicitly or adequately spelled out by a law. An injunction is used in place of monetary compensation for a past harmful action when there is no lawful provision for monetary compensation. The defendant in the case may be required to perform a positive act to demonstrate regret for an intentional or unintentional harmful act or to demonstrate goodwill or intentions for future actions. A defendant can be penalized or held in contempt for not heeding an injunction. Defendants have the right to appeal injunctions. Injunctions are issued in three forms: (1) temporary restraining order, issued when the court believes that a delay could cause irreparable harm; (2) preliminary injunction, issued to prevent or force an action until there is a final court judgment; and (3) permanent injunction, issued to prevent or force an action permanently.

4. Minow and Lipinski. 2003, p. 5.

5. *Faith Center Church Evangelistic Ministries v. Glover* 462 F.3d 1194, 1198 (9th Cir. 2006).

6. *Mainstream Loudoun v. Bd. of Trs. of the Loudoun County Library* 24 F. Supp. 2d 552 (E.D. Va. 1998).

7. *Kathleen R. v. City of Livermore* No. V-0153266-4 (Cal. Super. Ct. Jan. 14 1998).

8. State of Michigan: History, Arts and Libraries. Primer on Library Policies (July 2000). Available: www.michigan.gov/hal/0,1607,7-160-17451_18668_18689-54481—,00.html. Accessed: March 9, 2006.

Chapter 2

How to Develop Policies

DETERMINING WHEN TO DEVELOP POLICIES

Policy development involves decisions to create, revise, or delete policies in order to stay current with changes in the library, its environment, and the needs of its staff and client groups. Many library directors find that they need to revise current policies, add new ones, or delete policies that have become obsolete when they are working on long-range plans or the development of new programs. The mission of many public libraries has changed dramatically over the past decade. Whenever the library's mission, major services, or values change or are revised, look also for changes that may need to be made in policies. In fact, some public libraries even create a policy on policies, outlining why policies are developed, how they will be developed, and when policies will be reviewed and revised.[1]

New policy is developed to deal with recurring problems or situations or to address issues related to new services and technology. Generally, if a problem has arisen three or more times and been resolved each time on an ad hoc basis, there may be a need for a policy that will allow the situation to be resolved consistently in the future. For example, if serious complaints are repeatedly made about the way certain employees dress, there may be a need for a dress code. New policy can also be developed to deal with anticipated problems that might be expected to occur, such as user access conflicts that may arise when new electronic technologies are introduced.

Revise policies on an ongoing basis to accommodate significant internal and external changes to the library and its services. Collection development policy might need to be revised if, for example, a large acquisition shifts the balance of the collection as a whole or if schools served by the public library close their libraries. Avoid the temptation, or pressure, to revise a policy based on a single conflict or crisis. Having a set schedule for examining policies allows time for tempers to cool and permits revisions to be discussed based on issues and in the best interests of the patrons and community served.

Obsolete policies should be removed on a regular basis. These may include policies for programs or services, such as circulation of art prints or mail delivery of books, which have been discontinued. Many organizations retain outdated and obsolete policies, taking a laissez-faire approach that can lead to disillusionment on the part of those who must interpret and enforce policy. Furthermore, if a library simply has too many policies or rules—whether outdated or current—it may develop a reputation for being overly rigid or unnecessarily bureaucratic.

Achieving an appropriate number and balance of useful policies requires informed judgment. Libraries should adopt policies that relate uniquely to their own priorities, collections, services, and users. Each policy should be adopted for justifiable reasons, and these reasons should be known, understood, and explained to staff and patrons. The approach to policy enforcement should be flexible enough to allow for an occasional exception—instead of a policy revision—to be made when a genuine and understandable reason exists, or when an unfortunate or undesirable precedent is not likely to be set. Check that the policy supports the library's primary and secondary service responses or in some way furthers the mission of the library. Resist the urge to implement a new policy every time a patron complains about something, or you will quickly be overrun with policies, including many that are unnecessary or even contradictory. In fact, it is generally good practice to review policies and develop them on a schedule that allows for careful consideration and discussion of the issues. This avoids unpleasant surprises, helps to keep a well-intended policy from becoming an internal or external issue, and maintains the library's credibility with staff and the public.

Decisions on policy development should be made at least once a year during a review, sometimes referred to as an audit, of all policies by library staff, the administration, and the board. This is the time to note if new policies are needed and which existing policies should be updated or deleted. A written administrative statement may mandate an annual review of policies by the governing authority. Review library policies, determine the work to be done, and establish a schedule for dealing with the development of new policy or the revision of existing ones on a logical basis throughout the year. Do not try to develop several new policies at the same time as the review! Time is needed for research, consideration of the issues, discussion, and thought. Minor revisions to established policies, of course, will not require as much time as the development of new ones or major rewriting of outdated policies. Some state and regional library support organizations help small and medium sized public libraries by offering policy-writing clinics. These can be useful in getting the process going but do not substitute for local discussion of the issues and input into policies.

DEVELOPING EFFECTIVE POLICIES

Careful thought, discussion, and coordination are necessary for developing policies that will best serve the organization. To be effective, policies should be:

- Reflective of the mission, roles, and objectives of the organization; individual policies should dovetail so that they build on one another.
- Consistent, in order to maintain efficiency and fairness; contradictory policies counteract management goals.
- Flexible, to allow for some latitude in interpretation; content should be assessed and updated regularly.
- Supported by procedures and rules; procedures and rules are firm guides to action, exercising control and authority, whereas policies are flexible guides to thinking.
- Clearly written, so they are easily communicated to staff and users; a well-organized policy manual is a valuable aid to policy dissemination and use.
- Fully discussed by staff; staff must understand the policy and all of its ramifications in order to effectively and consistently follow the policy.
- Appealable through an established mechanism, even if that mechanism is informal.

STEPS IN POLICY DEVELOPMENT

It might be helpful to think of the following life cycle graphic when considering library policies (see Figure 2-1).[2] Policy statements are usually prepared by, even if they did not originate with, library staff. Although a board member or citizen may initiate the process, staff tends to be the first to recognize a situation that should be addressed by new policy. Staff and administrators develop and approve the proposed policy and present it to the library board or other governing authority for final approval. Board members are obligated to know good library practice, which will help them react to policy statements, challenge staff assumptions, and mold a policy that meets the needs of the library and the public. They may also be called on to defend and support the policy if a citizen challenges it. Once the need for a new or revised policy has been identified, the process can be broken down into eight steps.

Step 1: Research. Policymakers should consider the philosophy behind, and the situation leading to, the call for policy development. They should examine relevant documents such as the library's existing mission statement, documentation of the library's service priorities, existing policies, procedures, rules, and regulations as well as relevant external laws and policies of the parent organization. They should be aware of any constraints relating to the library's budget, staffing, resources, services, and patrons. While it may be helpful to examine similar policies developed by other libraries, remember that your library is unique and you should not simply adapt the policies of another library to fit yours. The Internet has made

Figure 2-1

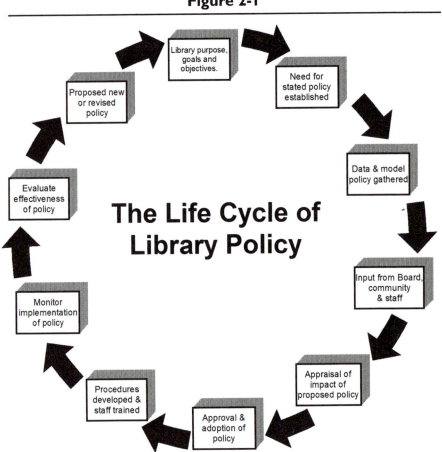

reviewing policies from other libraries easier, but library managers are urged to resist the temptation to copy.

Step 2: Writing. Because policy statements must be understandable to a range of readers, including patrons, the text must be clear, brief, as free of professional jargon as possible, and carefully edited for spelling and grammar. The policy should be as brief as possible—no longer than one or two pages whenever possible—in a format consistent with the other policies of the library. Several drafts will probably be necessary in order to create a satisfactory "first draft" for review.

Step 3: Library review. Depending on the library's size and organizational structure, the proposed policy may be reviewed in one or more meetings at one or more levels. At some point, it should be reviewed by the staff as a whole, the library director, and, if appropriate, citizen representatives or groups such as Friends of the Library. Copies should be distributed a few days in advance of a meeting so that reviewers have time to read and consider the draft. If consensus cannot be reached during initial discussions, further meetings may need to be scheduled; however, consensus may not be possible and is not required for the policy to move forward. After thorough discussion, the library director may need to make decisions that put the needs of the public and the organization above the preferences of the staff.

Make note of policies or sections of policies that are mandated (either by local, state, or federal law, or otherwise externally imposed), and, therefore, not part of the standard decision-making process. Groups working with the library to develop externally imposed policies will have less input, and consensus may not be achievable.

Step 4: Revision. After review and discussion, the text must be rewritten as many times as is necessary to reflect the consensus or the director's decision based on discussion when it was not possible to reach consensus. It may be necessary to discuss the ramifications or impact of suggested changes as well as how different readers may interpret terminology. Take care, however, to ensure that the review and revision process does not become cumbersome, wearing down the staff until they no longer have interest in the content of the policy or how it is interpreted.

Step 5: Library approval. The revised version may be approved during a meeting or simply circulated for individual staff members to initial. If the library has an advisory board rather than a governing board, approval from that group should be sought before submitting the policy to the governing authority for final adoption.

Step 6: Approval by governing authority. The proposed policy should be scheduled for presentation at the library board, city council, or commissioner's court meeting, and copies of the policy distributed a few days prior to the meeting. An executive summary or cover memo may outline the process followed and elucidate the need for the policy. The policy will be presented, discussed, and possibly revised further. Once it is approved, the policy should be signed and dated by authorized representatives of the governing authority. A useful guide for trustees who are involved in policy development is *The Successful Library Trustee Handbook* by Mary Moore.

Step 7: Distribution. The approved policy should be distributed to each member of the board, administration, and staff, and be added to the library's comprehensive policy manual. It should also be distributed and explained to new staff and patrons whenever appropriate.

Step 8: Periodic review. An annual review of all library policies will ensure the addition of new policies or the deletion of outdated or superfluous policies. Policies are not set in stone. As your community changes and as the library's roles, goals, and resources change, policies must be reviewed and revised to reflect the current situations. Changes to existing policies will go through the same steps as new policy development described previously. Periodic review on a "rolling schedule" will help ensure that no policy is ever seriously outdated or overlooked for consideration.

POLICY MANUALS AND DISTRIBUTION

Because they are the primary vehicles for communicating policies to a variety of library personnel and patrons, policy manuals should be compiled, organized, and formatted for optimal readability and usability. Ask new employees for feedback to ensure that they understand the policies and that the policy manual is organized for maximum usability. New eyes may find poorly worded sentences, jargon that requires clarification, or confusing concepts.

Policy manuals should be easily accessible to staff, patrons, and any others who are affected by the policies. Keep in mind that the Americans with Disabilities Act also requires that policies be made available in alternate formats that are accessible to people with disabilities. Consider having the policy manual printed in large print, which is easy to do if your policy manual is maintained electronically, and be prepared to have Braille and recorded versions available within a reasonable period if requested. Many libraries are choosing to provide their policy manual on the Internet, especially the parts that pertain to public services, so that patrons have easy access. This also makes it easier for staff to quickly locate the appropriate policy when questioned about a decision. Internal policies that deal with personnel issues, staff development, and behind-the-scenes issues are still public documents, but many libraries make them readily available only on the library's intranet. Keep in mind, though, that as public documents, these policies must be shared with patrons on request.

In addition to the types of policies described in this book, the library's policy manual should contain the library's mission statement, a statement about the primary and secondary service priorities selected for library service, and important supporting documents, such as the American Library Association's Library Bill of Rights. The entire set of policies should be organized for easy access to a specific policy and should include an index, if possible, and a table of contents. Fortunately, most word processing software includes an easy-to-use indexing feature that makes it fairly easy to create an index that will suit your needs. Policies should be formatted and numbered consistently throughout, with dates of adoption and revision noted on each policy. Each policy should be approved and signed by the library's governing authority.

The format of the policy manual should facilitate updating and distribution. Many libraries maintain electronic copies on the library's Web site and intranet, but many also compile policies in a loose-leaf notebook. This allows updated pages to be replaced individually, and specific policies can be reproduced and distributed as needed. It may be useful, and good public relations, to have a summary of important policies available as a brochure. However, copies of the entire manual should generally not be printed for wide public distribution because parts of the manual will always soon be obsolete. Of course, copies that are mounted on the library's Web site should also be updated as changes are made. Copies should be readily available for study by the public, and it may be useful to print copies for distribution of specific policies that are regularly needed. For example, the meeting room policy should be distributed with all applications to use the meeting room. Policies can also be distributed within an organization through letters, memoranda, and announcements, and posted on walls and bulletin boards for staff and patrons.

HOW TO USE MODEL POLICIES

This book offers models of most of the types of policies that will be useful in running a small or medium sized public library. Larger libraries, of course, also need most of these same policies, but may need others or may require policies that are more detailed. It is important to remember that no model policy will fit every library. Although they can borrow and share ideas with other libraries, library staff should not simply copy the policy of another library. It is important that issues and options, and the ramifications of the policy, be discussed by the local people—staff, administrators, governing authority, advisory groups, and the public—who will have to apply, support, and defend the policies. The proper wording of a policy will vary depending on the type of political structure that governs the library. Use these model policies, which are also provided on the CD-ROM included with this book, and any samples borrowed from other libraries, strictly as models. Always check with legal counsel and the governing authority for local style and proper language.

NOTES

1. Cook Memorial Public Library District. Policies and Procedures. Available: www.cooklib.org/Learn/Policies/pol_polproc.htm. Accessed September 26, 2007.
2. Curry, Betsy. 1984. *Georgia Public Library Trustees Handbook*. Atlanta: Georgia Library Trustee and Friends Association.

Part II

Policy Areas and Model Policies

Chapter 3

Personnel and Employment Practices

Most public libraries operate as a department of a larger governmental body (city, municipality, county) that sets personnel policies affecting working conditions of all who are employed or who seek employment with that parent institution. If personnel functions are handled centrally, library staff members who interview potential candidates, make hiring decisions, or evaluate and supervise staff must be familiar with established personnel guidelines. For such cases, the library may also wish to have a general written policy that states that the library will conform to all governmentally established employment policies.

The library's governing structure and local or state laws may affect some personnel policies. Is the library in a "right to work" state, where employees work "at will?" Are employees covered by civil service or union agreements? Especially in smaller libraries that may not have on-site human resource staff available, it is important to have personnel policies readily and easily available to all who may be affected by them. These policies may protect the library from situations that encourage or permit nepotism and favoritism. It is also helpful to include a statement of governance (what body governs library personnel issues) and an organizational chart that shows the chain of command.

If the library is large enough to operate an independent personnel office or is an autonomous agency, it is even more critical that all appropriate personnel policies be in place. Libraries that are organized and run by a foundation or are owned by a private federated club should consult additional sources, including Section 4 of *Library and Information Center Management* by Robert Stueart and Barbara Moran, for detailed information on staffing. Additionally, the American Library Association's *Library Personnel News* (which ceased publication in 2004) and *Library Worklife: HR E-News for Today's Leaders,* or general journals like *Workforce Management,* provide guidance on issues related to human resources and employment policies.

Current federal law requires that employers confirm U.S. citizenship or legal status for working in the United States, and the library's policies should indicate adherence to all legal requirements. This is an area that may continue to change as the U.S. Congress deals with issues of illegal immigration and workforce issues. It is also important to check with state labor authorities for other laws and regulations that may affect employment practices before developing or revising personnel policies. For the purposes of this book, it is assumed that the public library is part of a larger organization and, therefore, the model policies provided are suited to that situation.

MODEL POLICY: PERSONNEL AND EMPLOYMENT PRACTICES

The (name of library) is a department of (city, county, municipality). Personnel services are coordinated through the (city, county, municipality) personnel office. The (name of library) supports and adheres to all laws and policies dealing with equal employment opportunity, the Civil Rights Acts, the Americans with Disabilities Act, fair employment practices, fair labor standards, the Family Medical Leave Act, and other federal, state, and local legislation concerned with employment and hiring practices.

In accordance with appropriate federal laws, the (name of library) will confirm citizenship or the right for noncitizens to work in the United States. Additional policies pertaining to library personnel practices have been implemented and are included in this policy manual.

Employees of (name of library) are hired "at will," and within the guidelines of library and (name of city, county, municipality) policies and procedures conditions of employment may be changed without cause or notice. Likewise, employees are not contracted to work for a specific tenure of service and may terminate their employment relationship at any time with or without cause and with or without notice.

Approved by (governing body) on (insert date)

Signature of responsible representative

SEXUAL HARASSMENT

Background

Harassment on the basis of sex is a violation of section 703 of Title VII of the *Code of Federal Regulations.* If the library is part of a parent institution, such as city or county government, that organization will most likely have well-articulated sexual harassment policies in place for every entity within their political jurisdiction. Even so, the library may want to reinforce its commitment to providing an environment that is comfortable and safe by having its own policy regarding sexual harassment.

The policy may address sexual harassment by employees, but it may also protect employees from sexual harassment by library patrons. Staff has the right to work in an environment that is safe from unwanted and inappropriate advances from patrons. For advice on sexual harassment by patrons, review the article "Sexual Harassment and the Library Don't Mix" in the November/December 2005 issue of *Library Mosaics.*[1] You might also refer to the Spring 1997 issue of *Illinois Libraries* for a ten-step program to minimize the likelihood of sexual harassment and reduce the likelihood of lawsuits.[2] If the legal structure of your library is such that you are not a part of a larger political entity, you will want to refer to *The Librarian's Legal Companion*[3] to develop a harassment or sexual harassment policy for your library.

Issues

- Have your read the pertinent parts of the *Code of Federal Regulations*? 29 C.F.R. Section 1604.11 deals with sexual harassment. Are there state laws that deal with this issue?
- All public library policies with regard to sexual harassment should have a clear and detailed definition of sexual harassment. Does your governing organization have background material that you should review? The library's definition should be consistent with that of any parent organization.
- Does the library offer regular and ongoing training, especially for new hires, that includes information on prevention of sexual harassment? Training should include information about how to deal with sexual harassment, how to avoid it, and what steps to take if one is subjected to sexual harassment.
- Are you comfortable with all of the elements that can constitute sexual harassment? Sexual harassment includes any verbal, nonverbal, or physical actions of employees toward patrons, employees toward other employees, patrons toward employees, or patrons toward other patrons that intimidate, offend, or embarrass the recipient.

- Where else in library policies is sexual harassment addressed? References should be made from other policies to the library's policy dealing with sexual harassment and vice versa. For example, the policy might include reference to sections of the library's Internet policy that may be related to sexual harassment so that library employees may refuse to provide assistance to a patron if they believe that it will require the employee to view printed or computer screen materials that the employee finds to be obscene.[4] However, the library employee must immediately ask a supervisor for assistance with the patron's request.

MODEL POLICY: SEXUAL HARASSMENT

It is the policy of (name of library) to provide a place that is comfortable for employees and patrons to work and use library resources. In compliance with applicable federal and state laws, the library will be a place that is free of any form of harassment, including sexual harassment. Sexual harassment includes unwelcome sexual advances, flirtations, propositions, sexually degrading words to describe an individual, graphic or suggestive comments, or requests for sexual favors. It includes the display in staff work areas of sexually suggestive pictures or objects, including photographs or illustrations of nude or seminude figures. All employees are responsible for assuring that the workplace is free of sexual harassment and should promptly report incidents or possible incidents of sexual harassment to the library director. After investigation, any employee found to have engaged in sexual harassment will be subject to disciplinary actions that range from counseling and education up to and including termination of employment.

Patrons are not permitted to sexually harass other patrons or staff members. Library employees may refuse to assist a patron if they believe that such assistance will require the employee to view printed or computer screen materials that the employee finds to be offensive or interprets as harassment. The library employee must immediately ask a supervisor for assistance with the patron's request. Patrons who harass staff or other patrons will be asked to leave the library and, if appropriate, their behavior will be reported to the appropriate authorities.

Approved by (governing body) on (insert date)

Signature of responsible representative

- Be sure that you are familiar with the issues that balance an environment that is free from sexual harassment with the principles of First Amendment rights. In at least one case,[5] the court found that allowing patrons to access sexually explicit materials that was not illegal did not create a hostile work environment even when staff were called on to assist with tasks such as printing. However, in other cases, the Equal Employment Opportunity Commission has found that unrestricted access to the Internet that allows patrons to view and print sexually explicit material may constitute a hostile work environment.

- The library has a responsibility to take corrective action to ensure that its employees are not subject to sexual harassment by patrons. Section 1604.11(e) of the *Code of Federal Regulations* 29 specifically holds an employer responsible for sexual harassment by nonemployees if the employer knows, or should have known, of the conduct and fails to take immediate and appropriate corrective action.

- What are the consequences of sexual harassment for employees and patrons? To whom are reports of sexual harassment made? The policy should give an explicit explanation of the consequences of sexual harassment. For example, employees engaging in sexual harassment will be subject to discipline, up to and including, termination. Patrons engaging in sexual harassment will be asked to leave the library and reported to the proper authorities.

RECRUITMENT OF CANDIDATES FOR POSITIONS

Background

Staff is the mainstay of all library services, and we want to hire the best people possible. It can be very difficult and time consuming for any library to locate, screen, interview, and select qualified personnel, and even more so for some smaller libraries, especially if they are in rural or isolated areas. It is also important to recruit for a diverse workforce. Workforce diversity is more than simply being fair and equitable to all potential applicants. Persons from all segments of the community must feel welcome to apply for positions with the library. In order to ensure equal opportunity, federal and state laws mandate that certain procedures and policies be in place so that all qualified candidates for employment will be treated fairly and equitably. Some cities, counties, or library districts are also subject to local civil service requirements. Diversity, and equitable access to jobs, begins with the recruiting process and accurate, up-to-date job descriptions.

The Americans with Disabilities Act (ADA) covers the employment process as well as access to the library's services. Job requirements must relate to the work that the employee is expected to perform and cannot require arbitrary physical abilities (such as height or weight restrictions). Job descriptions should be written to clearly identify the essential functions of the job. Employers must also be prepared to provide reasonable accommodation that allows an otherwise qualified candidate with a disability to perform the job. Additional information on the employment process and the ADA can be found in Chapter 4 of *How Libraries Must Comply with the Americans with Disabilities Act (ADA)* by Donald D. Foos and Nancy C. Pack. Although the copyright is 1992, the information is still valid. For a broader look at legal issues related to employment, consult *The Essential Guide to Federal Employment Laws* by Lisa Guerin, released in 2006 by Nolo Press. The Job Accommodation Network (JAN) provides free information (call 800-526-7234) and consulting services about the employability of people with disabilities and job accommodation, as well as information regarding the Americans with Disabilities Act. The Web site at http://janweb.icdi. wvu.edu/ provides links to the law and other documents related to ADA, plus a variety of other resources, including sample self-evaluation documents to help organizations analyze programs and services for accessibility. JAN also provides assistance to employers seeking ways to accommodate employees with disabilities, with more than 80 percent of the accommodations costing less than $500.

Issues

- Are you aware of and familiar with current state and federal guidelines and regulations concerning employment practices?
- Are there any age limitations for hiring based on state or city regulations? In some cases, local regulations set a lower age limit (usually 16 or 18 years of age) for full-time employment.
- Are there any issues related to civil service or union rules that must be followed?
- Is the library responsible for recruitment, or does the responsibility lie within a central personnel office? If recruitment is not the responsibility of the library, library administration can still assist the personnel department by suggesting the best places to reach qualified minority applicants. Many personnel departments will not be familiar with specialized library journals, electronic resources, and associations.
- Are funds budgeted to advertise positions widely? When advertising positions, do you know how to reach qualified minority candi-

---

MODEL POLICY: RECRUITMENT OF CANDIDATES FOR POSITIONS

The (name of library) is committed to developing a diverse workforce while also selecting the most qualified persons available for library positions. When hiring new staff or promoting current staff, the library will systematically and aggressively make reasonable efforts to provide an equal opportunity for all employees and applicants. An applicant pool that is representative of the makeup of the community is desirable, however no person under the age of 18 will be considered for full-time regular positions. Positions will be advertised as widely as appropriate for the position and, when possible, advertising will be targeted to reach qualified applicants from minority groups and persons with disabilities. Reasonable accommodation, in accordance with the Americans with Disabilities Act, will be provided to all applicants. Funds will be expended, subject to budgetary limitations, to pay travel costs for candidates selected for interviews for position at the upper management level. Whenever possible, prescreening interviews will be conducted by telephone or video conferencing; however, when these methods are used, all candidates will be screened by the same prescreening method.

Approved by (governing body) on (insert date)

Signature of responsible representative

---

dates? Many specialized journals, periodicals, electronic resources, and joblines exist. Do ads include a statement indicating that your library adheres to all Equal Employment Opportunity guidelines and encourages members of minority groups and people with disabilities to apply?

- Have positions been identified where national searches are appropriate? Are funds available to help pay travel costs for qualified candidates who might not otherwise be able to travel to an interview? Have you considered alternative ways to interview (via conference call, videoconferencing, or at national or state conferences, for example) that might attract a more diverse group of candidates for positions?
- Are job descriptions current? Do position requirements relate directly to the tasks required by the job and as described by the job description? Have job descriptions been updated to include essen-

tial physical requirements, and are you prepared to make reasonable accommodation for job applicants as required by the Americans with Disabilities Act?

- What background checking will be done prior to hiring a candidate? Is the level of investigation reasonable to the scope of the person's work duties? For example, someone who will be regularly handling money might need to have a background check that includes a credit report, while the financial health of a shelving clerk probably isn't a major concern. Criminal background checks may be required for all positions that come in contact with children.

NEPOTISM

Background

Hiring relatives to work in the same institution or the same work area is called nepotism. Employment policies should include a policy that clearly delineates when relatives cannot be hired and under what circumstance people who are related can work for the same organization. The policy may also need to provide a definition of family, keeping in mind that close familial types of relationships are not always defined by legalities or blood. At the same time, legal rights and privacy issues must be considered. Some states have antidiscrimination laws that prohibit consideration of marital or familial status except where business necessity requires antinepotism rules be applied.

Within the library, it might be inadvisable to have relatives working within the same range of supervision (reporting to the same supervisor). It would generally be unacceptable to have someone supervise his or her own relative.[6] Larger organizations may be able to compartmentalize people who are related into different work areas, but this is less practical, and probably unattainable, in smaller libraries. The policy statement should also address how the library will deal with changes in status following employment. For example, how will the library deal with two current employees who marry while working together or who become related through the marriage of other relatives? Some libraries choose to include office romances in the nepotism policy or in a policy on staff relations. Office romances, especially in small libraries or where supervisory relationships are involved, can be very tricky to deal with, especially in the absence of an approved policy.

Generally, relatives can be hired to work in another department of the same governing agency (for example, the sibling of someone working for the library could be hired by the city water department). It is prudent, however, to have a policy in place that addresses how relatives will be treated during the job recruitment process. This protects the library from being forced to hire the mayor's grandchild or the spouse of the police chief. You may also wish to address how relatives of current board members will be treated, especially if the library is under the direction of a governing board.

Issues

- Do any state nepotism laws affect the library? In many jurisdictions nepotism is not illegal, even if it may be unwise. Does the library's governing organization have policies that deal with relatives working in the same department or work program? State laws that regulate nepotism with regard to marriage may not cover other relatives.
- How large is your organization? Can the organizational structure accommodate people from the same family working under different chains of command?
- How will you define relatives? Obvious relatives include spouse, children, parents, and siblings. What about aunts and uncles, grandparents, first cousins, and half-siblings or stepsiblings? Does the definition apply to the relatives of my spouse (for example, if I work for the library, could my husband's sister get a job there?)?
- Will persons residing in the same household, but not related through blood or marriage, be treated as if they were related? Today people may share living quarters with and without personal attachments. Consider carefully the privacy issues that relate to living arrange-

---

MODEL POLICY: NEPOTISM

The (name of library) will not hire the relatives of current employees. A relative is defined as the spouse, children, parents, grandparents, grandchildren, siblings, nephews and nieces, and aunts and uncles. The library may not employ two persons residing in the same household who present themselves to the community as "a family" at the same time, even though they might not be legally related through kinship or marriage. Relatives of employees working in other city departments are not given special consideration in employment. Relatives will be considered for positions if they meet the job qualifications; an employee's relative may be hired if he or she is the best candidate for the position.

Approved by (governing body) on (insert date)

Signature of responsible representative

ments. Weigh the impact of becoming too involved in someone's personal life against the need of the library to avoid even the appearance of nepotism or favoritism.

- How will the library handle office romances that begin between two people already hired? What happens if two employees marry each other? Does your state have any laws that prohibit discrimination based on marital status that may need to be considered?

PERFORMANCE EVALUATION

Background

It is important to determine how employee performance will be evaluated well in advance of the evaluation. Guidelines should be available for review by all who are affected by these policies. Many organizations of all sizes embrace the philosophy of immediate and continuous feedback for employees. Paula Peters' "Seven Tips for Delivering Performance Feedback" provides excellent advice for the difficult job of giving honest feedback.[7] Even though regular, informal feedback is recommended, formal periodic evaluations are still necessary to document an employee's performance in writing.

Everyone has the right to know how their job performance will be evaluated, when written evaluations will take place, and to have, as much as possible, objective and measurable goals against which their performance will be measured. An excellent overview of performance evaluation is available in Chapter 8 of *Library and Information Center Management* by Robert D. Stueart and Barbara B. Moran.[8] Detailed assistance on writing effective job descriptions, developing performance plans, and staff performance review methods and processes is available in *Performance Analysis and Appraisal* by Robert D. Stueart and Maureen Sullivan. Other excellent resources are Carol Goodson's *The Complete Guide to Performance Standards for Library Personnel* and *Human Resources for Results* by Jeanne Goodrich and Paula M. Singer, which includes work forms for developing performance plans and evaluation tools.

In some libraries, salary increases are tied to performance evaluations, and one statement may combine both policies. We have chosen to treat the issues separately because salary increases are not necessarily tied to performance and personal job improvement. Regardless, evaluations should be as objective as possible, based on established criteria. The employee should know in advance what is expected in order to meet or exceed expectations. The supervisor should provide the employee with a written draft of the evalu-

ation but also review the evaluation in person prior to finalizing the information and sending it up the chain of command.

A timeline for evaluation should be established. Often new employees
are in a probationary status for six months or a year. Evaluation may occur
more frequently than for established employees in order to ensure that the
new employee is doing a good job. If evaluations are tied to salary increases,
it is crucial that the evaluation occur prior to any deadlines for pay
adjustments.

Issues

- Does the library's governing authority have an overall orientation
  for new hires? Does the library have an orientation that introduces
  its policies, performance evaluation, chain of command, etc.? How

---

MODEL POLICY: PERFORMANCE EVALUATIONS

Within one month of employment, a job performance plan will be established for each employee and a written copy given to the employee.
The first job performance evaluation will be conducted at the end of
three months of employment. A second evaluation will be conducted at
the end of the six-month probationary period. For nonprobationary
employees, performance plans will be set and evaluations will be scheduled for a period of one year unless circumstances warrant a shorter
period for the review.

Upon completion of probation with a satisfactory performance evaluation, an employee will be considered for a merit raise. Subsequent
merit raises will be considered at the end of each 12-month evaluation
period. Merit raises are awarded only once in a year even if more than
one performance evaluation is completed during that time. Supervisors
have the responsibility to ensure that the timeline for employee evaluation is met so that salary increases can be awarded. No salary increase
will be awarded without an evaluation; therefore, employees should report the lack of evaluation to the library director if not completed within
ten days of the due date.

Approved by (governing body) on (insert date)

_____
Signature of responsible representative

---

will staff be oriented to the job for which they have been hired? A good checklist for new hires can be found in *Library Personnel News.*[9]

- Does the library or parent organization have an established process to evaluate job performance? What is the timeline? Is there a probationary period for new employees?

- How frequently are written evaluations performed? Are supervisors encouraged to provide feedback informally on a more frequent basis?

- Are there different evaluation criteria for professional, clerical, or other categories of staff? Are there civil service or union regulations that affect evaluation of staff?

- Are salary increases tied to periodic performance evaluations? What happens if an employee is not evaluated in a timely manner? Will merit increases be awarded without an evaluation?

SALARIES AND SALARY INCREASES

Background

Ways in which salaries are determined, how employee performance is evaluated and the impact of performance on salaries, and decisions about when and how salaries will be increased or decreased must be established in advance and be available for review by all who are affected by these policies. Knowing how salaries are set and under what conditions raises will be awarded is vital to good staff morale. Salary policies may also address overtime compensation, shift differential pay, special skills pay (for example, for fluency in speaking a second language), and other pay issues.

Issues

- Who is authorized to set salaries? Are salary ranges set for each position? Who can authorize hiring at a salary above entry level and what factors (education, experience, previous salary, difficulty in filling the position) permit hiring above entry level?

- Are unions, employee organizations, or other legal authorities involved in establishing salaries? Is there a local minimum or "living" wage that affects salaries?

- Does the library or parent organization have an established process to evaluate job performance? How frequently are written evaluations performed? Are salary increases tied to periodic performance evaluations? If job performance is satisfactory, are salary increases automatic? Is there a probationary period for new employees?

- Under what circumstances can an employee receive a salary increase greater than one step on the salary scale? What happens when an employee "tops out" on the pay scale?

MODEL POLICY: PERFORMANCE EVALUATION AND SALARY INCREASES

Salary ranges are established for each position classification by the (governing authority) and are posted in the personnel office and the staff lounge. New employees are generally hired at the base level of the salary range. When approved by the library director, new hires may enter at a higher salary range based on exceptional experience, relevant education, or other appropriate factors.

Within one month of employment, a job performance plan will be established for each employee and a written copy given to the employee. An informal evaluation will be conducted after 90 days of employment. At the end of a six-month probationary period a formal evaluation will be conducted and the employee will be released from probation, terminated, or, with approval of the library director, have the probationary period extended for another 90 days. Subsequent performance plans will be set, and evaluations will be scheduled, for a period of one year unless circumstances warrant a shorter period for the review.

Upon completion of a satisfactory performance evaluation, an employee will be considered for a merit raise. Merit raises are awarded once in a year even if more than one performance evaluation is completed during that time.

Longevity pay, annual merit bonuses, and cost-of-living increases are established by (governing authority) and are generally given across the board to all employees who meet the established criteria.

The (name of library) expects that staff will be able to perform required work within a 40-hour workweek. However, when staff is required to work overtime, with the approval of the library director or in emergency situations, compensatory time will be awarded for actual time worked. The (name of library) does not budget for overtime pay, which will be paid only under extenuating circumstances when authorized by the library director and approved by the (governing authority).

Approved by (governing body) on (insert date)

Signature of responsible representative

- Are funds available for longevity pay, merit bonuses, or extra pay for specific abilities (proficiency in a foreign language, for example), working outside of normal business hours (Sunday pay after 40 hours), hazardous work (emergency conditions), or premium work (being subject to call back during off time)?
- How is overtime pay handled? Are some employees exempt from overtime pay, subject to flat rate pay, or given compensatory time instead of overtime pay? Is compensatory time awarded at a rate other than one hour for each hour worked? Are you familiar with federal Fair Labor Standards Act (FSLA) rules and do you know which staff positions may be subject to them? FSLA does not require extra pay for weekend, holiday, or evening work. Additionally, "Section 13(a)(1) of the FLSA provides an exemption from both minimum wage and overtime pay for employees employed as bona fide executive, administrative, professional and outside sales employees."[10] FSLA rules can be confusing, so consult legal counsel if you are uncertain as to whether employees are exempt from FSLA or not.
- Are all employees subject to the same salary scales, provisions for salary increases, etc., regardless of the source of funds for their salary? Are there positions that are funded from sources other than the library's regular funding source (such as grants or temporary positions) that are exempt from the policies that govern pay increases, longevity pay, merit increases, etc.?

EMPLOYEE BENEFITS

Background

Employee benefits generate the next largest budget item, after salaries, for most libraries. Benefits can often be as important to employees as salary level and play a major role in recruitment and retention of staff. Every employee should be aware of all benefits available and know how to receive them. If benefits are different for part-time or temporary employees, or for someone in a position that is funded from sources such as grant money, these deviations from standard policy should be clearly identified. Keep in mind that although many small libraries pay the library director for part-time hours, as the chief administrator for the organization, the job may actually be considered as full time. Although the pay may be low, the classification may imply that the person has been hired to perform a specific job regardless of the number of hours per week actually worked. If the library is part of a larger governmental body, benefits are usually uniform for all departments of that governmental body, but some benefits may be at the discretion of the department.

Issues

- What benefits does the library's governing authority offer? Are optional benefits available (dependent health insurance, disability insurance), or are some benefits available as "menu" selections from which employees can choose?
- If the library is a department of a larger governmental body, what flexibility, if any, is accorded individual departments in administering the overriding policies? For example, can the library require that vacation requests be submitted a specific period of time in advance? Having the ability to require sufficient advance notice of vacation can be critical to ensuring that adequate staff remains to cover service desks.

MODEL POLICY: EMPLOYEE BENEFITS

Benefits such as health insurance, group insurance, vacation and sick leave, paid time off, employee retirement plans, child care or elder care supplements, carpool subsidies, and other miscellaneous benefits (travel expenses, tuition reimbursements, access to subsidized day care, etc.) are established and administered by (name of governing authority). The (name of library) may not alter these benefits without specific authorization from (governing authority).

Within the parameters established for all employees of (name of governing authority), requests for vacation leave must be submitted to the library director in writing at least two weeks before the date that leave will begin. Effort will be made to accommodate leave requests during holiday periods, but staffing needs may preclude approval of all requests. Sick leave may be used for doctor appointments, but, to ensure adequate staffing, must be submitted at least one week in advance except in emergencies. Sick leave may not be claimed while on vacation leave. A maximum of three days each year may be granted for other types of leave (bereavement or other emergency leave) upon approval of the library director.

Approved by (governing body) on (insert date)

Signature of responsible representative

- How are sick leave and vacation leave accrued? Under what circumstances are employees able to use these types of leave? Are other types of leave available (jury duty, bereavement leave, leave without pay)? How are they defined, and under what circumstances may these types of leave be used?
- Are there other types of benefits available, such as child care or elder care supplements, carpooling subsidies, reduced or free bus passes, free parking, tuition reimbursement, and service awards?

STAFF DEVELOPMENT

Background

It is important that all staff, at every level of employment (including volunteers), be provided with initial and ongoing training to improve job performance and gain new skills. Staff should be encouraged to renew and expand their skills through cross-training, continuing education, and specialized training. Policies regarding release time from work, paid time for training, and reimbursement of training and education costs help ensure that all staff understand the nature and extent of available support.

Membership and involvement in professional associations is another form of staff development. Staff should be encouraged to join and participate in these organizations even if budget limitations or local governmental policies do not allow dues and registration fees to be paid from the library budget. Of course, whenever possible, paid time and financial support will encourage even more participation. Participation and the assumption of leadership roles on staff committees and task forces are another form of staff development. Policy may set out guidelines for appointments, terms of service, and chairmanship.

Some states have certification requirements that mandate continuing education for library staff. Many governing bodies require continuing education and development of new skills as a factor in the evaluation process, including allocation of merit increases and consideration for advancement or promotion. Knowledge of these requirements and their inclusion in a written policy, job descriptions, and performance evaluations helps to ensure that funds are budgeted for travel, fees, substitute staff, and materials. *Performance Management and Appraisal* by G. Edward Evans includes additional information on staff development plans and their use in the evaluation of employee performance.

Issues

- Is any library staff member subject to state or local certification or continuing education requirements? Do you know the timeline for meeting any mandated continuing education requirements? Are continuing education, professional association involvement, and other training included in job requirements? Be sure to distinguish between staff development and required job training, which must take priority. For example, state law may require that the administrative assistant take a state-provided course in records management in order to ensure that appropriate records of government decisions are kept for the appropriate period of time.
- Will the library support formal education, such as obtaining a master's degree in librarianship, or voluntary post-master's certification programs, such as the Public Library Association's Certified Public Library Administrator Program?[11]
- What are the potential sources for training and continuing education? What training and staff development opportunities does the library's governing body provide? How far will staff have to travel to obtain training? What costs are associated with receiving training? What non-library-specific training is available locally and regionally (for example, computer training, management skills, foreign language)? Do you know what training resources, such as Web conferences, videoconferences, online classes, books, videotapes or DVDs, etc., are available? Are funds budgeted to rent or purchase items if they cannot be borrowed, or to pay class fees or licensing costs?
- Is personal and professional development included in job performance evaluations and/or a factor in receiving salary increases, merit raises, and promotions? Are sample staff development plans available for individuals to review?
- Does the library's governing authority have a policy regarding release time for training? Are restrictions placed on travel (e.g., permission is required to leave the county; no out-of-state travel; limited reimbursement, etc.)? Will travel be permitted if a similar training opportunity is available online?
- Are substitutes available to cover service desks while staff is away? Staff size, availability of substitutes, and other staffing considerations may preclude training that requires extensive travel or extended time away from the library. If this is the case, what alternatives are available?
- Will the library support involvement in professional associations by encouraging membership and providing financial support for in-

volvement in association activities? Do local laws and policies permit the library to reimburse all or part of association dues? Do local laws and policies permit, encourage, or specifically prohibit the use of staff time for association activities and for staff to hold office in associations? Are there other organizations and associations that, while not library specific, relate to the library's mission and roles (for example, local business clubs, the Chamber of Commerce, International Reading Association, or the National Association for the Education of Young People)? Will the library support membership in those organizations?

MODEL POLICY: STAFF DEVELOPMENT

The (name of library) is committed to having a well-trained and highly educated workforce. During the first week on the job, every new employee will receive a general orientation to the library. During that time, the employee and his or her supervisor will develop an individualized training plan and timeline based on the job requirements, experience, and educational needs for the particular position.

Basic dues for the state professional association will be reimbursed, funds permitting, for all permanent, full-time staff members (including paraprofessional and clerical staff who join appropriate organizations). If funds are not available to cover the entire cost of basic dues, each employee will receive a prorated share of available funds. The library director may also approve financial and other support for staff to join non-library-related organizations that further the library's service priorities (for example, the Chamber of Commerce or International Reading Association).

Every staff member is encouraged to have a written staff development plan prepared annually in consultation with his or her supervisor. All staff members are encouraged to attend job-related workshops and seminars to fulfill their staff development plan. Three workdays (up to 24 hours) of work release time are available annually for each full-time employee to attend optional job-related training and educational functions. Part-time employees will receive prorated release time. Funds will be budgeted as equitably as possible to cover the travel expenses and registration fees for this training.

Additional work time may be given to attend training that meets the employee's staff development plan. Travel expenses and registration fees will be reimbursed if funds are available, upon approval of the library director.

Professional and paraprofessional staff are encouraged to attend library science and related professional association meetings, such as the ALA annual conference, state library association conferences, and regional conferences. Funds are budgeted for this purpose, and staff wishing to attend conferences should indicate their interest to the library director early in the budget year. If there are not sufficient funds to cover costs for all employees wishing to attend conferences, funds will be given first toward the expenses of staff members who have official responsibilities or who are officers of the association. Remaining funds will be prorated so that as many staff members as possible have some financial support. Attendance at professional association conferences and meetings will be rotated as equitably as possible among staff members.

Professional staff is expected to stay familiar with current issues librarianship by reading professional journals and library literature. Funds are budgeted to purchase the major professional journals and books. Requests that the library purchase specific books, periodicals, videos and DVDs, audiotapes, and other materials specifically for staff development should be made to the library director (or other designated staff member). Funds are budgeted to purchase items that will be useful to more than one staff member. In some cases, videos or DVDs and audiotapes may be borrowed or rented for limited use.

In order that training may be shared with other staff, written reports will be required within five workdays of an employee's return from training. Employees may also be required to conduct programs, seminars, and similar activities for other staff. When necessary, one-on-one training between staff may also be required.

Approved by (governing body) on (insert date)

———————————————————————————
Signature of responsible representative

USE OF VOLUNTEERS

Background

Volunteers can add immensely to the quality of service that the library can provide. Volunteers act as public relations spokespersons for the library, becoming "friends" of the library. A volunteer program also offers a means for members of the community to give of themselves and give back to their community. Volunteers should be used to provide specific and selective ser-

vices and should not replace permanent, paid staff. It is important to remember that volunteers are not "free." Volunteers require training, supervision, development, and encouragement. The best volunteers will take their
job just as seriously as paid staff does, but regular, budgeted staff will spend
varying amounts of time recruiting volunteers, training them, and supervis-
ing their work.

Issues

- Do union rules, local laws, and the policies of the library's governing authority permit the use of volunteers?
- Have you identified the ways in which volunteers could contribute
  to the library and its services? Remember that volunteers bring many
  different skills to their service and people volunteer for many different reasons. Will Manly offers an interesting look at the topic in
  his article "Is Love's Labor a Loss for Libraries?"[12]
- Will volunteers be required to undergo a criminal background check
  or drug testing prior to working with children, money, or patron
  records?
- Do you have a process for reporting volunteer time? Have you considered ways to avoid any negative effect on the budget from using
  volunteers? Volunteers should supplement, not supplant, permanent paid staff.
- Who will recruit, train, and monitor volunteers? Job descriptions
  must be available for all volunteer positions. Potential volunteers
  must be interviewed, selected, and trained for positions in much
  the same way as paid staff. Volunteers have a lot to offer libraries,
  but need the same supervision and guidance as paid staff. Can you
  recruit a diverse group of volunteers? Bonnie McCune makes a great
  case for "broadening and strengthening the library's ties to the community the library serves" and "offsetting the limited diversity in
  paid staff positions that exists within many libraries" in her article in
  Colorado Libraries.[13]
- Will those who have volunteered be considered when paying positions are available? Some libraries avoid hurt feelings or problems
  with favoritism by stating up front that volunteers will not be considered for paid employment, especially during the period while
  they are volunteering. Other libraries look at volunteers as a valuable pool of potential applicants who already have some job training
  and familiarity with the organization. Regardless of potential future
  employment, all volunteers need to have their work recognized and
  appreciated.

- Will children and teenagers be used as volunteers? Young people can provide great enthusiasm and energy, but volunteering should not be a substitute for child care or summer camp. Youth volunteers usually require closer supervision, continued motivation, and more social interaction. Do child labor laws limit the number of hours or restrict the times a young person can work? Do those laws apply for nonpaid work? A parental permission form and disclaimer of liability is highly recommended for youth volunteers.
- Are community service restitution "volunteers" to be used? These are people required by a court or other law enforcement agency to perform community service. These "volunteers" may be very motivated to provide short-term, intensive services.
- Can staff volunteer for the library in any capacity? Fair labor laws or the policies of the library's governing entity may prohibit a staff member from volunteering to perform any activity for which they would normally be paid. However, staff may be able to volunteer to work in areas outside the scope of their normal duties (for example, a reference librarian might share her hobby during a children's program) or for other city or county departments.

MODEL POLICY: USE OF VOLUNTEERS

The (name of library) welcomes and encourages members of the community to volunteer their time and talents to enrich and expand library services. Volunteers are expected to conform to all policies of (name of library) and the rules outlined in the volunteer handbook, and they are selected and retained for as long as the library needs their services. Volunteers may be used for special events, projects, and activities, or on a regular basis to assist staff. Services provided by volunteers will supplement, but not replace, regular services, and volunteers will not be used in places of hiring full- or part-time staff. Volunteers may apply for paid positions under the same conditions as other outside applicants. In accordance with labor laws and the policies of (governing entity), paid staff may not volunteer their services to the library except with written permission from the library director. Staff may volunteer in other departments of city government outside the library.

Approved by (governing body) on (insert date)

Signature of responsible representative

TERMINATION OF EMPLOYMENT

Background

People leave their jobs for a variety of reasons, sometimes voluntarily and other times due to termination through firing or layoffs. Employees who resign to take another job can be a valuable source of information about what is not working right within your organization. To ensure a smooth transition of job responsibilities following a resignation, employees should be expected to provide reasonable notice and to do what they can to complete unfinished projects or transfer responsibility to another staff member. Those following the established procedures for resignation may be entitled to specific benefits. Library policy may also wish to address letters of reference or recommendation for departing employees. This can be a tricky issue because employers are increasingly being subjected to lawsuits if they provide negative information about former employees.

Policymakers must be familiar with any regulations regarding termination of employees. You should know whether employment is "at will" or subject to explicit or implied contracts. In many cases, employees who are subject to termination because of substandard performance must be afforded opportunity to correct the deficiencies in their work and may be able to appeal the management decision. Managers and supervisors need to be familiar with and ready to follow policies in order to avoid potential legal actions or delays in filling the vacated position.

Budget cuts may require that some employees be laid off, and policies will establish what benefits they may be entitled to as part of the layoff. Employees who are fired may be entitled to a grievance process or other rights. Some governing authorities provide additional benefits, such as payment for accrued sick leave, for employees who are retiring.

Policies make clear how terminations will be handled under the various situations and make the process of leaving equitable and more pleasant for everyone. The library's governing authority may establish general policies, which must be adhered to by all departments.

Issues

- If an employee is leaving for another job, how much advance notice must be given in order for the employee to have left in good standing? Reasonable notice may differ for specific positions depending on the complexities of the job and staffing levels. For example, it might be reasonable to ask for three weeks' notice for professional-level positions, but only one week for shelver and aide positions. Is less notice required if the employee is transferring to another divi-

sion or department of the same governing authority? If reasonable notice is not given, are some benefits denied? What benefits must be accorded by law (vacation pay, continued insurance coverage)?
- Will the departing employee receive a final performance appraisal prior to the last day of employment? Is an exit interview, where the departing employee can provide feedback about the organization, encouraged? Consult *Human Resources for Results* by Jeanne Goodrich and Paula M. Singer for a sample exit interview form.
- What conditions must exist for an employee to be dismissed? Do

---

MODEL POLICY: TERMINATION OF EMPLOYMENT

Employees who resign to accept employment with another business or to leave the workforce must give written notice two weeks prior to the last work day in order to leave in good standing. Employees who leave in good standing will be paid for unused vacation and compensatory time on their final paycheck and will be eligible for rehire in the future. An exit interview will be scheduled with the library director on the last day of employment. All library property, including keys and identification cards, must be returned before issuance of the final paycheck.

Employees may be terminated for substandard work without notice during the probationary period. After the probation period, employees will receive oral and written counseling to improve substandard work before dismissal if work does not improve. Serious offenses, such as theft, use of drugs or alcohol while at work, and physical assault, may result in immediate dismissal without counseling. Employees who are terminated may file a grievance with (governing authority) within five days of termination. A grievance appeal must be made in writing.

If budget cuts necessitate a reduction in staffing levels, the library director will determine which positions can be cut to create the least overall negative effect on library services. The director's plan will be submitted to (governing authority) for approval before implementation. Longevity will be a primary factor in retaining staff, and whenever possible, staff will be moved into vacant positions for which they are qualified. Employees who are laid off will be paid for all unused vacation, compensatory time, and sick leave.

Approved by (governing body) on (insert date)

Signature of responsible representative

you know the policies of the library's governing authority and any procedures that must be followed? Are there different policies for terminating an employee during a probationary period? Are there actions (such as theft, misuse of funds, time, or library resources, violent behavior, excessive absence, harassment) that can lead to immediate dismissal?

- If budget cuts require a reduction in the workforce, how will decisions be made as to which positions will be cut? What rights and benefits are accorded those who are laid off? What outplacement resources are available within the organization and the community to aid the employee's transition?

- Do union rules, or agreements with employee groups, affect policies about terminations? Are any positions designated as serving at the pleasure of the director or another official? Are hourly employees subject to different rules than salaried staff? Are grievance procedures in place for employees to contest decisions about layoff or firing?

DRUG-FREE AND SMOKE-FREE WORKPLACE

Background

The use of unlawful drugs cannot be tolerated in the workplace. The use of legal drugs, including alcohol, that impair an employee's ability to do a good job, or that lead to increased absenteeism, may be considered a violation of the policies of the governing authority. Possession of illegal drugs can also result in health and safety issues for the staff and public. Parent institutions may also have implemented smoking bans and restrictions on where staff and patrons can smoke. Staff who work with children may be held to a higher standard because of the relationship of trust and their ability to influence minors.

Employees who step forward to get help for drug problems may be treated differently than employees who are trying to cover up their problem. Staff who drive as part of their job or who work with heavy equipment or dangerous materials may be subject to random drug testing or drug testing following any on-the-job accident. For more information on this subject consult "State Policy Adoption and Content: A Study of Drug Testing in the Workplace Legislation."[14]

Issues

- Does the library, or its governing authority, offer drug and alcohol abuse counseling through the health benefits or employee assistance program? Will an employee who recognizes that he or she has a problem and seeks help be allowed to seek treatment?

- Is an employee who is charged with or convicted of a crime that involves the manufacture, sale, or use of an illegal drug subject to termination? Is the employee required to disclose his or her arrest and/or conviction for drug-related offenses to the library administration?
- Are there state or local laws related to smoking in public areas? Has the parent institution or local government initiated smoking bans in the workplace? Does the parent institution offer smoking cessation treatment for employees? Are these programs covered by the library's health insurance or other health benefits program?

MODEL POLICY: DRUG-FREE AND SMOKE-FREE WORKPLACE

Employees of the (name of library) may not engage in the unlawful manufacture, distribution, possession, or use of illegal drugs and controlled substances in the workplace. Employees who violate the terms of this policy statement will be subject to immediate dismissal.

The library and its governing body recognize that the use of illegal drugs, or the abuse of legal substances such as prescription drugs or alcohol, may be a symptom of chemical dependency or mental health issues. Employees who pursue treatment under the library's health care program will be granted sick leave, vacation leave, or emergency leave. In compliance with local ordinances, and to protect the health of all employees and patrons, smoking is prohibited within the library and within 15 feet of the building. Smoking is not permitted in private offices. The library encourages employees to participate in smoking cessation programs available through the health care program, and sick leave may be used to attend smoking cessation classes or for health care appointments related necessary to quit smoking.

Approved by (governing body) on (insert date)

Signature of responsible representative

NOTES

1. Moore, Victoria. 2005. Sexual Harassment and the Library Don't Mix. *Library Mosaics* 16, no. 6 (November/December): 18–19.
2. Uhler, Scott F. and Rinda Y. Allison. 1997. A 10-Step Program: Reducing

the Likelihood of Sexual Harassment and the Possibility of Successful Sexual Harassment Lawsuits. *Illinois Libraries* 79, no. 2 (Spring): 64–65.

3. Tryon, Jonathan S. 1994. *The Librarian's Legal Companion.* New York: G.K. Hall.

4. "Obscenity" is a legal term, and is defined by the Miller standard. In *Miller v. California* (413 U.S. 15, 1973) the Court states: "a work may be subjected to state regulation if (a) whether 'the average person, applying contemporary, community standards' would find that the work, taken as a whole, appeals to the prurient interest; (b) whether the work depicts or describes, in a patently offensive way, sexual conduct specifically defined by the applicable state law; and (c) whether the work, taken as a whole, lacks serious literary, artistic, political or scientific value."

5. *Mainstream Loudoun v. Loudoun County Library* 24 F. Supp. 2d 552 (E.D. Va. 1998).

6. For an opposing viewpoint on nepotism, see by Robinson, Charles W. 2005. Anti-Nepotism. *Library Administrator's Digest,* 40, no. 2 (February): 1.

7. Peters, Paula. 2000. Seven Tips for Delivering Performance Feedback. *Supervision* 61, no. 5 (May): 12–14.

8. Stueart, Robert D. and Barbara Moran. 2007. *Library and Information Center Management.* Westport, CT: Libraries Unlimited.

9. Checklist for New Employee Orientation. 2000. *Library Personnel News* 13, no. 1–2 (Spring/Summer): 15–16.

10. U.S. Department of Labor. Fact Sheet #17A: Exemption for Executive, Administrative, Professional, Computer & Outside Sales Employees Under the Fair Labor Standards Act (FLSA). Available: www.dol.gov/esa/regs/compliance/whd/fairpay/fs17a_overview.htm. Accessed September 17, 2007.

11. Certified Public Library Administrator Program. CPLA Application. Available: www.ala-apa.org/certification/cplaapplication.html. Accessed September 18, 2007.

12. Manley, W. 2006. Is Love's Labor a Loss for Libraries? *American Libraries* 37 no. 2 (February): 64.

13. McCune, Bonnie. 2005. Diversity and Volunteers. *Colorado Libraries* 31, no. 3 (Fall): 43–44.

14. Lamothe, Scott. 2006. State Policy Adoption and Content: A Study of Drug Testing in the Workplace Legislation. *SAGE Public Administration Abstracts* 32, no. 4 (January): 25–39.

Chapter 4

Staff Conduct

The staff is the greatest asset of the library; without them the books, materials, equipment, and building are of little value. Staff has an obligation to maintain a high standard of ethical behavior. Because of their position with the library, some privileges may be available to them that are not afforded to the public. The public may also have the perception that staff receives special privileges that are, in fact, not granted them. Policies dealing with staff conduct and behavior ensure that every staff member knows the parameters and is aware that breach of conduct will be dealt with in a fair and consistent manner. Policies also help staff know their rights and provide a consistent way for sharing that information with the public. Affirming publicly that staff does have rights, as well as responsibilities, is important in case questions of appropriate conduct are raised. The policy may also lay out the appropriate path for complaints about staff conduct.

Additionally, staff dress, demeanor, and conduct set the tone for library patrons. If the library is to be seen as a friendly, open, business-like agency, staff must adhere to appropriate guidelines for conduct. Guidelines for conduct also help create an environment conducive to quality job performance and provide opportunities for each staff member to know what is expected of him or her.

Unfortunately, problems may make it necessary to conduct criminal background checks on staff and volunteers, especially those who will be working with children or who will be handling cash. It may be prudent to include a statement about background checks and problems that may arise in the library's policies. Some librarians purchase liability insurance to provide coverage in case of problems they may encounter as a supervisor or in dealing with volunteers and children. Staff should also be aware of issues such as the unauthorized "practice of law" that may manifest while trying to help patrons use reference materials.

CODE OF ETHICS

Background

Ethics are the principles of conduct and the moral values that govern the actions of an individual or a group. Although ethics are not synonymous with law, that is, they are not written, approved, and codified by a legislative body, ethics may, in the case of public employees, overlap with law. For example, the ethical standard in public libraries is to retain transparency in our operations. It is ethical to provide an open forum for the public to observe the board of trustees in action. It may also be a legal requirement that all meetings be posted and open for observers.

Principles of ethics are created to respond to actual and/or anticipated conflicts that occur in the real world and establish that, as a group, we recognize our obligation to society above our own self-interests. In public service organizations, honesty and integrity are the cornerstones of trust. A code of ethics also helps staff understand the values of the profession, even at times when the implementation of those values are at odds with one's personal feelings or beliefs. In fact, as the preamble to the American Library Association's Code of Ethics states, "Ethical dilemmas occur when values are in conflict." Because of these conflicts, codes of ethics can be controversial and should be thoroughly understood. A good reference for discussion is available from the Center for the Study of Ethics in the Professions, online at http://ethics.iit.edu/codes/coe.html. To help library staff understand issues related to ethical dilemmas, ALA's Committee on Professional Ethics provides scripts for skits that explore the issues.

For librarians and library staff, the American Library Association has established a code of ethics, revised in 1997 and amended in 2008, which is available on the Web site, www.ala.org/ala/oif/statementspols/codeofethics/codeethics.cfm. Additionally, some state library associations have either endorsed the American Library Association code or supplemented it with one of their own. Some state and local governmental bodies also establish codes of ethics for public employees.

Although library trustees are included in the American Library Association Code of Ethics, they have also recognized their ethical obligations and established their own code of ethics, which is set forth by and available through the Association for Library Trustees and Advocates, a division of the American Library Association.[1]

Issues

- Public employees are held to a high standard of conduct. The American Library Association Code of Ethics establishes high expectations for the profession. Public authority cannot enforce ethical guidelines, although state and local regulations may afford penalties for specific violations that may deal with ethical behavior. For example, the Code of Ethics stipulates that librarians must protect each user's right to privacy; most states also have laws mandating the confidentiality of patron records and affording penalties for violating that privacy. Do you know what laws in your community might enforce or relate to the ALA Code of Ethics or state library association statements on ethics? Ethics also generally prohibit public employees from accepting gifts that might influence their decisions. Many jurisdictions provide penalties for not adhering to this principle of ethics.
- Agree on a working definition of ethics. Richard Rubin recommends the following definition: "Ethical considerations are those involved in deciding what is good or right in terms of the treatment of human beings, human actions and values. It involves determining what people 'ought' to do, in distinction from what individuals may be forced to do, as in when one is legally required to act in a certain way."[2]
- Adherence to a code of ethics sets a professional apart from someone who is just doing a job. Do you agree that every library staff member, regardless of his or her educational degrees, salary, or position, is a library professional?
- Discuss how the tenets of the American Library Association Code of Ethics or statements on ethics by the state library association or other organizations will help the library director, board members, and staff understand the practical philosophy that supports the reasons for behaviors outlined in other policies. Our obligation is to the patron and service to the public. Use some of the skits provided through ALA's Committee on Professional Ethics to explore the issues.
- Endorsement of a code of ethics reminds us of this obligation and reinforces the organization's commitment to the highest quality of service and ethical treatment of people. A recent study conducted

---

MODEL POLICY: CODE OF ETHICS

The (name of library) endorses the American Library Association Code of Ethics and the (name of state library association) "Statement on Ethics" and expects that all staff will strive to maintain the highest levels of personal and professional integrity. Additionally, the trustees for (name of library) will follow the code of ethics established by the American Library Trustees Association (ALTA) in carrying out the duties and responsibilities of their office.

Public employees are held to a high standard of ethical behavior. No staff member may accept or solicit any gift or service that is offered to influence the employee's action, seeks to curry special privileges or favors, or is given to reward the employee for doing his or her job. Token items, such as food or flowers, may be accepted and shared with other staff. Items of value must be refused or returned to the giver. In exceptional cases where the item cannot be returned, the library director will donate the item to an appropriate local charity such as Goodwill. Staff is also prohibited from using their position for private gain and from transacting library business with any entity in which they have a financial interest (see also policy on "Selling and Soliciting in the Library").

Staff will receive training and opportunities to discuss case studies in areas of librarianship that might present ethical dilemmas. Staff is encouraged to discuss any concerns about their own handling of potential problems with their supervisors or the library director before or after a situation has occurred.

Approved by (governing body) on (insert date)

Signature of responsible representative

by the Texas Library Association (TLA) indicated that while almost 70 percent of Texas librarians were aware of the TLA Code of Ethics, far fewer were aware that ALA has a Code of Ethics.[3] How will you ensure that staff are aware of and understand the code of ethics established for the library?

- Are there local ordinances related to conflict of interest, use of office for private gain, or rules related to acceptance of gifts by public employees? These rules, if applicable, or the concepts they regulate should also be incorporated into a policy on ethics.

- Has staff received training in potential problem areas and do you have an ongoing process of continued discussion about situations that have or might present ethical problems?

DRESS CODE

Background

The way in which we dress sets the tone for many aspects of our work. While staff should be encouraged to dress for comfort and safety, some guidelines let staff know what is acceptable and what is discouraged or prohibited. Style of dress is very personal and many people use the way they dress and the jewelry or accessories they wear to make a personal statement. The library director has no authority to mandate personal beliefs or to regulate dress outside of the library, but the library, as a public institution, is generally not an appropriate place to make personal statements that intentionally or deliberately offend or inflame the public who come into the library.

Dress codes should be clear and unambiguous, and should be discussed thoroughly with new staff members to ensure that there is no misunderstanding about appropriate dress. In general, courts have held that employers have accepted justifications for establishing dress codes, including safety, health, business atmosphere, avoiding alienation of customers, and to minimize dissension and conflict. However, when establishing a dress code, an employer must take care not to unreasonably restrict dress and must be careful to enforce the dress code in a consistent and nondiscriminatory fashion. Recognize that what is considered acceptable attire, including body piercing, facial jewelry, and tattooing, changes over time, and fashions change. The pendulum swings both ways—business casual was very common in the 1990s and early 2000s, but as office wear became too casual many companies, and even universities, returned to a more formal dress code.[4]

If a dress code is established as policy, it is important that the code be consistently, uniformly, and fairly enforced. Irregular enforcement or uneven enforcement may result in the inability to enforce the dress code at a later date. Also, while it is probably impossible to set forth guidelines that cover every conceivable issue that may arise, it can be difficult to enforce compliance for something that is not included in the policy, and the courts have not upheld dress codes that are overly restrictive.[5]

Issues

- If the library is part of a larger governmental body, is there an over-riding dress code? Are you familiar with the prevailing business dress code for your community? Some areas of the country have dress codes that are more casual (in the South, for example, it is often acceptable for men to forgo ties during the summer). Smaller communities may view a casual style of dress as being "more friendly." Library staff should dress comfortably but suitably for the position held and the type of work performed. Children's librarians, for example, may be more comfortable wearing clothing that allows them to sit on the floor during story times, and teenagers may find librarians who are wearing casual clothing to be more approachable. Are there collective bargaining agreements in place that address appropriate attire?

- Standards should be tolerant to individual styles of dress, ethnic culture, and religious requirements. Staff with disabilities may also need to dress differently than one might expect for a business. Are you familiar with dress requirements for special situations? These situations may require leniency in style of dress, but no situation should permit staff to dress in a sloppy or unclean manner. Staff can also be expected to dress appropriately for their gender (mores are more tolerant toward women in masculine attire than they are toward men dressing in skirts and dresses), although some "states may protect dress as it relates to sexual preference."[6]

- Are you aware of current fashion trends that might temporarily change the way staff dresses? Will T-shirts be acceptable attire for any staff? If so, may staff wear T-shirts that promote causes, cultural icons, or statements of belief? Be careful about allowing slogans that support some causes while restricting others. Are you familiar with current slang, including words in foreign languages, that may appear on T-shirts?

- How tolerant is the community toward alternative fashions, such as body piercing, tattoos, and unusual hair fashions? Jewelry can also create image problems if it is excessively flamboyant, consists of obscene or illegal images (such as private body parts or drugs), or interferes with the staff member's ability to work. Be careful that regulations related to jewelry don't conflict with First Amendment rights. The courts have ruled that the personal display of an unobtrusive and minor religious symbol, such as a necklace with a cross, would not interfere with a library's purposes.[7]

- Personal hygiene can be a very touchy problem. A staff member who does not bathe frequently enough, has unclean hair, or uses excessive amounts of cologne creates an unpleasant and unprofessional environment. This managerial or supervisory problem must be dealt with tactfully. Keep in mind that some odors may be indicators of health problems, and the staff member may not even realize that there is a problem.

- Heavy odors, even those that are pleasant in moderation, can also trigger allergies or physical illness in others. Some organizations have instituted "fragrance-free" policies out of concern for indoor air quality. However, fragrance is ubiquitous in our lives and it can be extremely difficult to enforce such a fragrance-free policy with staff, much less with visitors and patrons.

- Does the work in some job categories require or allow a more lenient dress code? Some libraries distinguish between staff who work with the public and those who are behind the scenes out of the public eye, although in most small and medium sized libraries any staff member may be called into service to cover a public desk or meet with a citizen. Jobs that are typically filled by students or that require working in a messy environment often allow for more casual dress, but a dress code should mandate that casual does not mean sloppy, unsafe, or disruptive. Will volunteers also be subject to the dress code?

- Are there times when leisure clothing or costume would be appropriate? Some libraries encourage staff to dress "Western" for rodeo days, dress in costume for Halloween, or wear reading and library related T-shirts and jeans to kick off summer reading programs. Some libraries also designate Fridays as casual days, permitting staff to wear jeans or other casual attire. If casual or costume days are established, clothing should still be clean and appropriately modest (no belly dancer costumes or swimsuits). Keep in mind that casual should never mean sloppy!

- Have you considered the implications of the dress code so that requirements can be enforced in a consistent and nondiscriminatory manner? For example, it may be difficult to enforce a dress code that states "business casual attire" without defining what business casual means. A policy that requires women to wear hose might be discriminatory if men are not required to wear socks. Consider the ways in which the code might create problems and word the policy carefully. For example, a policy that states "no blue denim" may unnecessarily restrict the wearing of skirts and jumpers that are otherwise acceptable when the issue is really blue denim pants.

MODEL POLICY: DRESS CODE

Public image plays an important role in developing and maintaining support for the (name of library). In order to maintain a public image consistent with a professional organization, each staff member's dress and grooming will be appropriate for a business environment and in keeping with his or her work assignment. Health and safety standards must also be considered in dressing for work.

Clothing and accessories must be neat and clean, and should not draw inappropriate or disruptive attention to the individual. Staff members working with the public must dress appropriately for a casual business environment, defined as professional attire that is neat and tailored. Staff who primarily shelve materials, work outdoors, or whose work is confined to the back office areas may dress more casually, but shorts, halter tops, and bare feet are never permitted. T-shirts or other attire that promote political or religious causes, campaigns, or issues may not be worn. Obscenities, euphemisms or slang words for foul language, and foreign phrases that could be interpreted inappropriately are also not permitted. Jewelry and body art that is visible to the public should also not display obscenities or offensive language.

Every staff member must wear a library issued name badge at all times while on duty. Staff working in public area may not wear radio or cassette player headphones. Questions regarding appropriate attire or exceptions to the dress code must be directed to the library director.

Approved by (governing body) on (insert date)

_____

Signature of responsible representative

STAFF USE OF LIBRARY MATERIALS AND EQUIPMENT

Background

Staff has access to library materials and equipment to a greater degree than is afforded to the public. This access brings with it a higher degree of responsibility for ethical behavior. Staff must keep in mind that the needs of the community come first. They are not entitled to special privileges, such as lengthier checkout periods, due to their employment, although the library board or governing authority may wish to confer some degree of privilege as a benefit of employment. Additionally, ethics policies and regulations may preclude offering staff any benefit or service not within the scope of their employment agreement (salary, health insurance, etc.) that is not accorded to the general public.

Issues

- Is staff required to check out all materials for personal use outside of the library? Staff checkout adds to the circulation figures (library staff can also be library patrons) and maintains control over inventory. Additionally, requiring that all materials be checked out avoids allegations of theft and protects the staff from a potentially harmful situation.
- Are fines forgiven for overdue materials checked out by staff? This can be a reasonable perquisite if it is not abused. However, doing so should not violate any ethics policies. What constitutes abuse of circulation periods, and what action will take place if a staff member keeps material out for too long?
- Is staff required to pay fees for personal use of equipment (such as projectors, digital cameras, etc.) if fees are charged to patrons?

MODEL POLICY: STAFF USE OF LIBRARY MATERIALS AND EQUIPMENT

Staff must exercise extreme caution in the access and use of materials and equipment placed in their trust. Library employees are prohibited from using library facilities, equipment, supplies, or other resources for personal use, except to the extent that such resources are available to the public. Library materials or equipment taken for personal use must be checked out if they are to be removed from the library or if the item(s) will be kept away from the normal location for more than four hours. Large quantities of material should not be held out of the collection for extended periods for staff use.

Staff will not be charged for overdue fines or reserves, but will be subject to disciplinary action if materials are not returned and discharged before the system generates a second overdue notice. Staff may not make personal copies on the photocopier using the bypass key. Violation of any part of this policy may be considered theft of property or services and subject to disciplinary or legal actions.

Approved by (governing body) on (insert date)

Signature of responsible representative

- Will staff be permitted to make personal copies with the copier by-pass key or code? Even if the copier does not have a per-copy cost associated with it, paper and toner are used, and excessive staff copying depletes resources intended for the general public and for the daily operations of the library.

SELLING AND SOLICITING IN THE LIBRARY

Background

Staff and patrons have the right to work in or use the library without being subject to sales and solicitations by others. Selling and solicitation by patrons may be included in a policy dealing with distribution of materials in the library. Generally, it is best not to turn the library into a swap meet or bargaining floor.

Policies regarding interactions with other staff may be more lenient than are rules for interacting with patrons. Some staff may be prohibited, by the nature of their position, from having employment outside the library or from selling or buying items with the people under their supervision. In any case, appropriate selling or solicitation must be defined. Staff members who do not wish to avail themselves of offered items or services must be protected from real or perceived harassment. Care must be exercised to avoid any suggestion of improper or undue pressure on employees to purchase items from their supervisor(s) or fellow employees.

Issues

- Is there a staff lounge or other appropriate place for library employees to post announcements or solicitations? Are there local or state laws that govern staff interactions while on and off duty? Some organizations have strict interpretations about "public property" and provide a staff lounge for use only in taking a break and prohibit posting of personal notices, sales notices, or announcements that are not work related. Extra care must be taken to ensure that supervisors are not overtly or unintentionally creating an environment where subordinates feel obliged to make purchases.
- Do policies of the library's governing authority regulate outside employment by any categories of staff? How might staff who work outside the library interact with library patrons? For example, a clerk who also sells beauty supplies may meet customers at his or her home but should not handle business transactions at the library. Outside employment should not interfere with the employee's ability to perform library work.

> ## MODEL POLICY: SELLING AND SOLICITING IN THE LIBRARY
>
> It is recognized that library employees may engage in the sale of goods or services outside of their employment with the library. However, it is never appropriate to solicit business from staff or patrons during library work time. Soliciting business from patrons during off-work time while on library property is not permitted; however, staff may offer a business card if one is requested. Information regarding personal business may be distributed to other employees by placing ads on the staff bulletin board, posting information in the staff lounge, or by leaving catalogs or brochures in the staff lounge. Oral and/or written invitations to product parties or distribution of information may not be made through interoffice mail. Display of items for sale is not permitted on library property.
>
> Approved by (governing body) on (insert date)
>
> _____
> Signature of responsible representative

- Does the library's policy on use of meeting rooms permit selling in the meeting room? If so, staff should be able to apply for and use the meeting room as a private citizen under the same conditions stipulated for the public.

POLITICAL ACTIVITIES BY EMPLOYEES

Background

Everyone has the right to hold political opinions and to promote his or her political beliefs. However, such activities should be limited to off-work time and may not be appropriately pursued while representing the library. Library employees should never subject staff and patrons to proselytizing or lobbying. Additionally, in larger organizations, top-level staff may be precluded by their employment agreement from participating publicly in *any* political activity, even while off duty. (In part, this is because some organizations do not consider the director and other top-level staff to ever truly be "off duty.") Special care must be taken that staff do not appear to be lobbying or politicking on matters of local interest, especially those that affect the library, unless doing so is explicitly authorized by the governing body.

Issues

- Are there local ordinances or state laws that govern political activity by public employees that would include library employees? In some cases, management staff above a specific level are precluded from any political activity, even on their own time, especially when the activity involves local politics.
- Are the library and its staff subject to rules from a union or bargaining group? Does the library have a policy on distribution of materials in the library? Does it permit the distribution or posting of political information? Staff may be entitled to distribute information, as private citizens, in the information center or on a bulletin board under the same conditions as the public.
- Does the library have a Friends group or foundation that serves as a political advocacy group for the library? Often such groups can advocate when staff can't, but care must be taken to ensure that staff don't unwittingly get caught up in these activities.
- Bumper stickers, especially on library vehicles, may create problems. Who can decide what, if any, messages will appear on library vehicles? In general, the library cannot restrict personal expression on private vehicles, although in some cases organizations have tried to do so if the vehicle is parked in an employee parking lot.

MODEL POLICY: POLITICAL ACTIVITIES BY EMPLOYEES

Employees may engage in political activities on their own time. However, (jurisdictional authority) limits the employees' right to express their political opinion during work hours or as a representative of the library. Prohibited activities include, but are not limited to, wearing campaign or political buttons, distributing campaign or political literature except as permitted in the library's policy on "Distribution of Free Materials," and expressing political opinions while on work time. T-shirts or other attire that promote a particular political issue, person, or cause are not appropriate (see also "Dress Code"). Bumper stickers may not be applied to library property or library vehicles unless specifically approved by the library director.

Approved by (governing body) on (insert date)

Signature of responsible representative

DISCOUNTS ON STAFF PURCHASES

Background

Because libraries can buy books and other materials at a substantial discount, some libraries permit staff to make personal purchases through the library account. Care must be taken to see that this privilege does not result in undue time spent placing orders and collecting from staff. Patrons and staff in other city or county departments may also feel that the library should order materials for them if this privilege is not structured carefully. If this is a service the library wants to provide for other city or county departments, policy should establish conditions to avoid any improper use of public funds and to minimize staff time used for personal purchases. Care must also be taken to ensure that this privilege does not violate any ethics codes.

Issues

- Do the policies of the library's governing authority permit personal items to be ordered through the library's vendor with payment being made by the staff member?
- Does the library have a staff association? Often the staff association can establish its own account with a library vendor (Baker & Taylor or Ingram, for example), and association officers handle the orders and payment, removing the financial mechanics from the library's bill.
- Does the library or staff association want to handle cash, or must

---

MODEL POLICY: DISCOUNTS ON STAFF PURCHASES

Library staff members may order books and other library materials for personal use at a discount through the staff association. Discounts cannot be guaranteed, and books, once ordered, may not be returned unless received in damaged condition. Payment must be made, by check, within two workdays after the item is received. Abuse of this policy will result in loss of the privilege to purchase books through the library staff association. This privilege is limited to library staff and may be discontinued at any time at the discretion of the library director.

Approved by (governing body) on (insert date)

Signature of responsible representative

payment be made by check? Cash makes it harder to ensure proper credit and maintain a paper trail if problems arise.

- Does the library wish to offer this perquisite to employees of other city or county departments? Will doing so create a burden for library staff or interfere with their ability to carry out their own work?
- Does providing discounted purchasing for staff violate any ethics codes that cover library staff?

STAFF RELATIONS AND CELEBRATIONS

Background

We frequently spend more time with our coworkers than we do with our families. Coworkers should be encouraged to enjoy one another as individuals, required to respect everyone's abilities, and expected to treat one another with dignity and fairness. Parties and celebrations can be a time to pull people together, but, if not handled properly, these events can cause resentment and friction. No one should ever be required to participate in staff celebrations, contribute to gift funds, or in any way be coerced into socializing.

Issues

- Does the library have a staff association that organizes celebrations and staff events? Does that group have written guidelines to ensure that every staff member is treated equally in social events?
- Are there any policies or rules developed by the library's governing agency that restrict or prohibit recognition of birthdays, use of staff time or library funds for parties, etc.? Be sure that you are familiar with any ethics policies related to giving and accepting gifts that may be part of the larger organization. In some cases, state law may regulate the acceptance of gifts by public officials, even from other public employees.
- Can staff rooms and library meeting rooms be used for staff functions, or must all socializing be done off library property?
- Do you want to establish guidelines to reduce the number of parties and group functions? Depending on how large the staff is (do not forget volunteers!), individual celebration of birthdays can get out of hand.

MODEL POLICY: STAFF RELATIONS AND CELEBRATIONS

Good staff relations and the development of a cohesive work team benefit from some socializing. Therefore, the (name of library) encourages a reasonable amount of socializing and staff celebration so long as these events do not interfere with the normal flow of work. Birthdays should be celebrated one time per month, with all birthdays for that month recognized at the same time. Staff parties to celebrate holidays will be scheduled at times with minimal impact to service, and all service desks must be covered during parties. Every staff member is welcome to attend any party held during work hours on library property. Parties scheduled outside of work time and off library property are considered personal parties, but, in the interest of good staff relations, party planners are encouraged to include all staff members in the festivities.

Gifts between individual staff members are not prohibited, but group gifts should be given equitably. Solicitation for contributions for group gift should be done anonymously by routing an envelope. Supervisors may not accept gifts except for token, inexpensive items such as coffee mugs, pens, and candy, from the people they directly supervise.

Approved by (governing body) on (insert date)

_____
Signature of responsible representative

PURCHASING

Background

Staff who are involved in the ordering and purchasing of items, goods, and services for the library are generally bound by a high level of oversight to ensure that public dollars are spent fairly and in the best interests of the public. In larger libraries, purchasing may be restricted to a few staff members who receive special training to ensure that state and local laws and regulations are followed. In smaller libraries, several people may be involved in purchasing and procedures may be lax or flexible. Keep in mind that some purchases, especially for larger amounts of money, may need to go through several people to provide "checks and balances," but the library may also have a petty cash fund or provide purchasing (credit) cards for some staff.

Issues

- Who is authorized by your governing body to act as a purchasing agent for the library? Has that person (or persons) received training related to bid requirements, approval limits, contracting, and other issues (such as minority vendors, vendor requirements, etc.)?
- How will bidding and authorization of purchases be handled? Is any of the purchasing process handled by another entity within the library's governmental structure?
- Is there a purchasing card, similar to a credit card, available for small purchases, or does the purchaser need to obtain funds from petty cash? What are the criteria that an employee should meet to be eligible to use the purchasing card (job description, tenure, etc.)? Will employees be trained on the proper method for keeping a transaction log of purchases made with the purchasing card? What items, regardless of cost, are not allowable for charge to the purchasing card? How will the petty cash account and credit card purchases be monitored and audited?

MODEL POLICY: PURCHASING

Only the library director, the office manager, and department managers are authorized to obligate or expend funds on behalf of the (name of library). Purchases for more than $100.00 require approval from the library director. Purchases of goods or services costing more than $500.00 shall require a minimum of two bids unless the library director has determined that there is only one source for the purchase. Department managers are responsible for ensuring that funds are expended as determined within the budget. To facilitate purchases that are less than $500.00, credit cards will be issued to department managers. These cards may be used only for official library business and must be surrendered upon termination of employment or at the request of the library director. Prior to payment of credit card charges, the office manager will approve the monthly statement of charges. Purchases that are greater than $500.00 but less than $5,000.00 may be made only by purchase order. Any purchases that are greater than $5,000.00 require the approval of the library's board of trustees.

Approved by (governing body) on (insert date)

Signature of responsible representative

EMERGENCY AND DISASTER PREPAREDNESS

Background

We have all come to recognize the need to be ready for the unexpected. Whether the emergency is a local crisis, a natural disaster, or the result of unforeseeable conditions, staff should know what is expected of them and how to handle the crisis. Keep in mind that common sense must always be exercised, as it is impossible to foresee every condition and every need in an unforeseeable situation. A policy on dealing with emergencies should provide guidance as to what defines an emergency or disaster, who is responsible for declaring the emergency, and what happens to protect human life, assist those who are injured, and, to the extent possible, protect public and private property. When developing a policy for dealing with emergencies, you will want to consider local conditions—severe winter storms or frequent tornadoes may require more specific guidance in some areas of the country.

Following 9/11 and the Hurricane Katrina and Rita disasters, it is imperative that every library is prepared not only for dealing with an emergency, but also for dealing with the aftermath. If your library does not have a disaster plan in place, use resources like Beth Dempsey's article, "Responding to Disaster"[8] and *Disaster Response and Planning for Libraries*, 2nd edition, by Miriam B. Kahn for more detailed information.

Issues

- What constitutes an emergency? Emergencies are not always of monumental proportion, such as floods or earthquakes, but may be as simple as having no heat in the library during the dead of winter. If the library is part of a larger organization, does that organization have a policy for dealing with emergencies?
- Does the library, or its governing body, have a full-scale emergency preparedness plan? Have you discussed emergency preparedness and responses with local disaster and emergency preparedness agencies? Are you familiar with guidelines for reacting to a variety of emergency situations? Do you have emergency kits, including battery-powered emergency radios, available?
- Does staff know how to deal with suspicious packages that are left in the building? What happens if a bomb threat is phoned in to the library?
- Under what circumstances should the library be evacuated? To where can patrons and staff safely be evacuated? For example, it may be best to encourage people to remain in the library during a weather-related emergency rather than trying to send people home.

The basement may or may not be the best location for containing staff and patrons if there were a chemical spill near the library.

- Are there guidelines in place if people must be contained inside the library building for an extended period of time? It may be necessary in some areas of the country, for example, areas prone to floods, tornadoes, etc., to have a designated shelter area with a reserve of survival supplies, such as bottled water, light snacks, etc.
- Who has the authority to close the library due to a localized emergency? To whom does this closure need to be reported? Who will decide whether to close for the day or simply delay opening? How will this information be communicated to staff? Do the media need to be informed, and, if so, who will relay information to reporters?
- Has staff received training on how to deal with emergencies? Does the library conduct regular fire drills or other tests to evacuate the building? Has a gathering place been designated so that management can ensure that all staff is accounted for?
- Are emergencies to be handled differently if they occur while the library is closed?
- While many emergencies are resolved quickly, how will employee pay be handled if an emergency closes the library for a lengthy period of time? Can staff be reassigned to other work locations? Are some staff expected to report to work during an emergency while others are told not to report?
- How will unattended children be handled if the library is going to close early due to an emergency? Even children who are old enough to be in the library without parental supervision may need guidance and assistance during an emergency. Is staff permitted to transport children to a safe area or to the child's home in an emergency?
- Who has emergency phone numbers for key staff and other officials who need to be notified of an emergency at the library? What reports need to be made following an emergency or disaster, and who is responsible for making this report? What damage assessments will be made following the emergency, and who is responsible for compiling those assessments?

MODEL POLICY: EMERGENCIES AND DISASTERS

The library director (or designee) may close the (name of library) when, in his or her best judgment, conditions are such that they pose a safety risk or danger to staff and patrons. Department managers will alert the library director (or designee) when conditions warrant closure. Conditions that warrant closure of the library include those that endanger the health or safety of the staff or public. Staff members who are sent home will be paid for the remainder of their normal work shift.

If the building must be evacuated, the staff member in charge must ensure that all members of the public and staff have left the building. The building will then be secured to the extent possible (doors locked, security system armed, etc.) based on the current situation. The library director and the police department are to be informed of the evacuation and closure as quickly as it is safe to do so.

Staff should take care to ensure that children under the age of 16 have safe passage home if the library must close. If a parent or guardian cannot be contacted, two staff members (or a staff member and volunteer) must stay with the child until transportation can be arranged. If possible, contact the police. Under only the most severe circumstances, when police and other safety officers are not available and the situation appears to be long-term, will staff transport a child in their own or a library vehicle.

Emergency kits, including basic first aid supplies, a flashlight and batteries, biological hazard gloves and masks, and a battery-operated radio, will be maintained at the circulation desk and in the director's office. The kits will be checked monthly to ensure that all items are available and supplies are replenished as needed. In case of a disaster requiring shelter, e.g., tornado, flood, etc., staff should direct other staff and patrons to the basement where basic survival supplies are maintained.

In the event that inclement weather or other conditions make it unsafe to open the library, the library director will notify staff that they should not report to work or that the library will open on a delayed schedule. Staff members who are notified that they should not report to work will receive their regular pay. Staff on sick or vacation leave during an emergency closure will have their time charged to those pay accounts. Depending on the exact nature of the emergency closure, key staff may be required to report to work. Failure to report to work when directed may result in disciplinary action. The library director may also assign staff to work at different locations or for other city departments during times when the library is closed.

Following any emergency, department managers must assess any damage to their areas of operation and submit a report to the library director. The library director will provide a report on the emergency and its handling to the board of directors at their next meeting.

Approved by (governing body) on (insert date)

_____

Signature of responsible representative

NOTES

1. American Library Trustee Association. Ethics Statement for Public Library Trustees. Available: www.ala.org/ala/alta/altapubs/PDFaltaethicsstatement.pdf. Accessed September 26, 2007.
2. Rubin, Richard. 1991. Ethical Issues in Library Personnel Management. *Journal of Library Administration* 14, no. 4 (September): 1–16.
3. Hoffman, Kathy. 2005. Professional Ethics and Librarianship. *Texas Library Journal* 81, no. 3 (Fall): 7–11.
4. Damast, Alison. 2007. Return of the Dress Code. *Business Week Online*, August 29, p. 15.
5. Strict Dress Code Blocked by Judge. 2007. *New York Times*, July 4, p. A11.
6. Findley, Henry et. al. 2005–2006. Dress and Grooming Standards: How Legal Are They? *Journal of Individual Employment Rights*, 12 no. 2: 165–182.
7. Judge: Dress Code Unconstitutional. 2003. *American Libraries* 34, no. 9 (October): 17.
8. Dempsey, Beth. 2005. Responding to Disaster. *Library Journal* 130, supp. (December): 6–8.

Chapter 5

Access to Library Services

Libraries are more than collections of books and other materials in a building. The library provides services and programs that can range from public meeting places to book discussions to assistance with homework. Policies that clearly explain what library services and programs are available, to whom, and under what conditions will go far toward ensuring fair and equitable access to everything the library can offer to everyone in the community. The library should also establish its primary service responses or priorities, based on the Public Library Association's (PLA) *The New Planning for Results: A Streamlined Approach* and the 2007 *Public Library Service Responses*, or a similar planning process. Your policy manual should include a mission statement that supports those service responses. A synopsis of the PLA service responses is included in Resource H of this book.

AMERICANS WITH DISABILITIES ACT

Background

The passage of Public Law 101-336, the Americans with Disabilities Act of 1990 (usually referred to as the ADA), by the United States Congress in July 1990 was viewed by many as the "Emancipation Proclamation" for the millions of Americans who have one or more physical or mental disabilities. This comprehensive law requires changes in a variety of areas, including transportation, telecommunications, employment, and public accommodation.[1] So many years after the act's passage, it may seem obvious that libraries must comply with the section of the Americans with Disabilities Act dealing with public accommodation, but your policies should demonstrate the library's commitment to access for all patrons. (Employers, including libraries, must also have nondiscriminatory job application procedures, qualification standards, selection criteria, and conditions of employment, but these issues are addressed in the employment policies of the library or by the governing body that oversees the personnel needs of the library. If you have not read the ADA, copies are available on the Internet through several sites, including the Job Accommodation Network, http://janweb.icdi.wvu.edu/. The U.S. Department of Justice also provides an ADA Information Line, toll-free at 800-514-0301.) Additionally, over time federal agencies and other organizations have enhanced the resources available to help businesses do a better job complying with the letter and spirit of the law. One resource is the *ADA Best Practices Toolkit for State and Local Governments*, updated in 2007 and available online at www.usdoj.gov/crt/ada/pcatoolkit/ toolkitmain.htm, which "is designed to teach state and local government officials how to identify and fix problems that prevent people with disabilities from gaining equal access to state and local government programs, services, and activities. It will also teach state and local officials how to conduct accessibility surveys of their buildings and facilities to identify and remove architectural barriers to access."[2]

All government facilities and all entities that serve the public must make their buildings and services accessible to persons with disabilities. Physical barriers should be removed and auxiliary aids and services must be provided to individuals with disabilities. Reasonable accommodation must be made to ensure that, whenever possible, persons with disabilities can use library services and gain access to public areas without assistance or intervention. If areas or services cannot be made accessible, other methods to deliver the same service must be provided (for example, retrieving items stored on high shelves, providing library forms and documents in alternative formats, or relocating a program to an accessible area). Although it is a little dated, additional information on making library facilities and services accessible is available in *The Americans with Disabilities Act: Its Impact on Libraries* edited by Joanne L. Crispin. This resource includes a detailed self-evaluation survey. *The ADA Library Kit: Sample ADA–Related Documents to Help You Implement the Law*, edited by Kathleen Mayo and Ruth O'Donnell, offers sample community surveys, accommodation forms and notices, compliance plans, and staff training information. "The Spirit of the Law: When ADA Compliance Means Overall Excellence in Service to Patrons with Disabilities" by Kent Oliver details the comprehensive program executed by the Johnson County Library in Kansas. In *Planning for Library Services to People with Disabilities*, Rhea Joyce Rubin has created a planning process to help libraries consider all of the issues related to ADA.

In addition to making facilities accessible, libraries have a legal responsibility to make content available to patrons with disabilities. In the past, this primarily involved providing auditory or braille versions of library-created documents or providing sign interpreters at library meetings and programs. The increased availability of digital or electronic content may now offer other alternatives for providing access, including providing alternative text for visual images on Web sites, providing tools that permit the size of text to be changed on a screen, or permitting headphones to be used with speech synthesizing software. *The Library's Legal Answer Book* by Mary Minow and Tomas A. Lipinski includes an extensive chapter on digital resources and patrons with disabilities that offers additional information on how to meet the needs of disabled patrons while complying with the law. A concise look at adaptive technology is provided in the article "Assistive Technology: 10 Things To Know" by Janet Hopkins,[3] and there are any number of resources for helping to make Web sites accessible.

The Americans with Disabilities Act provides the legal basis to end discrimination, and a policy supporting ADA demonstrates that the library is committed to providing access to its facilities and services. Training for staff and the inclusion of people with disabilities on library advisory committees, governing boards, and related citizen input groups will encourage lasting and real changes.

Issues

- Have you read the Americans with Disabilities Act of 1990 and are you familiar with its requirements? Has the library completed an ADA self-evaluation, as required by the law, and is a compliance plan in place? Has the plan been updated and reviewed recently? Have you reviewed recent documents related to compliance with the ADA?

- Is a procedure in place for persons with disabilities to request accommodation or provide input or complaints about services? (See also the policy on "Public Participation in Library Decision Making.")

- Do you understand the laws related to service animals? The ADA requires that most businesses allow people with disabilities to bring their service animals into any areas where customers are generally allowed. Not all service animals are guide dogs for the blind, nor are they always dogs. The ADA defines a service animal as any guide dog, signal dog, or other animal trained to provide assistance to an individual with a disability regardless of whether the animal has been licensed or certified by a state or local government.

- Do you know what areas of the library building might pose problems for persons with disabilities? Have you examined ways to correct or adjust those problems or to offer the same service in a different, more accessible location in the library?
- Have you included local agencies, organizations, and disability groups in the planning process? Do you have up-to-date contact information on those resources? Do you know how to locate sign language interpreters, braille services, etc.? Have you included funds in the

---

MODEL POLICY: AMERICANS WITH DISABILITIES ACT

The (name of library) strives to provide equal access equal access to employment opportunities and to all library facilities, activities, and programs in adherence to the Americans with Disabilities Act of 1990. The (name of library) does not discriminate on the basis of disability in the admission or access to, or treatment or employment in, its library programs or services. The library will take appropriate steps to ensure that communications with job applicants, library patrons, and members of the public with disabilities are as effective as communications with others.

The library has completed a self-evaluation study and a compliance plan, both of which are available for review in print and alternate formats. The library welcomes input from persons with disabilities about ways the library can more completely serve them, and every effort will be made to accommodate the needs of persons with disabilities. Individuals with service animals are welcome in areas where pets or animals are not normally permitted. Library materials are provided in various formats and, to the extent possible, equipment and visual aids are provided to assist in using library resources.

Questions about ADA compliance and complaints or suggestions about accessibility of library facilities, activities, and programs should be addressed to the library director, (provide address and telephone number) or to the (parent organization's) ADA coordinator.

Approved by (governing body) on (insert date)

Signature of responsible representative

budget to pay for interpreters, braille services, etc., if they are requested?

- Has staff received training on the ADA, and do they know how to offer accommodation, if requested? Are basic library informational materials, such as the policy manual, registration cards, and general information brochures available in alternate formats (e.g., braille, large print, recording)?

- Does the library or its parent organization have a designated ADA coordinator? To whom should complaints or questions about compliance with the ADA be directed? How does a library patron or potential applicant request accommodation?

DATA PRIVACY POLICY

Background

Protecting privacy and confidentially have long been basic tenets of librarianship, and many states have laws related to confidentiality of patron library records. As more information is available in electronic files, concerns about misuse of personal information, identity theft, and "data mining," have led many organizations to implement policies specifically related to privacy and to outline how personal information that is obtained as part of the regular course of business will be used. The implementation of radio frequency identification (RFID) technology is adding to privacy concerns and has led the American Library Association to add privacy and confidentiality guidelines specifically for this technology.[4] For a full review of the issues related to technology and privacy, consult the many articles in "Policy and Library Technology" by Walt Crawford, the March/April 2005 issue of *Library Technology Reports*, or *What Every Librarian Should Know about Electronic Privacy* by Jeannette Woodward.

Because much of the data collecting technology is based on patrons opting in to use services or is connected to the use of publicly accessible resources, this concern is different from and broader than confidentiality of patron record laws. Technology has added complexities to the library's ability to protect privacy. For example, automated circulation systems generally delete information after it is no longer relevant (i.e., the patron has returned the item borrowed). Computers electronically track sites visited, the type of information requested, and information submitted via online forms. This information may be stored by "cookies" or held in the computer history. While computers can be set to delete history and clear the cache, it can be difficult, if not impossible to guarantee privacy in all areas of the computer.

Additionally, it is impossible to guarantee the security of any computer network. While the library has a strong obligation to provide as much protection as possible, complete security cannot be assured. However, as Walt Crawford points out, "If your library proceeds with a new technology that *does* affect privacy and confidentiality, and you haven't addressed those issues in advance, there's a good chance someone else will address them for you."[5]

Issues

- Does state law address confidentiality of patron records? Have those laws been updated to reflect new technology and the ways in which the technology is used?
- Do you have a policy in place to cover confidentiality? Has the library board adopted the ALA statement, "Privacy: An Interpretation of the Library Bill of Rights?" Also review ALA's "Resolution on Radio Frequency Identification (RFID) Technology and Privacy Principles," a copy of which is included in Resource D of this manual. Both documents will help library managers and governing authorities understand some of the issues libraries are facing.
- Are laws in place that specify how long specific government records, such as library card registration forms, must be maintained? Does the library have a plan in place to destroy records once they are no longer needed?
- Does the library share patron registration information with any other organization, government department, or business? For example, are new patron names and contact information regularly forwarded to the Friends of the Library for use in soliciting memberships?
- What type of information is regularly collected about patrons? How is that information used? How is it stored? Who has access to the information once it is collected? What safeguards are in place to protect stored information?
- Are there library services that can be accessed without revealing personal information? Does the library's Web site collect information for statistics and use data? Does the library request contact information for questions or comments submitted via library Web pages? For example, what information does a patron give when submitting an interlibrary loan request via the library's online catalog or when submitting an "Ask the Reference Desk" question?
- Are there services that patrons can opt-in to use that link to their private information? For example, some online catalogs allow patrons to maintain a list of books they have read or a "wish list" of books they want to read. Patrons may also be able to indicate that

they wish to receive e-mail reminders when new books arrive on a topic of interest.

- Does the library utilize any radio frequency identification (RFID) technology? Have you read "RFID in Libraries: Privacy and Confidentiality Guidelines" released by the American Library Association?
- How will you alert patrons to changes in the type of information collected by the library or changes to the way information will be used?

MODEL POLICY: DATA PRIVACY

The (name of library) is committed to protecting the privacy of our patrons. We will limit requests for personal information to that which is necessary to conduct library business. Personal information gathered, such as name, address, telephone number, e-mail address, photograph, driver's license number, etc., will be used only for the purposes of identification and accountability for library materials. Information related to materials borrowed or used will not be disclosed except as required to retrieve items that are overdue or to collect fines and fees owed to the library. The library occasionally conducts promotional campaigns to inform the community of our services. The library at those times use patron e-mail or postal address for the library's internal mailing lists.

Nonpersonal information about visits to the library's Web site or use of electronic resources may be collected. This information is used for system administration and to calculate usage statistics. No personal information collected is connected to usage information.

Personal information will not be sold, leased, or otherwise shared with any other organizations or outside parties, unless specifically required by law. Information about library users, materials borrowed, or services utilized are private, subject to the provisions of The USA PATRIOT Act and state laws related to confidentiality of patron records. This information will be secured, and we will attempt to notify library patrons of any breaches in the security that result in theft of records.

Changes to the library's privacy policy will be posted on the library's Web site and at the library circulation desk and will be e-mailed to those patrons who have provided an e-mail address as part of their contact information.

Approved by (governing body) on (insert date)

Signature of responsible representative

PUBLIC PARTICIPATION IN LIBRARY DECISION MAKING

Background

To provide sufficient opportunity for the public to express opinions and provide input into library operations, policies, and procedures, both through policy and by practice, the library should encourage communication through a variety of methods. Meetings, such as those of the library board, should be announced ahead of time, and visitors should be welcome. If the board is a governing board, state laws on open meetings may require that meetings be open to anyone. Provide as many different avenues for public input as possible. Remember that younger patrons may prefer electronic communication methods, while older patrons may rely on mail and telephone conversations.

Written and oral communications should receive prompt response from the library director or other appropriate staff member. If you truly want to know what the community is thinking, keep your doors as open as possible and acknowledge calls and letters, even if you cannot make the desired changes or appease the complainant. Citizens should be part of any formal planning process and their participation in the development of library programs, services, and policy should be welcomed and encouraged.

Issues

- What kinds of public meetings are held that might offer an open forum for citizen input? How can these meetings be advertised and announced? Are meetings, particularly library board meetings, subject to any open meeting regulations? Meetings of governing boards are generally required to be posted and open to citizens wishing to attend. State law may also regulate advisory boards, but even if they are not subject to open meeting regulations, anyone who wishes to attend should be welcome.
- Are people truly welcomed when they call for information about meetings, or when they attend them? A cliquish group will discourage participation by citizens. Too many rules about attendance (such as signing up too far in advance, submitting information ahead of time) will discourage some people from showing up.
- When are meetings and public forums scheduled? Do the times and days encourage attendance by as many affected citizens as possible? Care should be taken not to exclude any group of citizens. Opportunities for general public input should be placed at the beginning of the agenda. It is discouraging to make visitors wait until the end of the meeting to express their opinion. Some method for

control of the meeting, such as *Robert's Rules of Order or Sturgis Standard Code of Parliamentary Procedure,* should be used.
- How will the library director respond to telephone calls from citi-

---

MODEL POLICY: PUBLIC PARTICIPATION IN LIBRARY DECISION MAKING

The (name of library) shall provide a variety of mechanisms for members of the public to present their questions and concerns about its programs, services, and other library-related matters. Residents and others who have an interest in the library are welcome at any open meeting of the library board either as observers or to present information and concerns to the board.

Library board meetings will be held in compliance with state laws governing meetings of regulatory groups (cite appropriate law). Any member of the public who wishes to speak to the board is asked to register on arrival, indicate group affiliation if speaking on behalf of anyone other than self, and to limit comments and general information to five minutes. Library administration and the board welcome written documentation to support or restate information and concerns, but written documents are not required. Any group or individual wishing to place a library-related item on the official agenda for action should contact the library director one week in advance.

When public information gathering forums are planned, care will be taken to schedule forums at times that are convenient to potential participants. If necessary, several forums may be scheduled to allow maximum input into library service decisions. Sign interpretation will be provided if requested 24 hours in advance.

Telephone calls, letters, and visits to the library director are encouraged, and the director maintains an open-door policy. Appointments to meet with the director are encouraged, but not required. The library director or appropriate staff will respond to letters and telephone calls within five workdays. Comments placed in the library's suggestion box will receive a personal response, if desired. Responses to questions and comments of general interest may also be addressed in the library newsletter.

Approved by (governing body) on (insert date)

Signature of responsible representative

zens? Do you have an open-door policy that welcomes citizens to visit without an appointment? Are telephone calls and visitors screened? Other methods to encourage input and comments might include suggestion boxes, library newsletters, a complaint hotline, or informal gatherings (brown bag lunches, coffees, etc.).

HOURS OF OPERATION

Background

Staffing levels and the budget will play an essential role in determining how many hours the library can be open each week. Hours of operation should be established to meet the needs of library users and to maximize accessibility of the collection, services, and staff. Keep in mind that schedules may need to change seasonally based on community needs (fewer evening hours in summer, Saturday hours during the school year, holiday closings). Additionally, hours of operation may be extended beyond the traditional hours of business to include after-hours telephone assistance.

Once hours are established they should be reviewed on a regular basis but should not be frequently or arbitrarily changed. The written policy should establish general practices but need not indicate exact days and hours of operation. Remember that the policy sets general guidelines. If exact days and hours are included in the policy, the policy will need to be revised and reapproved every time library hours change.

Issues

- Are there state, regional, or local regulations or standards regarding the minimum number of hours the library must be open? Do regulations stipulate that the library must be staffed by a specific number of employees when open? Do rules require that paid staff volunteers run the library for a stipulated period of time?
- Do you know what days and hours the community wants the library to be open? Have you surveyed the public to establish priority use times and potential times of high use? Does the library need to change hours seasonally or to meet specific short-term needs? While staffing may not be sufficient to keep the library open all hours that are desired, the schedule should be established to best meet the needs of the community, not the staff.
- Does the library have times when temporary staffing shortages occur? How difficult is it to fill vacant positions? Are qualified board members or volunteers available to cover service desks when paid staff is not available due to staff vacancies, illness, vacation, or other absence?

> **MODEL POLICY: HOURS OF OPERATION**
>
> The (name of library) will be open a minimum of (establish number) hours each week. The library director, with the approval of (governing body), will determine the days and daily hours of operation. Summer and holiday schedules will be established to maximize staffing during periods of heavy and light library usage. Regular and holiday schedules for the calendar year will be posted on the library's Web site.
>
> The library will close on the holidays approved by (governing body) and at other times deemed necessary by the library director with the approval of (governing body). Except in the case of emergencies, notice of closings will be posted in the library two weeks in advance and will be reported to the local news media.
>
> Regularly scheduled hours of operation will be established to best meet the needs of library users and will be evaluated by survey and/or public input on a regular basis.
>
> Approved by (governing body) on (insert date)
>
> _____
> Signature of responsible representative

- Is assistance available for remote users of library resources, such as the online catalog and databases, after normal business hours?
- Who has the authority to close the library in case of an emergency, such as bad weather, shortage of staff, or when problems with the building occur? How will the public be notified about changes to the posted hours whether due to an emergency or because of other factors?

PUBLIC USE OF COMPUTERS

Background

Today, libraries provide many services via computers, not least of which is the online catalog of library holdings and access to electronic databases. Even though computers have become ubiquitous in our society, libraries also remain one of the few places where everyone and anyone can have access to computers to learn their use, improve computing skills, try out software, or perform tasks at little or no cost. Computers also provide access to a growing range of library resources, including downloadable e-books, audiobooks, and video files. Even with more computers in the library and the prevalence of laptops, smart phones, PDAs, and wireless Internet access, most libraries find that staff spends a lot of time dealing with issues related to access to the library's computers and how the public is using those computers.

Any library that provides computers for public use needs a written policy that establishes guidelines for equitable and fair access, maintaining expensive and often irreplaceable equipment, and reducing the need for staff intervention. Many libraries make stand-alone, non-networked computers available to the public for word processing, self-education, and use of software packages; however, for some patrons the library remains the only place where free access to the Internet and other sources of electronic information is available.

This policy focuses on providing equitable access to computers for personal use. A more thorough look at use of the Internet by the public and acceptable use policies is included in Chapter 8, "Reference and Information Services." The complexities of networked computer systems and the rapid rate at which technology is changing and improving make it essential that all policies dealing with computers, the Internet, networked resources, and access to electronic information be reviewed regularly.

Issues

- Have staff and volunteers received adequate training and time to learn and maintain their own computer skills? Will staff provide any training for patrons on basic computer skills and/or to troubleshoot software problems?
- In addition to the library's online catalog, electronic resources, and the Internet, for what other purposes might the public want to use library computers?
- Has the library's governing authority reviewed and adopted the Library Bill of Rights and its interpretation, "Access to Electronic Information, Services, and Networks?"
- How available are computers in your community? Do young people have significant access to computers at school? Are there businesses in the community that rent computer access time or will the library be the only available place for public use of computers?
- What software is available for use on the public-access computer(s)? Will patrons be permitted to load additional programs for their own use? Will the library accept donations of software, and if so, will donated software be upgraded with library funds? Does staff understand the difference between freeware, shareware, and licensed products subject to copyright?

MODEL POLICY: PUBLIC USE OF COMPUTERS

The (name of library) provides a variety of computers for public use. Online library catalog computers access the library's holdings and do not provide access to other resources, including the Internet. Stand-alone computers and software programs are provided to permit patrons to improve computer skills, test new computer programs, and enhance self-learning through self-improvement and testing software (Typing Tutor, GED, etc.). Software is purchased according to the collection development policy to support specific areas of library service. Recommendations for additional software purchases are welcome and will be handled according to the collection development policy. The library does not attempt to have the latest version of any particular software program. Programs are selected, updated, and discarded according to the collection development policy. Computers are also provided that offer access to the Internet and to the library's online databases.

The library will establish and post a schedule of sessions for general computer orientation. During the general orientation, library staff will explain correct operating procedures and discuss rules for use of the computer(s). All users will be required to sign a user agreement form, indicating that they understand the rules and procedures established for computer use and will comply with relevant copyright laws. Library staff cannot provide training on computer technology or software; however, online tutorials and self-instructional videos or DVDs may be available for some software programs. Community groups that provide software training may schedule free public classes with the approval of the library director, and the library will promote those classes, when available.

Users agree to observe all copyright and licensing laws and will not duplicate any computer programs or documentation unless expressly labeled as being "in the public domain" or "shareware." No personal software may be loaded on library computer hard drives without written permission from the library director. No private files may be stored on the library computer(s), and any files left on the computers will be deleted. Users will supply their own recording media (diskettes or portable storage devices) when needed, but must check to ensure that the computer being used can support the desired storage media.

Computer time may be reserved for one-hour blocks of time up to one week in advance. No more than one hour per day may be reserved. When no reservation has been scheduled, the computer(s) is available on a first-come, first-serve basis for one hour. Computer time and res-

> ervations are available to all patrons, regardless of age, who have a current user agreement on file. Generally, no more than two people should be sharing the computer at the same time, and each user must have signed a user agreement form.
>
> Approved by (governing body) on (insert date)
>
> ————————————————————————————————
> Signature of responsible representative

- Will any of the computers include disk drives that allow patrons to save files? If so, will patrons be required to supply their own storage devices, such as diskettes, or will they be available for purchase? Will patrons be permitted to use jump drives or other portable storage devices to load and save information?
- Will fees be charged for printing? Any charges should be consistent with fees charged for similar services in the library (fax, photocopies, database searching) and should generally be based on actual costs to provide the materials or service.
- Do you know what level of computer use is anticipated? Can patrons reserve computer time either through a computer reservation software system or at a service desk? Will time be limited to allow access to patrons who are waiting? Will "express" computers be available for quick use without reservation? Is sufficient staff available to take reservations for computer time, orient new users, and assist with problems? Has any part of the reservation system been automated?
- How will patrons be informed about rules and procedures related to the use of the library's computers? Do you want each user to sign an agreement, indicating that the person understands the rules, knows basic techniques of computer use, and will be responsible for damage caused by negligence or misuse? Can general orientation sessions be scheduled, or will staff review correct operating procedures and rules on an individual basis?
- Will computer users be required to have a valid library card? Is a library card required for the computer reservation system? Will those without library cards be accommodated (remember that travelers often visit public libraries to use the computers)?

INTERNET ACCESS

Background

The Internet has dramatically changed the way libraries operate. In most areas of the country, even the smallest, most remote library has access to a multitude of electronic resources via the Internet at a relatively low cost. Uses of the Internet can be for functions as varied as instant messaging and chatting with friends or colleagues to more traditional library functions such as searching online catalogs from other libraries to researching reference questions and reading newspaper articles. For many libraries, the Internet has become a major way to communicate with colleagues, vendors, and patrons.

A written policy establishes the conditions under which the Internet will be made available to the public. It establishes who on staff will have personal accounts, how much time might be devoted to monitoring listservs and blogs, and how access will be granted to library patrons.

If patrons will also have direct, unmediated access to the Internet, policy guidelines can be included here to determine the extent of access and establish the parameters of acceptable use of the Internet. Many libraries feel more comfortable, however, having a separate "Internet Use" policy that establishes guidelines for acceptable use. A more thorough examination of acceptable use of the Internet by patrons is included in Chapter 8.

While many of the issues in this section deal with staff use of the Internet (and therefore could have been included in Chapter 4, "Staff Conduct"), the discussion is included here because staff access and patron access are closely related. The Internet has become an essential tool for all aspects of staff work as well as a critical resource for many patrons.

It is important to remember that the Internet is another library resource and is not inherently more valuable than other resources. However, the Internet and access to its resources, good and not so good, can cause a lot of discussion and controversy. An excellent report that looks at many of the issues related to the Internet is *Access, Internet, and Public Libraries: A Report to the Santa Clara County Public Libraries* prepared by Thomas E. Shanks and Barry J. Stenger for the Markkula Center for Applied Ethics and updated in March 2002. The report is available at www.scu.edu/ethics/practicing/focusareas/technology/libraryaccess/homepage.html. Additional policies on using electronic information resources are addressed in Chapter 8.

Issues

- If possible, every staff member should have an e-mail account for library business use. Not only does this help staff keep up with the

MODEL POLICY: INTERNET ACCESS

The Internet is a valuable tool available for providing library services. The (name of library) provides access to the Internet through individual staff accounts for professional staff, public service staff, and other staff as necessitated by job responsibilities. Staff is encouraged to use the Internet for business communications, to conduct research for patrons and library programs, and to monitor appropriate listservs and blogs. To ensure that a broad range of information is shared and to conserve time, staff will be assigned to monitor library-related listservs and blogs and to relay important information to other staff.

Staff may use Internet resources to answer reference questions and to supply information for patrons. The library will accept requests for materials, reference questions, or other communications via its general e-mail address from patrons normally served by the library. Personal use of Internet accounts by staff is not prohibited, but any personal communications must include the following disclaimer: "Views expressed by the writer do not necessarily reflect those of (name of library)." Personal use of the Internet should not be conducted on staff time and personal files should not be maintained on the library computers. Library Internet accounts may not ever be used for illegal or commercial purposes.

As part of the library's mission of providing access to information of all types in a wide range of formats, the (name of library) provides access to the Internet for staff and patrons. Patrons may also access the Internet via personal laptops using the library's wireless connection. Information exchanged electronically should not be considered secure. Patron use is subject to the library's acceptable use policy. Parents are responsible for monitoring their children's use of library computers and the Internet.

Approved by (governing body) on (insert date)

———————————————————————————

Signature of responsible representative

technology and changes in the technology, but increasingly e-mail is the major method for routinely communicating with staff. If all staff members will not be provided with e-mail accounts, which staff positions will get accounts? Will accounts and passwords be shared? Shared accounts, or accounts for specific positions (for example, librarian@yourlibrary.org) invite security risks and make accountability difficult to maintain but may be unavoidable for a variety of reasons.

- Will patrons be given access to the Internet through library computers? Providing this service will usually assist in meeting many facets of the library's mission. If so, include policy decisions related to patron access in this policy and also in your policies on reference and information services. Will the library provide full access to the Internet for patrons? Some libraries offer limited public access via menu selections through the library's online catalog.
- Is staff speaking as individuals (rather than on behalf of the library) when posting to listservs or answering e-mail?
- Will staff be assigned specific listservs and blogs to monitor? This avoids unnecessary duplication of effort, reduces time spent reading listservs and blogs, and establishes responsibility for sharing information with other staff.
- Most libraries now accept e-mail from patrons and many patrons have e-mail accounts and prefer to contact the library with reference questions, requests for materials, or other communications in this way. Who will be responsible for receiving and distributing such messages? Will the library accept e-mail questions and requests for information from nonresidents? The implications of providing "global" library service can be staggering. Can library staff handle the workload? The most prudent course is usually to begin conservatively and expand services as warranted and as staff can handle increased workload and problems.

LIBRARY PROGRAMS

Background

Library programs supplement and extend the information found in library materials and resources. Programs offer an alternative way for people to obtain and assimilate information, promote the use of library materials by focusing on topics of interest to the community, and may address the library's selected service priorities. Additionally, programming can increase traffic into the library and increase circulation of materials related to the program. The library and its staff may develop programs, or the library may choose to support programs developed by community organizations and interest groups. Policies related to programming should work toward meeting the library's established goals and selected service responses. Policies should promote as open an environment as possible, so consider carefully the benefits or impositions that result from requiring advanced registration, fees, or limits on audience size. Programs sponsored or cosponsored by the library should always be open to anyone wishing to attend, as distinguished from groups making private use of the meeting room (see the policies on "Use of Meeting Rooms" in Chapter 9).

Issues

- Will the library support and encourage programs developed and cosponsored by community groups and organizations, or will programs be limited to those developed and presented by library staff?
- Has the library endorsed ALA's "Library-Initiated Programs as a Resource" interpretation of the Library Bill of Rights?
- How does programming help the library meet its selected service responses, its mission, and its goals? Who will be responsible for planning and overseeing library programs? Are funds budgeted to help with setting up programs, including funds to pay presenters, performers, and speakers? Can volunteers present programs for children, including preschool storytimes? Can refreshments be served?
- Can people with disabilities be accommodated in library programs in compliance with the Americans with Disabilities Act? Compliance includes access to the facilities where programs are held and interpretive services or alternative formats for handouts.
- What types of programs will be approved for library sponsorship or cosponsorship? Who will determine whether the library will cosponsor programs developed by outside groups? Do you have a policy on religious programming and decorations? Can outside presenters solicit business before, during, or after their program? For example, a program on financial planning may be very informative; can the person presenting the program solicit business verbally, by leaving brochures and business cards, or by having a sign-up sheet for follow-up contact?
- Who is responsible for advertising and publicity if the program is to be cosponsored by the library and an outside organization or business? The library has more control over how the program is advertised if staff is responsible. Extra caution must be exercised if a business or organization will be using the name of the library in its advertising to ensure that it does not appear to be a library sanctioned program or that the library is properly credited for its support.
- Will registration be required, encouraged, or discouraged? Will registration be permitted for certain types of programs, such as children's story times, to facilitate program planning? Can attendance be limited to a specific number of attendees? How will staff handle crowds

that exceed the capacity of the meeting room? Will fees be permitted for any programs?

- Will attendance at programs be limited to residents of the library's service area or to patrons holding valid library cards, or will programs be open to anyone interested in attending?

MODEL POLICY: LIBRARY PROGRAMS

Programs are an extension of the services provided by (name of library) and programs are offered for citizens of all ages. Programs are defined as a planned activity or event that may be developed and presented by library staff or may be cosponsored by the library and other community organizations. Library programs are open to the public without charge.

Library staff will present preschool story time programs on a regular schedule throughout the year. Other programs for children and young adults will be planned, staff time and budget permitting, during school holidays and summer vacations. Each year the library director will establish a budget for hiring performers and purchasing materials to support children's programming.

Programs for adults may be scheduled throughout the year as interest warrants. Speakers from community groups and businesses may be invited to present programs on topics of general interest or of a timely nature. No funds are budgeted to pay speakers or performers, although gifts and grant funds may provide funds. Presenters may not directly solicit business before, during, or following a program, although cards and brochures may be left on the display table for attendees to pick up. No fees may be charged to attend any library sponsored or cosponsored program.

Library programs are generally open to anyone wishing to attend. If space restrictions or program requirements limit the number of people who may attend, preference will be given to residents of (the library's jurisdiction). Persons attending library sponsored or cosponsored programs are expected to adhere to the library's policies on patron conduct.

By separate action, and reaffirmed herein, the (name of jurisdiction) has endorsed the American Library Association's Library Bill of Rights and its interpretation, "Library-Initiated Programs as a Resource."

Approved by (governing body) on (insert date)

Signature of responsible representative

AGE REQUIREMENTS IN THE CHILDREN'S AREA

Background

A number of libraries are establishing policies that restrict use of the children's room, children's area, or children's department to children or adults accompanied by a child. Some have also instituted policies that prohibit adults from attending children's programs unless a child accompanies them or from using the bathrooms in the children's area. This policy is often perceived to be necessary because of a precipitating incident or as a preemptive move developed out of concern for children's safety.

Consider carefully whether the library, as a public building, is serving the public by limiting access to specific areas of the building or to specific services. Many adults have legitimate reasons for accessing materials in the children's collection or for wanting to attend a children's program. Programs and materials for children may better serve adults who are mentally handicapped. If the library decides to limit access, be sure that a method is in place for exceptions and for determining a legitimate use without subjecting the patron to a lengthy interview and cross-examination. A basic tenet of librarianship precludes questioning patrons about the reasons for their use of library resources, and this must be balanced against concerns for child safety.

If you feel there is a need for this policy, consider expanding it to allow adults who are using the children's collection while excluding adults who are simply loitering in the area. Keep in mind, however, that sometimes during the school day the children's area may be the only quiet area. While we all want to ensure the children are safe in our community, excluding adults from a specific area of the library may not have the desired result. If a restrictive policy is in place, caution must be exercised to ensure that decisions about perceived intentions are not based on outward appearances.

Issues

- Is the children's area isolated from the rest of the library, creating extreme safety issues when it is not fully staffed? Can staff monitor the area sufficiently to avoid requiring a restrictive policy? Can other staff observe the room at times when adults might be in the department, but use by unaccompanied children is low (for example, during the school day most use would be by younger children who are with an adult)?
- Consider whether a completely restrictive policy is necessary or whether the policy can be written to discourage "loitering" by adults in the children's area. What do local and/or state laws say about loitering in a public place?

- Do many parents, homeschool teachers, educators, and university students use the children's collection for research, class work, or their own work? How will the policy impact their use of the children's collection?
- What constitutes a "legitimate" use by an unaccompanied adult? For example, is it sufficient for an adult to indicate that he or she is doing research for a class? If the purpose is to monitor adults who are in the area, a simple check-in process might be sufficient (however, be sure that this record of use is maintained or destroyed in compliance with confidentiality laws).
- Is the policy being considered because of an isolated incident or perceived problem? Check with legal counsel to be sure that establishing this policy does not set up a perception of security beyond what the library is prepared to ensure.
- Consider carefully whether you want to restrict unaccompanied adults from observing at children's programs. Often mentally disabled adults enjoy listening to stories at story time or lonely grandparents like to see children enjoying a program. Library school and education students are also often required to observe public programming with children.

MODEL POLICY: AGE REQUIREMENTS FOR USE OF THE CHILDREN'S AREA

In order to make the children's room at (name of library) as safe and comfortable as possible for young people, use of the children's room is restricted to children under the age of 13 and their parents or caregivers. Adults, including teachers and university students, who have a legitimate need to use the children's collection must check in at the children's desk. Adults who are in the children's area without a child or who are not actively using children's library materials will be asked to leave the area. Persons over the age of 13 who wish to attend or observe at a children's program must speak with the children's librarian prior to entering the program room.

Approved by (governing body) on (insert date)

Signature of responsible representative

NOTES

1. 42 United States Code Chapter 126 §12101–12213—Equal Opportunity for Individuals with Disabilities (See 62a).
2. U.S. Department of Justice. ADA Best Practices Tool Kit for State and Local Governments (July 26, 2007). Available: www.usdoj.gov/crt/ada/pcatoolkit/toolkitmain.htm. Accessed February 22, 2008.
3. Hopkins, Janet. 2006. Assistive Technology: 10 Things to Know. *Library Media Connection* 25, no. 1 (August/September): 12–14.
4. Minow, Mary and Tomas A. Lipinski. 2003. *The Library's Legal Answer Book*. Chicago: American Library Association.
5. Crawford, Walt. 2005.Policy and Library Technology. *Library Technology Reports* 41, no. 2 (March/April): 24.

Chapter 6

Use of Materials

The library's collection offers vast resources in many formats, often provid-ing access to information that is not readily available anywhere else in the community. Much time and money goes into selecting, cataloging, shelving, circulating, and maintaining library materials. These items are placed in libraries to be used by patrons who may either borrow the materials or use them in the library. Additionally, more and more resources are available for use remotely from home, office, and everywhere that anyone has access to the Internet. Policies are often established to determine who can borrow or use items and under what conditions. Fees may be established for special usage of some materials or for nonresident users, and fines may be consid-ered necessary to encourage the timely return of items or for revenue re-covery. These policies may be encompassed into a general circulation policy with statements related to each issue, or they may be dealt with separately.

Patrons have the right to use library materials without public scrutiny or comment on their choices. Within the limits of current legal requirements, patrons also expect to have records of their use of library materials kept confidential. Even the fact that the patron is a registered borrower should be confidential information (and may legally be so in some jurisdictions). The Children's Internet Protection Act (CIPA), the USA PATRIOT Act of 2001 and subsequent updates, Deleting Online Predators Act (DOPA), and other federal legislation will affect how information about patron use of library materials is handled, and library staff needs to be aware of these requirements. However, even within the scope of meeting law enforcement requirements, policies pertaining to the use of materials should be as non-restrictive as possible to be certain that the taxpayers who support the library have as complete access and full use as is feasible. Related to these issues is the question about what data will be voluntarily gathered about a patron. If the library will use technology to enhance customer service features, consider also developing a policy related to data privacy (see Chapter 5).

REGISTRATION OF PATRONS

Background

Libraries are generally tax-supported institutions open to all who meet certain eligibility requirements. Eligibility requirements should be as simple as possible to ensure that everyone in the jurisdiction that is entitled to service feels welcomed and encouraged to use the library. Each person desiring to borrow materials must register for service, but registration policies should be kept as straightforward and inclusive as possible.

The age at which children can register, or be registered, for borrowing privileges is a widely debated issue. In most jurisdictions, parents or legal guardians must accept responsibility for items charged out to a minor. Therefore, many libraries require a parent's signature on a child's card. If parents are ultimately responsible for materials checked out by their children, libraries should encourage people to register as library users as early in life as possible. Registering young children for library cards may also support the library's mission and service priorities. Successful library card campaigns aimed at registering young borrowers have even resulted in up to a 30 percent increase in circulation.[1] More than a few libraries have even registered unborn children for their first library card!

The age of majority for legal responsibility is usually 18 years old, unless a teenager has become legally emancipated. Therefore, persons under the age of 18 cannot be held legally responsible for library materials. Many libraries would like to issue adult borrower cards, or cards that do not require parental permission, to young adults before the age of eighteen. Weigh carefully the fact that while the library may not have any legal recourse in collecting fines and overdue materials, teenagers need the independence that comes from not having to ask a parent to sign for their library privileges. As libraries are turning to collection agencies to collect unpaid fines and fees, consider also the complications that may arise when the agency contacts a parent who was unaware that his or her child had registered for a library card. Additionally, consider the implications of any relevant confidentiality of records laws, intellectual freedom issues, and the Library Bill of Rights before requiring that teenagers have a parent's signature to obtain a library card. In some jurisdictions, even though the parent has signed for the child's card, only the cardholder can initiate a review of the borrower record.[2] In other jurisdictions, the parent or guardian is considered to be a joint owner of the library card with all rights and responsibilities related to the card.

Issues

- What is the source or sources of funds used to support the library? Library service may be paid for through property taxes, but taxing districts boundaries may differ from the boundaries of the city limits. A special library tax district may encompass a broad area. Anyone paying taxes to support the library is usually entitled to receive services.
- Has the library board and governing authority adopted the Library Bill of Rights and its interpretation, "Free Access to Libraries for Minors?"
- Who is entitled to borrowing privileges at no charge? Are there categories of nonresidents who are also offered borrowing privileges at no charge (local government employees, students in local schools and colleges, etc.)? Will owners and employees of businesses that pay taxes be permitted to borrow materials? How will children register, and at what age can a minor register for a card without a parental signature? How frequently will cards expire and require reregistration? Are cards with shorter expiration dates provided to temporary residents (such as winter or summer visitors)?
- Do state or regional laws or rules require that you extend borrowing privileges to residents of any other jurisdictions due to reciprocal borrowing agreements, statewide library cards, or funding? Does the library or its governing body desire to permit noneligible library users to borrow materials at no charge or by paying a fee? How will the fee be established and by whom? Does paying a fee permit full library service, or will noneligible users be limited in their use of resources and services? Some libraries offer only telephone reference or other high-use services to residents, stipulating that nonresidents have paid for borrowing privileges only when they purchase a library card. If fees are to be charged, it is best to establish the conditions under which fees may be levied through the policy, but do not include the fee schedule since fees may change as costs and taxes increase.
- What information is required as part of the registration process? Will any voluntary information be requested for demographic or statistical purposes? How will the information be used? Exercise caution in

MODEL POLICY: REGISTRATION OF PATRONS

The (name of library) is supported primarily by taxes paid by residents of (city, county, state, or other jurisdiction). Library cards are provided at no additional charge to residents of (jurisdiction). Additionally, city employees, students attending schools in (city), and anyone owning real property within the (jurisdiction) may obtain a library card at no charge. Members of the armed services temporarily residing in the library's jurisdiction may also receive a library card without charge. Others may apply for borrowing privileges by paying the current fee established by (governing body). Library cards are valid for one year.

The library has a responsibility to protect the taxpayers' investment in the collection of the library; therefore photo identification and verification of residence is required to obtain a library card. Identification can be established through a current driver's license, school identification card, or other valid picture identification issued by a governmental agency. If no valid picture identification is available, the circulation supervisor may accept other reasonable forms of identification that establish identity. A parent or guardian must assume responsibility for materials borrowed by a person under sixteen years of age; therefore it is the adult's identification that is required for registration of a minor. Youth over the age of 16 but younger than 18 may sign for their own library card; however, parents will receive a letter indicating that their child has applied for a card and that they are responsible for materials borrowed.

If proof of residence is not provided, the library card will be mailed to the address provided. Library cards may not be forwarded to a second address and will not be distributed in person without proof of residency. Demographic information may be gathered in order to plan library services. This information is used in the aggregate (no identifying information is compiled or reported) and is not stored or disclosed in any way that would identify the person registering. State and federal rules and laws pertaining to confidentiality of records and privacy protect information provided on the registration form.

Information about use of library materials and services will be disclosed only under court order or in keeping with federal legislation.

Approved by (governing body) on (insert date)

_____

Signature of responsible representative

requesting personal information unless having it serves a vital purpose and can be kept confidential.

- What documentation of identification and residency will be accepted? Are methods available to accommodate persons who do not have more common forms of identification? What alternative methods of establishing identification and place of residence are acceptable? It is important that documentation not be unnecessarily restrictive, especially when a specific group might be excluded from obtaining borrowing privileges (for example, accepting only a driver's license may exclude some elderly people who no longer drive; requiring a utility bill or tax statement may exclude renters; requiring a utility bill or rent receipt would bar someone who is homeless but living in a shelter from receiving a card). Lawsuits have been filed on behalf of homeless people who live in shelters when libraries have borrowing policies that are too restrictive,[3] so consider carefully the intent behind the library's procedures. Identification may also be necessary to use special materials or services (for example "behind the desk" books, specialized online searching services, reserve shelf, computer access).

CONFIDENTIALITY OF LIBRARY PATRON RECORDS

Background

The freedom to read is one of the basic axioms of the library profession. Implicit in that axiom is the freedom to read, listen, view, and gain access to materials and information without concern that one's habits, choice of materials, or borrowing record might face public scrutiny. Federal law does not directly protect the privacy of public library patrons, although the Supreme Court has ruled that the Constitution implies the right to privacy.[4] Law enforcement agencies, special interest groups, the media, and others may seek to obtain personally identifiable information about library users. Interest by others in the library materials a patron chooses to use reflects a dangerous and fallacious assumption that what a person reads, listens to, or views equates with his or her beliefs, behavior, or potential actions. Ethically and, in many states, legally, the library must seek to protect the privacy of library users and may release information only under clearly defined circumstances. Federal regulation about information that must be released to law enforcement agencies has changed significantly since September 11, 2001, especially with the passage and subsequent reauthorization of the USA PATRIOT Act.

Under limited circumstances, and following proper legal procedure, library records and information about patron use of library resources and services may be released, but this action should be based solely on the execution of a properly prepared court order. Privacy-related legislation is introduced every year in the United States legislature; be sure that you are keeping up with any new laws that affect confidentiality of library records. The USA PATRIOT Act was reauthorized in March 2006 with even more stringent requirements. The American Library Association provides information on its Web site, www.ala.org/ala/oif/ifissues/usapatriotactlibrary.htm, about the act and its impact on libraries. ALA also has developed model policies and procedures for responding to requests for library records and user information from law enforcement agencies and other third parties.

Depending on state laws and how they are worded, the library may be required to or prohibited from giving parents access to their child's library records. Some states explicitly or implicitly give parents the right to review the records of their minor child, while others either don't address the question or suggest that parents should be granted access to these records. Issues may also arise in cases where a noncustodial parent wants access to the records of their child, although "no state makes any distinction between a custodial and noncustodial parent."[5] In developing policies related to minor children's records, some libraries distinguish between the financial records—what fines a child has, what books are considered lost and subject to payment—and content records—the specific items a child has borrowed or requested. From a practical standpoint, many circulation systems now allow the cardholder to check his or her own record remotely and parents who hold their children's library cards will have access to those records. In the absence of clear guidelines from state laws, it is especially essential that the library policy address parental access to records.

The American Library Association has approved a number of policy statements, including its "Policy on Confidentiality of Library Records and Privacy: An Interpretation of the Library Bill of Rights," that should be considered while formulating this policy. It may be useful for the library's governing board to adopt them or refer to them for support as part of the local policy. ALA also provides guidelines, model policies, and procedures to help libraries respond to demands for library records from law enforcement agencies and other third parties.

Issues

- Forty-eight states and the District of Columbia have laws that affect the confidentiality of library records. The attorneys general of Hawaii and Kentucky, the two states lacking laws, have ruled that library records are confidential and may not be disclosed under the laws governing open records. Do you have a copy of the pertinent laws readily available to you? Although many states do have laws concerning library records, some do not. Mary Minow and Tomas A. Lipinski provide an excellent outline of the four general elements to look for in state laws that govern privacy in their book *The Library's Legal Answer Book*, which will help library staff and administrators understand what to look for in state statutes.

- Even without a specific state law, "all states come under the jurisdiction of federal laws—in this case, the Freedom of Information Act of 1974 and the Privacy Act of 1974."[6] Are you familiar with these statutes and with the USA PATRIOT Act? Regardless of state laws, if there is a conflict with the USA PATRIOT Act or other federal regulations, federal will supersede state laws.[7]

- Has your governing body reviewed the American Library Association's "Policy on Confidentiality of Library Records"? Have you read the American Library Association's "Suggested Procedures for Implementing Policy on Confidentiality of Library Records"? Have you read the American Library Association Code of Ethics? A copy is provided in Resource A of this manual. This code states, "Librarians must protect each user's right to privacy with respect to information sought or received, and materials consulted, borrowed, or acquired."[8] Adopting the code and endorsing the ALA policies can become especially critical in supporting the rights of privacy for library patrons if your state does not have a law guaranteeing confidentiality. If local government or library policies are not in agreement with the ALA statements, be sure that you understand the ways and reasons they differ. Even if your state has laws addressing confidentiality of records, consider endorsing these statements because they may provide an extra measure of support.

- Have you reviewed the ALA publication "Model Policy: Responding to Demands for Library Records?" It was published as an insert in the September 2007 issue of *American Libraries* and provides procedures for dealing with third party and law enforcement requests for library records and user information.

- Does your state library association have statements or policies on intellectual freedom? Such documents may endorse or support the principles of the American Library Association, but usually also represent areas of concern in your state. Consider adopting any state statements on intellectual freedom and privacy of patron records. State library associations may also direct you to state and local organizations, laws, and regulations that may support or affect your poli-

MODEL POLICY: CONFIDENTIALITY OF LIBRARY PATRON RECORDS

The policy of the (name of library) is to preserve the privacy of its patrons' circulation, borrower registration, and usage records and to treat them with confidentiality. These records include, but are not limited to, patron registration data, circulation records, overdue and reserve records, participation in library sponsored programs, record library visits, and/or any data that contain information that links a specific patron to specific materials or services used. Each patron has individual control over his or her borrower's card, and presentation of the card permits access to information about the borrower's current circulation record.

Except during the actual period of transaction (circulation, maintenance of record on unpaid fines, reservation of materials), the library administration purposes, records will be expunged when the information is no longer needed or upon expiration of any records retention requirements. The library has no control over any data that a library computer user sends to another computer server during an Internet session. Transactions are erased regularly; however, data can remain on the hard drive and confidentiality of this data cannot be assured.

In compliance with (cite appropriate law, if applicable), no information will be released to any person, agency, or organization, except in response to a valid court order or subpoena, properly presented to the library administrator. As provided for in state law (cite law if appropriate), records may be released without a court order to law enforcement officers in an emergency situation solely to identify a suspect, victim, or witness to a crime.

Nothing in this policy shall prevent authorized library personnel from using library records in the administration of their regular duties. Staff will not disclose personal information we collect from you to any other party except where required by law or to fulfill your service request.

Library resources and services may not be used to conduct illegal activities. Nothing in this policy prevents the library from exercising its right to enforce the approved rules of behavior, to protect its facilities, computer network, and equipment from harm, or to prevent the use of library facilities and equipment for illegal purposes.

Any employee or volunteer who discloses information in violation of this policy commits an offense and is subject to disciplinary action and may be subject to criminal prosecution.

By separate action, the (name of library) has endorsed the recommendations of the American Library Association's Policy on Confidentiality of Library Records and the (name of state library association) "Statement on Intellectual Freedom."

Approved by (governing body) on (insert date)

_____

Signature of responsible representative

cies. In the absence of state laws regarding the confidentiality of patron records, check for opinions from your state attorney general or legal precedence in your state. Generally, this information will be most easily available through the state library association or your state, regional, and/or system library.

- Under what exceptions or circumstances can patron records be revealed and to whom may they be released? Most laws permit disclosure of information when it is ordered by subpoena or court order. Common sense, and usually law, also permits library records to be released "because the library or library system determines that disclosure is reasonably necessary for the operation of the library or library system."[9] What penalty is stipulated for violations of confidentiality laws? Be careful about the wording used in the library's policy and obtain legal counsel if necessary. The desire to help law enforcement officers fight serious crimes, including child abductions, may conflict with state laws and library policy.[10] Know how you will deal with these conflicts. A good resource is ALA's "Confidentiality and Coping with Law Enforcement Inquiries: Guidelines for the Library and its Staff."[11]

- How are borrower cards for juvenile patrons handled? If cards are issued in a child's name, is the child's right to privacy protected even though a parent or legal guardian is financially responsible for the materials checked out on the card? Some states do permit information about a minor child's record to be released to a parent or guardian. How will you balance confidentiality of the child's record with the parent's right to monitor and guide his or her own child's reading habits? Are juvenile library cards issued as "joint accounts," accessible by either person named on the card? Does presentation of the borrower's card imply that the presenter has the right to look at the patron records for that card?

- Does your circulation system eliminate patron records when they are no longer needed for circulation control? If your circulation system is computerized, it should be programmed to delete information that links an identifiable patron with a particular item after the item is no longer charged out to the patron. If your circulation system is manual, care must be taken to completely block out or remove information that identifies the patron who used the material. Lack of adequate control or security could result in legal liability for the library and its governing authority.

- Check your procedures regarding mailing overdue notices, notification of reserves, and other processes or services that might inadvertently violate a patron's right to confidentiality. Postcards that identify the items being held or the materials overdue must not be used, and messages left with others or on answering machines should not disclose the title, subject of materials, or amount of fines or fees owed. Documents that record the reading habits of children during summer reading clubs or similar activities must also be kept confidential unless the release of such information is authorized by a parent or legal guardian. In some states, even informing the school that a child has participated in a library program might be a breach of confidentiality laws.
- Know the penalties for violating your state's law regarding confidentiality (if applicable), and train staff and volunteers in the importance of maintaining confidentiality. Have legal counsel for the library review your policy for legal language and compliance with your state's laws.

CIRCULATION OF MATERIALS

Background

The library collection exists to be used by its patrons. Most of the use will occur outside the library building. That is, patrons may visit the library to look for materials, but they will want to take the items home, to school, or to an office to actually use them. One of the library's primary functions is to loan material for use for a defined time period. A circulation policy sets out that time period, often called a "checkout" period, and outlines service parameters related to borrowing of materials. The policy should be specific enough to protect the collection and assets and provide a framework for effectively organizing library use without being overly restrictive or discouraging.

Issues

- Who may borrow materials for use outside the library? Do you have a policy that establishes who may register for a borrower's card?
- Is it possible for patrons to borrow material if they do not have the borrower's card available for presentation? Consider the amount of time it may take staff to retrieve library card information against the customer service issues related to helping a patron use the library without having to make a return visit. What identification is needed if the borrower's card is not available?
- Can someone use another person's card? Unless you ask for identification or know the patron personally, it may be best to assume that

---

MODEL POLICY: CIRCULATION OF MATERIALS

The (name of library) has established policies that facilitate the borrowing of library materials for use outside of the library building. A patron must present a valid borrower's card in order to remove library materials from the building. The person presenting a valid borrower's card is assumed to have the authority to use that card unless it has been reported lost or stolen.

Library materials will be loaned to anyone holding a valid library card for the loan period established by (name of governing body). Materials that are not returned by the due date will be subject to fines, as established by the schedule approved by (name of governing body).

Borrowing privileges will be revoked by the library director or his or her designee if the circulation policy is abused. Abuse of the circulation policy includes failure to return materials on time, failure to pay fines that exceed the threshold established by (name of governing authority), or intentionally damaging materials. Disputed claims, such as materials that are claimed returned but have not cleared from the patron record or items that a patron claims not to have borrowed, will be accepted and removed from the patron record no more than twice a year. Fines and records of overdue materials are maintained for a minimum of seven years and are subject to the library's policy on "Fees and Recovery of Overdue Materials."

Approved by (governing body) on (insert date)

Signature of responsible representative

the person who presents the card has the right to use it, assuming that the card has not been reported lost or stolen.

- What penalties have been established for failure to return materials on time? What if an item is never returned or is returned in damaged condition? Are there exceptions to fiscal responsibilities? For example, in the case of catastrophic loss such as a major fire or natural disaster where a person's house is destroyed, will fines be waived?
- How will you handle contested claims in which the patron claims an item was returned but the item cannot be located in the library, or if a patron insists that he or she did not check out an item that shows on his or her record? Some libraries track these claims and allow for a reasonable number, which is set out in the policy, assuming that mistakes are made but setting a limit to how often that can be legitimately claimed.
- How long will fines and records of overdue materials remain on a patron's record? Does the library's governing authority have any laws or regulations that cover the length of time that fines and other financial obligations remain viable?

FEES FOR SERVICES

Background

It is within the mission of the library to provide the widest range of services without additional cost to all users. As much as possible, all library services should be funded by budgeted revenue derived from taxes or other public monies, trust funds, or donations. Your policy should not reflect actual fees or it will have to be updated every time costs change. Therefore, this policy will be brief, however it should indicate the library boards ideas about establishing fees.

Some libraries adhere strictly to a policy that stipulates that only those services that can be supported by the budget will be offered. No fees will be applied to extend special services or to provide service enhancements. If budgets are cut or costs rise unexpectedly due to price increases or higher than anticipated usage, some services may need to be reduced or eliminated.

Sometimes charging a fee is the only way the library is able to provide a service or to provide expanded or enhanced services that meet the needs of only a small group of patrons. You must balance the value and need of the service against the patron's ability to pay for them. Basic library services should always be tax supported, but on-demand or specialize database searching, reserving materials, use of meeting rooms, and other supplemental services may be available only if costs can be recovered. Fees should be determined on a cost-recovery basis, which may include staff time, subscription costs, printing costs, consumable materials, postage, and utilities.

Many libraries have found that services that generate revenue, even only at cost-recovery levels, set up the expectation by the library's funding source for a certain amount of income to be generated by the library each year. This may make it difficult, even impossible, to stop charging for a service once you have begun to do so. Conversely, it can be difficult to begin charging for a service that was previously provided without additional charges if costs for or use of the service are higher than anticipated.

Issues

- What is the library board's philosophy regarding fees? Does your governing body require that fees be collected for some services? Are there state or regional laws or regulations defining basic library services for which fees cannot be charged?
- Has the library adopted the American Library Association's Bill of

---

MODEL POLICY: FEES FOR SERVICE, 1

The (name of library) has as its mission the provision of free and open access to information in varied formats. However, there are limits to what can be provided with budgeted funds. The (governing authority) has determined that some services will be provided on a cost-recovery basis, passing the cost of these expanded services on to the user. Fees are established and charged when the service clearly benefits an individual user, prevents reuse of materials, or requires extraordinary staff time to provide, e.g., printouts from library databases, meeting room use, proctoring exams.

Fees may also be established for supplemental services that are not within the scope of the library's basic mission or to enhance a service that is provided as an alternative to an existing free service, such as postage for notification of reserved materials and rental copies of bestsellers. Fees will be reviewed and established by the (governing authority) annually and a schedule of fees will be posted on the library's Web site and at the circulation desk.

Approved by (governing body) on (insert date)

Signature of responsible representative

Rights and endorsed its interpretation dealing with "Economic Barriers to Information Access"?

- Do fees deposited into an account allow the library to purchase more services or materials to support the services that generate the funds, or are the fees deposited into a general government fund from which the library's budget is funded? Are revolving funds, which funnel funds generated back into the program that generated them, permissible? Some fees may be more palatable to patrons if they support library services (for example, "rental" collections that allow more copies of bestsellers to be available) or are for personal services to a limited group of people, such as proctoring an exam or duplicating photographs from the library's archives.
- Will charging a fee reduce or limit demand for a service that would otherwise be extremely popular? Would uncontrolled demand deplete limited resources? To what extent will fees interfere with the ability of children and economically disadvantaged patrons to get the information and resources they need?
- Often libraries charge a fee when a new service is implemented (e.g., a specialty databases, downloadable audiobooks). These fees should be eliminated as soon as the service or materials become part of basic library services, as determined by general professional practices in your area, or when the budget permits. Libraries may also charge fees for out-of-area service requests, such as photocopying articles from the local newspaper, providing genealogical research through local resources, etc.
- How are fees established? Can you determine costs in order to set reasonable fees for the service provided? It is important to know

MODEL POLICY: FEES FOR SERVICE, 2

The (name of library) has as its mission the provision of free and unlimited access to library service and information. All services are paid for by local taxpayers and supplemented by funds from donations and trusts. It is expected that the library budget will fully fund all services and materials. No services will be offered that cannot be fully supported by the budget.

Approved by (governing body) on (insert date)

_____
Signature of responsible representative

how much a service will cost in order to determine if fees are necessary and to justify or explain how they were established. If you don't know the cost to provide a specific service, refer to *Staffing for Results* by Jeanne Goodrich and Diane Mayo to learn how to calculate costs for staff time.

FINES AND RECOVERY OF OVERDUE MATERIALS

Background

Fines are frequently assessed to encourage the prompt return of borrowed items. The amount of the fine is usually established by the library's governing authority and may differ for different types of materials or for the age of the borrower (fines on children's materials may be lower than for other materials; fines for DVDs may be higher than for books). When items are lost or never returned, the library generally charges a fee for the item, which may be based on the original purchase price or a replacement cost, and may charge a processing fee.

Uncollected fines can account for a large amount of money owed to public libraries. Of more concern to many librarians is the value of materials that are checked out but never returned. Attempts to recover materials and collect fines, in effect providing stewardship to the public's property, must be weighed against both the positive and negative publicity that might be generated by such attempts. The more aggressive the attempts, for example, arresting delinquent borrowers, using collection agencies, small claims court, etc., the more carefully the effect on public relations must be considered and the more support the library must have from both its governing authority and the community for retrieving materials and collecting fines and fees.

Sometimes someone other than the borrower may request information about overdue fines and outstanding materials in order to clear up fines on others' behalf (children, settling estates, insurance claims). Confidentiality laws and the right to privacy preclude disclosing more information than is necessary to clear fines. Caution must be exercised to ensure that personal reading habits are not disclosed.

Issues

- Do you know how much of the collection of the library is lost each year by patrons who do not return materials and do not pay for lost items? Does the economic impact consider processing costs, includ-

MODEL POLICY: FINES AND RECOVERY OF OVERDUE MATERIALS

Library materials are purchased for use by all citizens of (jurisdiction). The (name of library) establishes regulations for the loan of materials, including circulation periods, renewal processes, and fines for late return. The (governing body) believes that the individual who chooses to keep materials past the due date, or who refuses to settle unpaid fine or fees, compromises to some extent his or her right to privacy. The library will attempt to recover overdue materials and will notify patrons of unpaid fines and fees according to procedures established by (governing authority). Information regarding overdue and nonreturned materials and past-due fines and fees maybe disclosed by the (name of library) to third-party collection agencies when that agency has entered into an agreement with the (governing body) to recover materials or to collect fees and fines. The library will also provide sufficient information to allow any individual other than the holder of the borrower's card to settle unpaid fines or fees on that card. However, authors, titles, or subjects of lost or overdue materials will not be disclosed without presentation of the borrower's card.

Approved by (governing body) on (insert date)

———————————————————————————

Signature of responsible representative

ing the staff and database costs to withdraw the lost item and to obtain and process a new one? The average real cost of processing a book can easily be anywhere from $30 to $50! What costs are associated with more aggressive attempts to retrieve materials (fees to collection agencies, additional staff, increased printing and postage), and are the costs justified when compared with the value of materials that might be returned and fees that might be collected? Have you considered carefully the public relations impact (both positive and negative) that might ensue from more aggressive collection attempts?

- Are you familiar with state and local laws on confidentiality of library records, and does the library have a policy on confidentiality of records? Are there circumstances that might require that someone other than the patron know what materials have fines accrued or have not been returned in order to clear records?

- Does your library use an outside agency or organization to assist in the recovery of overdue materials or the collection of fines and fees?[12] Are there state or local laws that permit the use of outside agencies (law enforcement agencies, private collection agencies) to collect fines or recover the cost of materials that have not been returned? If your library does not receive the funds from fines, weigh carefully the public relations factors if you use a collection agency to recover fine monies. Consider having the governing body (city, county, etc.) be the agency actually entering into the contract with a collection agency.

RECIPROCAL BORROWING PRIVILEGES

Background

No single library can meet all of the needs of its users. Budgets, space, and the explosion of information make it impossible for any single library to own every book or item published, electronically or in print format. Sharing resources and materials extends the ability of the library to serve its customers and strengthen its collection without having to purchase every item potentially needed by a patron. Reciprocal borrowing agreements extend library privileges to walk-in patrons who wish to use the resources of another library without waiting for interlibrary loan. Such agreements may also provide access to resources at college and university libraries that might otherwise not be available to public library patrons.

Local taxing districts have expressed more concern in recent years that reciprocal borrowing agreements reflect a balanced relationship. One library should not be expected to support inordinately a library that is not providing basic services to its primary patrons. Reciprocal borrowing also generally applies only between libraries and is not used to extend services to areas that have chosen not to provide library services, have reduced hours and services significantly enough to impact basic services, or that have ceased to operate a library. Care should be taken to ensure that libraries in borrowing agreements offer complimentary services that expand the services of both libraries. Some imbalances may be compensated for through regional, state, or federal programs.

Issues

- Are the limits of the collection as defined by the mission statement of your library? Use the American Library Association's Planning for Results process to determine the primary service responses your library will emphasize. These service responses, supported by the library's collection development policy, will help you determine the priorities and boundaries of the collection.

- What other libraries are available within a reasonable distance from yours? Do patrons regularly travel between jurisdictions for work, school, or recreation? Will the collections in other libraries provide resources not available locally?
- Are there statewide or regional standards for basic services? Does the region or state have policies regarding interlibrary cooperation? Are other jurisdictions interested in cooperative agreements or reciprocal borrowing? Are local governing authorities willing to support sharing of resources? Is there a way for communities that are not supporting local library services to contract with your library for

---

MODEL POLICY: RECIPROCAL BORROWING PRIVILEGES

Recognizing that no library collection can meet all of the informational, recreational, or educational needs of members of its community, the (name of library) enters into agreements with other libraries to expand the range of materials available to our citizens. Reciprocal borrowing privileges may be extended to patrons of any library that extends privileges to residents of (your city, county, other jurisdiction). Reciprocal borrowing agreements must be approved by the (name of governing entity). Residents of (your jurisdiction) may request a current list of libraries with which reciprocal borrowing agreements exist. Due to differences in borrower registration procedures and circulation systems, borrowers may be required to register with the lending library but any nonresident fees will be waived. Privileges will not be extended, or may be limited, to persons who have lost library privileges in their own home library due to overdue materials, unpaid fines, or other unresolved problems. In addition to providing reciprocal borrowing privileges, the (governing authority) may also enter contracts to provide library service to residents of communities that do not have library service. However, reciprocal borrowing privileges will not be extended to residents of communities that significantly cut hours or reduce services after entering into the reciprocal borrowing agreement.

Approved by (governing body) on (insert date)

Signature of responsible representative

services? New directors or managers who are not familiar with co-operative agreements, or who are establishing a brand new library, may find helpful background information in *Public Library Start-Up Guide* by Christine Lind Hage.

- How will cooperative agreements increase demand for library services and materials? Can staff handle the increased traffic and any administrative or bureaucratic responsibilities?
- Will citizens from other jurisdictions be able to use your library if they have lost privileges in their own library due to abuse of library services or unpaid fines? How will you confirm active, nondelinquent status? Do patrons use their local library card or do they need to apply for a card at the borrowing library?

INTERLIBRARY LOAN

Background

Because no library can meet all of the needs of every patron, nor can any library purchase every book a patron might need, a system of interlibrary borrowing and lending has evolved. Interlibrary loan permits the local library to borrow materials from other libraries, providing patrons with access to materials from libraries across the state and around the country. For many small and medium sized libraries, interlibrary loan is a critical service that enhances all levels of service.

Interlibrary loan differs from reciprocal borrowing because the latter formalizes agreements between specific libraries to permit patrons to have borrowing privileges at both libraries. With reciprocal borrowing, the patron visits the library in person to search for and borrow materials. Interlibrary loan is a formal agreement that allows the library to borrow materials on behalf of its patron from any participating library that agrees to lend the items. Interlibrary loan is usually handled by mail, and lending libraries are usually compensated for their services from state and federal funds. Interlibrary loan is not a substitute for spending local funds to develop a collection to meet the ongoing needs of local patrons and, generally, newer titles, bestsellers, and very popular items may not be borrowed through interlibrary loan. Items owned by the library but checked out to another patron generally should not be requested through interlibrary loan unless the item is long overdue and unlikely to be available.

The proliferation of distance education, with graduate and doctoral students depending on local public libraries to provide highly specialized materials, has increased the demand for interlibrary loan in many communities. Online catalogs, electronic databases, and the Internet have greatly affected interlibrary loan. Some items, like periodical articles, once had to be located, photocopied, and mailed for patron pickup. Now many periodical articles are available immediately through electronic databases. However, Internet access to online catalogs, online bookstores, and sophisticated search engines have also made it easier for patrons to discover many small press and obscure, hard-to-find materials that may be requested through interlibrary loan. Requests may come in through fax, e-mail, and online links through the library catalog, in addition to in-person or telephone requests.

Changes in technology, our profession's philosophy on document delivery, and patron's expectations for instantaneous access are affecting how interlibrary loan is handled. Peer-to-peer lending, requiring that one library send the material to another library before it reaches the patron, is being replaced by direct delivery and direct return. Larger libraries and university libraries are utilizing purchase on demand as an alternative to interlibrary loan, often having the book sent directly from an online retailer to the borrowing patron. Although your library may or may not be involved in changing the mechanics of interlibrary loan, a policy is needed to support access to the service and establish local principles.

If your library also participates in the interlibrary loan process as a lender, you may need to support this in a written policy, including reference to any restrictions on lending. For example, the library may choose not to lend rare or irreplaceable materials to other libraries. A policy may also establish limitations on this service, restricting the service to library cardholders who have clear records. The borrowing library is responsible for the borrowed material, so many libraries do not provide the service to patrons with large fines or nonreturned materials on their record.

The American Library Association offers *The Interlibrary Loan Code for the United States*, a document revised in 2001, which establishes the principles that facilitate the process of borrowing or lending materials. This document and its supporting materials, including a sample ILL form, help libraries understand the procedures and practices of interlibrary loan.

Issues

- Will interlibrary loans be restricted to residents of the library's jurisdiction, or will materials be borrowed for anyone, including non-residents who purchase services, with a valid borrower's card? Will the library process interlibrary loan requests for someone who does not have a library card but who wants to use the materials in-house? Requests from children should be given the same consideration as those from adults.
- On average, what is the turnaround time (include in-house process-

MODEL POLICY: INTERLIBRARY LOAN

The (name of library) participates in the national interlibrary program that permits the library to borrow materials for its patrons from other libraries. This interlibrary loan service is available to all patrons whose record is clear of fines and overdue items. Materials will be requested for patrons who do not hold a current library card, but use will be limited to in-house. Books and photocopies of articles from periodicals not owned by (name of library), or that are otherwise unavailable, may be requested for loan through interlibrary loan. Requests for periodical articles, including newspapers and reports, will be checked against the library's electronic databases before the request is forwarded to ensure that the requested information is not available. Audio and film recordings, microfilm, and genealogy materials may be requested but are often difficult to obtain. Items owned by the library but checked out to another patron or otherwise temporarily unavailable may not be borrowed through interlibrary loan unless the item requested is more than two months overdue.

The (name of library) does not charge for interlibrary loan service; however, the patron is responsible for charges or fines imposed by the lending library. Every attempt will be made to borrow items from libraries that do not charge fees for loaning materials. If a patron does not wish to borrow an item if charges are imposed (such as insurance fees, lending fees, photocopying charges), this must be stipulated when the request is made. Fines for overdue materials and processing costs for lost items will vary with the lending library and are the responsibility of the patron.

The library may restrict the number of items requested by an individual patron or "meter" the number of items referred through interlibrary loan when necessary to ensure fair, equitable, and timely service within the constraints of budget and staffing. This action will be taken only in consultation with the patron, and alternative sources for service will be suggested. Requests that staff determine may violate copyright laws will not be accepted. Photocopies received through interlibrary loan will be stamped with a notice of copyright.

Approved by (governing body) on (insert date)

———————————————————————————

Signature of responsible representative

ing time plus time from the interlibrary loan center) for interlibrary loan service to your library? Will requests be accepted if the patron needs the materials more quickly than the average time for receipt? Accepting a request for an item that is unlikely to be received, while of use to the patron, may needlessly expend staff time that could be used for other services.

- Who will pay postage charges to return items borrowed through interlibrary loan? Some libraries budget for this, while others require that the patron pay return shipping costs. Is this charge permissible under state or local rules? Will overdue fines be assessed even if there is no penalty to the library? If an item is lost, will the patron be charged according to the lending library's fees? Processing costs and material replacement fees will vary greatly.

- Are you familiar with copyright laws that might regulate the number of articles that can be photocopied from a periodical for a patron? Does the library have a policy regarding copyright? What databases are available through the library? Generally, libraries will not request articles that are available online, and databases must be searched prior to placing the request.

- Will requests be limited to a maximum number of items at one time? Internet search engines and access to the online catalogs of libraries around the world have allowed patrons to identify numerous titles that might be of interest to them. Can your staff handle numerous requests from the same patron and still serve others? Are there items that typically cannot be borrowed through interlibrary loan? It can be difficult to obtain audio and video recordings or DVDs, paperbacks, reference books, microfilm, and genealogy materials through interlibrary loan.

- If the library is participating in the interlibrary loan process as a lender, do you want to include the boundaries of participation in this policy? Participation as a lender may incur costs, including staff time, photocopying, mailing supplies, and postage, that may not be recovered.

PROTECTION OF COPYRIGHT

Background

Copyright protects the creator or legal owner of original creative work, including books, articles, film, and music. Since libraries deal with these items on a daily basis, they also deal with copyright and the potential for copyright infringement. Copyright law is complex and includes provisions for fair use of protected materials. The library has an obligation to inform patrons about copyright laws with regard to photocopying of printed materials, duplication of audio and video materials, computer disks and other electronic formats, and public performance of audio and video materials. In general, the borrower or user has the ultimate liability if the library has made a diligent attempt to inform the patron about copyright law and to ensure compliance, particularly if use of the materials is unmediated by library staff. At minimum, be sure that copyright notices are posted on copiers, scanners, and printers, and that staff understand copyright basics. If library staff assists with using photocopiers or with downloading material from the Internet, the doctrine of "vicarious infringement" may apply.[13] Even though the library did not commit the infringement, staff may have contributed to the infringement by helping the patron to download music from a file sharing service, for example. "Under current law, libraries may be granted safe harbors from liability for copyright infringement resulting from certain actions only if they have copyright policies in place."[14]

In an era of easy "copy and paste," libraries must spend time educating patrons about copyright issues. Additionally, staff must comply with copyright laws when using materials for public programs, such as showing films at story times or to placing images on the library Web site. Failure to make diligent effort to comply with the copyright laws could result in costly litigation. *The Library's Legal Answer Book* by Mary Minow and Tomas A. Lipinski includes an extensive chapter that addresses many questions, and provides answers, about copyright and library patrons.

"A copyright policy acknowledges your institution's commitment to abiding by copyright law and provides guidelines to assist the members of your institution's community in doing so."[15] The policy should address the copyright law and principles of fair use. It should also direct patrons and staff to resources that further explain exceptions to copyright and how to ensure compliance.

Issues

- Does the library have a copy of Circular 21, "Reproduction of Copyrighted Works by Educators and Librarians," available from the Library of Congress?
- Is a statement about copyright placed on and near the photocopier(s), warning patrons that material being copied may be subject to copyright? Are other pieces of equipment in the library that are capable of reproducing materials (scanners, opaque projectors, cassette duplicators) also labeled? Articles in electronic databases are also covered by copyright and some libraries choose to include a copyright

statement in their computer or Internet use policies. Although law mandates no specific wording, the American Library Association suggests the following:

> Notice: The Copyright Law of the United States (Title 17 U. S. Code) governs the making of photocopies or other reproductions of copyrighted material. The person using this equipment is liable for any infringement.

- Are all copies of copyrighted materials made on behalf of a patron stamped with a notice of copyright? Again, the law does not specify wording for the copyright notice, but the American Library Association has developed sample statements that libraries can copy or adapt.
- Have staff and volunteers received training and information about copyright law, and do they know how to determine if materials can be copied or performed publicly? Staff is generally not liable for illegal copying if the photocopier is unsupervised, that is, if staff does not make the copy for a patron.
- Do you know which DVDs or other films in the library collection, if any, were purchased with public performance rights? If not, check with the supplier. When in doubt, assume that there is no right for public performance. Licenses are available that permit the library to show, or allow to be shown, films in the library, but this license would not cover patrons using films elsewhere for public performance. Does your meeting room policy include information related to the use of copyright-protected material by outside groups?
- Copyright also applies to items placed on the library's Web site. Although copyright law does not prevent linking to copyrighted material, the method of linking may create a violation if protected materials, such as photographs or other images, are used to create the link. If this is an issue, be sure to learn about the subject. Gretchen McCord Hoffman's article "What Every Librarian Should Know About Copyright Part II: Copyright in Cyberspace" in the Fall 2002 issue of *Texas Library Journal* provides a basic overview and her book *Copyright in Cyberspace 2*, published by Neal-Schuman, provides more details.
- Does the library own or have access to copyright-free art for use by patrons and staff? Does staff refrain from duplicating copyrighted materials for publicity items, decoration, use in children's programs, etc.?
- Have staff been informed and encouraged to refuse to comply with requests to copy materials that are subject to copyright protection?

MODEL POLICY: PROTECTION OF COPYRIGHT

It is the intent of the (name of library) to comply with Title 17 of the United States code, titled "Copyrights," and other federal legislation related to the duplication, retention, and use of copyrighted materials. A notice of copyright will be prominently placed on the photocopier(s) and any other library equipment, such as cassette recorders and overhead projectors, that are capable of duplicating or reproducing copyrighted materials. Library staff will refuse to duplicate any materials if doing so would violate copyright and will, when asked, inform patrons if materials being borrowed are subject to copyright restrictions (see also, "Interlibrary Loan"), and staff will refuse any request that would violate copyright regulations. Policies and procedures for use of the library's meeting room will include provisions related to use of copyright protected materials.

The library does not purchase audiovisual materials with public performance rights, and DVDs, videos, downloadable video, and other films are loaned for personal and home use only. The library has purchased a public performance license that covers material from specific producers in order to show films in the library meeting rooms. Library staff will follow copyright law in selecting and using materials for public performance at programs. Organizations using the library's meeting rooms are also covered by the license and must follow copyright laws.

Original or copyright-free art will be used to produce library publicity items or for creating displays and decorations.

Approved by (governing body) on (insert date)

_____

Signature of responsible representative

In general, a person may make one copy of printed material for their personal use, but rarely can an entire book be copied.

NOTES

1. Jones, Patrick. 2002. *Running a Successful Library Card Campaign*. New York: Neal-Schuman.
2. District of Columbia Confidentiality of Library Records Act of 1984 (D.C. Law 5–128).
3. Homeless Patrons Win in Worcester. *American Libraries Online* (Septem-

ber 15, 2006). Available: www.ala.org/ala/alonline/currentnews/newsarchive/2006abc/september2006a/worcester.cfm.

4. Minow, Mary and Tomas A. Lipinski. 2003. *The Library's Legal Answer Book*. Chicago: American Library Association, p. 166.

5. Minow and Lipinski. 2006, p. 186.

6. Million, Angela C. and Kim Fisher. 1986. Library Records: A Review of Confidentiality Laws and Policies. *Journal of Academic Librarianship* 11, no. 6 (January): 346–349.

7. Minow and Lipinski. 2003, p. 168.

8. American Library Association. Code of Ethics of the American Library Association. 1997. Amended January 22, 2008. Chicago: American Library Association Council. Available: www.ala.org/ala/oif/statementspols/codeofethics/codeethics.htm.

9. Vernon's Annotated Revised Civil Statutes of the State of Texas (Tex. Rev. Civ. Stat. Ann.) REF KFT 1230 .A3V4, Article 6252-17a.

10. The Naperville (IL) Public Library faced a situation in 2004 in which the state laws on privacy prevented the library from providing police with information to identify a suspect in a criminal case. The city is now working to change the law to permit "law enforcement officers who are actively engaged in the performance of their duties involving a criminal investigation to obtain information from a library in an emergency situation solely to identify a suspect, victim, or witness to a crime."

11. American Library Association. Confidentiality and Coping with Law Enforcement Inquiries: Guidelines for the Library and its Staff (April 2005). Available: www.ala.org/ala/oif/ifissues/confidentiality.htm. Accessed October 1, 2007.

12. For a discussion of the various issues related to using a collection agency, read: Hill, Nanci Milone. 2006. Are Collection Agencies the Answer? *Public Libraries* 45, no. 6 (November/December): 18–23.

13. Minow and Lipinski. 2003, p. 62.

14. Hoffman, Gretchen McCord. 2003. What Every Librarian Should Know about Copyright, Part IV: Writing a Copyright Policy. *Texas Library Journal* 79, no/ 1 (Spring): 12–15.

15. Hoffman. 2003.

Chapter 7

Collection Development

The most visible parts of a library are the staff, who assist patrons in determining their information needs, and the collection, which is the strength of public libraries. There is no other place in a community where the public can find the assortment of materials and topics in so many formats. Materials cost money to select, acquire, maintain, use, and dispose of; therefore, staff should carefully evaluate items before adding them to the collection. Decisions are made for books, media, electronic materials, and other resources.

A well-written collection development policy provides a statement of intent for the library's intentions about building a solid collection that meets the community's needs. It provides a planning process that allows the library to examine the strengths and weaknesses of the collection and plan for improvement. By providing guidance, the policy helps the staff make decisions about how much emphasis to place on specific subject areas, as well as make decisions about the audiences being served and the depth of coverage provided by resources in the collection.

Policies that outline how materials purchased with public dollars are selected allow staff to focus limited funds on those that fulfill the library's mission and established service priorities. The selection policy may also delineate the kinds of materials, such as textbooks, educational toys, or rare books that will not be included in the library's collection. Policies about gifts, donations, and deselecting and discarding of items establish clear guidelines to avoid overwhelming the library shelves with unusable items while also avoiding public relations problems and hurt feelings.

Many libraries have decided to outsource part of the selection, acquisition, and processing process. The decision to put some of the collection development process into the hands of others makes it even more important to have good policies in place. Staff working with the contractors will need clear guidelines and current information about the collection and its needs in order to provide appropriate parameters and ensure that the community's needs are being met.

At some point, items in the collection need to be removed because of age, lack of use, or other factors that make the item irrelevant to the collection. The selection policy provides guidance that allows staff to make informed, consistent, and defensible decisions about what to remove from the collection and when to do so. Selection policies can also provide an objective basis for evaluating items that may be the target of complaints by individuals or groups that do not think the item is appropriate for the library's collection. Issues related to the collection—what is included as well as what is not included—can cause some of the most visible public relations issues for a library. Therefore it is wise practice for every public library to have at least a short collection development policy that has been developed with input and approval from representatives of the community (through the library board and governing authority).

Libraries may choose to write a single comprehensive collection development policy that deals with all of the aforementioned issues, or they may choose to deal with each topic in separate policies. Policies will usually include general statements that provide an overview of the characteristics of the collection (current materials for popular reading, support for lifelong learning) as well as some specific indicators that offer insight into the unique characteristics of the community that are reflected in the library collection (Spanish language magazines, support for homeschool families). If the library has more than one location, the collection development policy may also delineate the scope of branch collections in relationship to the main library collection.

SELECTION OF MATERIALS

Background

The collection, including periodicals, electronic databases and online information sources, and nonprint or media materials, serve as the backbone of library services. Determining what to add to the collection, what to retain in the collection, and what to discard from the collection is one of the major responsibilities with which the staff is charged.

A selection policy serves as the blueprint from which the staff allocates funds and makes decisions. It will include a great deal of information that establishes the parameters of the collection and the level of service the collection will provide. In addition to a statement about the library's mission and institutional objectives, a materials selection policy should include information about the clientele served by the library. The policy should consider the types of programs the collection will support. For example, is the primary responsibility of the collection geared toward meeting the general informational and recreational needs of the community, or does the collection also support formal education? It should make reference to appropriate intellectual freedom documents and policies adopted that support the freedom of choice in reading and viewing. The statement should identify formats to be included in the collection, establish limitations of the collection, and determine areas in which the library will not make purchases. The policy will also set forth who has responsibility for selection decisions, what criteria will be used in making selection decisions, and how limited funds will be allocated to ensure that the needs of the entire community are considered in purchasing decisions. It should also address how complaints or concerns about materials, both those included and those not included in the collection, will be handled.

Be cautious about promising a "balanced" collection in the library's policy. Such a statement may imply to the public that the library will have an equal amount of information on any subject or cover all viewpoints, regardless of how farfetched and inflammatory they may be. It may also imply that the library will have material at all educational levels when, in fact, the library will have only basic information on a subject. Instead of offering a "balanced" collection, what public libraries must strive for is a diverse collection that reflects major viewpoints on a variety of subjects. Be cautious, also, about using budget limitations as the rationale for not having particular items, titles, or types of materials in the collection. Items that may in reality not be within the scope of the collection might then be given as gifts.

A collection development plan determines the depth and breadth of the collection and explains the types of materials that will and will not be added to the collection. Smaller libraries with limited budgets will probably find that their interests are best served by a brief collection development plan. Libraries with larger budgets or multiple branches may want detailed plans for long-term development, including guidelines by classification area. For that type of plan, refer to the collection development plan for the Hedberg Public Library in Janesville, Wisconsin. Available online at http://

hedbergpubliclibrary.org/policies.php, this policy was updated in 2005 and runs about 62 pages. The plan includes detailed guidelines for major subject areas and types of materials.

Issues

- What is the mission established for your library? Have you selected service responses for your library from among those developed in the Public Library Association's *The New Planning for Results: A Streamlined Approach* or a similar planning process? Knowing which service responses fit with the mission of your library is vital to establishing a collection development policy. A library that has established Basic Literacy or its 2007 equivalent, Learn to Read and Write, as a major service response will develop its collection very differently than will one that has selected Cultural Awareness (Celebrate Diversity) as its major role. Materials that support the primary missions of the library will receive more attention and funding than the secondary roles played by the library.
- Do you know the needs of the community served by the library? What demographic information (education, income, age groups) have you collected to assist in determining community needs?
- What other library or informational resources are available locally? Other nearby libraries, including school and college or university libraries, may affect your collection. What resource sharing options exist? Does the library have a policy on reciprocal borrowing privileges? You may not need to collect as extensively in some areas if another library nearby has a strong collection and makes that information available to your patrons. Many libraries, especially in closely knit communities or regions where patrons regularly travel between communities, have established cooperative collection development agreements. These agreements establish the scope of specific library collections to ensure that patrons have access to more in-depth collections within the broader community. For example, the public library in the county seat may focus more attention on law and legal resources while the library in an historic area is the source for local history and genealogy materials.
- Have you surveyed the collection to determine its strengths and weaknesses? Do you have circulation statistics for representative periods in the past? Do you know what materials are used in the library but not accounted for in the circulation statistics? If you need help evaluating your collection, refer to *Managing and Analyzing Your Collection: A Practical Guide for Small Libraries and School*

Media Centers by Carol Ann Doll and Pamela Petrick Barron for help. In addition to providing techniques for using the library's automated circulation system to gather data, Doll and Barron also provide guidance for alternate "paper and pencil" methods for determining average age of materials in subject areas, collection percentages, collection use, and other data.

- Has the library board or its governing officials considered endorsing the American Library Association's Library Bill of Rights, Freedom to Read, and Freedom to View statements? Resource G includes these freedom statements, while Resource C includes copies of the Library Bill of Rights and a number of interpretations that deal with collections. Among these are statements related to evaluation of library collections, diversity in library collections, and "Access to Library Resources and Services Regardless of Sex, Gender Identity, or Sexual Orientation." These statements strengthen support for the purchase of materials that may offend some segments of the community. Even if the governing body chooses not to endorse these documents, they may decide to reference them as supporting local decisions on selection of materials.
- What major selection tools will staff use to assist them in making purchasing decisions? If the library does not own or subscribe to sufficient standard tools, can they be borrowed from regional systems, neighboring libraries, or the state library? If staff is not doing most of the selection because this has been outsourced, do you have clear guidelines in place about how selection decisions will be made?
- Will materials be purchased only if reviews are available for the item? Is staff qualified to evaluate materials for which reviews are not available? Will certain items (local histories, patron requests, popular series) be purchased or accepted as gifts without reviews? Keep in mind that if the library collects cutting-edge technologies and formats, you may want a separate, more specific, policy that outlines how decisions will be made. This policy may only be needed until the format becomes commonplace.
- Will the library purchase multiple copies of high-demand items? Frequently the policy will indicate that additional copies are ordered based on reserves or anticipated reserves. Does the library provide an opportunity for patrons to request that the library purchase specific titles?
- Will the library purchase textbooks to support school curriculums? Are there any standing orders in place that require dedicated funds every year? Are there any formats that generally will not be pur-

MODEL POLICY: SELECTION OF MATERIALS

The (name of library) provides materials and services to support the informational and educational needs of the citizens of (jurisdiction). As part of its planning process, the (name of library) has selected two primary service responses that support this mission: Stimulate Imagination and Get Facts Fast. Secondary service responses selected were: Make Informed Decisions and Celebrate Diversity. These functional service responses will be considered in the development of the collection and will receive priority in the allocation of resources and funds.

Selection and purchase of library materials rests with the library director who may delegate some responsibilities to other staff members. Staff will adhere to accepted professional practices when making selection decisions. The recreational, educational, and informational needs of the community, as they fit within the selected services responses, will be considered in selecting materials.

Prior to the beginning of each budget year, the director will determine how budgeted funds will be allocated among the major collection subdivisions, e.g., adult nonfiction, fiction, youth collection, reference, periodicals, and nonprint. Circulation statistics and counts of in-house use of materials will be maintained to assist in decision making. Average cost per item, as determined by the previous year's purchases and reports in library and publishing journals, will also be considered in allocating funds.

Materials will be selected based on positive reviews in professional journals or actual examination and evaluation of materials. Popular demand, such as bestsellers, school bibliographies, or local interests, may also be used as the criterion for selection of materials. Items that must be updated every year may be placed on a standing order list to ensure timely delivery. Suggestions from the community for items to be considered for purchase are strongly encouraged, but materials must meet selection criteria.

The (name of library) does not attempt to acquire textbooks that specifically support local curricula, but it may acquire textbooks for general use by the public. Multiple copies of popular books, e.g., bestsellers, resume guides, or tax preparation, may be purchased to meet short-term demand. Paperback books will be purchased when available to meet short-term demand. The library will attempt to have information available in a variety of formats, such as book, nonbook, pamphlet, magazines, etc., when available and practical. Generally, only one copy of materials in other formats—DVD, compact disc, computer programs, etc.—will be purchased unless long-term high demand is anticipated. Film and audio recordings will be selected for potential long-term use that meets general interests. Regardless of an item's popularity, the library may choose not to select it if the available format is not durable enough to withstand reasonable library use or if it would require excessive staff time to maintain.

Objections to items in the collection should be made in writing to the library director. (See also the "Request for Reconsideration of Materials" policy.) Materials that no longer meet the needs of the community and no longer support the library's collection will be withdrawn and disposed of in accordance with the library's "Deselection of Materials" policy.

Approved by (governing body) on (insert date)

Signature of responsible representative

chased because the format is inappropriate for library use (for example, consumable workbooks), do not withstand heavy library use (for example, comic books or pop-up books), or require more staff attention than can be provided (for example, jigsaw puzzles, art prints, or clothing patterns)? You may prefer to detail the types of materials the library will purchase and leave it understood, explicitly or implicitly, that other formats or types of material will be purchased only under special circumstances.

- Will funds be expended to purchase popular or mass-market DVDs and music (for which demand rises and ebbs quickly), or will limited resources restrict the collection to specialty items for which most patrons would have only occasional need (sound effects, wedding music, recorded speeches, etc.)? Will the library continue to purchase traditional audio and film formats, such as compact discs and DVDs, if funds are also being expended for downloadable audio and video files? Will hard copies of books available electronically be purchased? Many libraries have stopped buying encyclopedias, for example, because they are now provided electronically, or they may purchase only one dictionary for the reference collection because they also subscribe to the *Oxford English Dictionary* in electronic format.
- Will the library maintain special or unconventional collections? Art prints, sculpture, educational toys, and other items may fit within

the mission of the library but require a great deal of staff time to handle. They may cost more to acquire, process, and replace, and they may be subject to greater loss or theft than other items. Toys and puzzles quickly become soiled or damaged and need to be cleaned and sanitized. Some libraries have accepted collections of cake pans, prom gowns, small tools, and fishing rods. These collections can gain a great deal of publicity for the library and may serve a real community need, especially in small towns. Remember, though, that once begun, a special collection can be difficult to maintain. Replacing, maintaining, and adding to a special collection may divert funds from the library's primary collections.

GIFTS

Background

Gifts of money, books, audiovisual materials, and other items can add significantly to the library's collection and services. While money is extremely flexible, new and used books and other materials may not have much value monetarily or to the collection.

A written policy establishes guidelines for what items the library is willing and able to accept, how gifts will be handled and acknowledged, and how items can be disposed of, if not needed by the library. It also establishes the gift as a transfer of property from the donor to the library, said gift becoming subject to policies related to other library property, such as what happens when an item that is added to the collection is no longer useful.

Equally important, a policy will guide staff and patrons in knowing what items are not appropriate for the library, helping the library avoid becoming a repository for items that cannot find a home elsewhere or that will incur substantial investments of time or money. Donors want their goods to go where they will be useful, so the policy also serves as a public service tool, alerting donors to seek other places to donate items that won't be used by the library.

It is perfectly reasonable to decline to accept donations if the value to the library (in time, money, and space) does not balance or outweigh the cost of sorting, processing, adding records to OCLC (Online Computer Library Center) or other databases, and storing the donated items. Remember, the cost to catalog and prepare a book to be placed on the shelf can easily exceed the value of the book. In addition, shelf space has a value, which can be calculated. Donated items should also meet the criteria established in the policy on "Selection of Materials," and may be rejected if the item would not have been acquired with library funds had they been available (for example, due to negative reviews, lack of local interest, or unsuitable format).

The majority of items donated to the library will be used books and magazines that are being recycled from a personal collection. The reality for most libraries is that staff is very limited, and it is easy to seriously underestimate the amount of staff time required to sort, evaluate, process, and distribute gift items. If you don't know what it costs to process gift books, consider using one or more of the work forms provided by the Public Library Association's *Staffing for Results*, available online at www.elearnlibraries.com/workforms/ to figure it out.

Few donated books from personal collections have any significant monetary value, but some titles may fill gaps in the collection if they are in good condition. For example, copies of older books in popular series may have been lost or discarded, but as they are still popular, especially when a new title is published, donations can fill in missing books and be a true benefit. Occasionally the library may receive new books, special collections, and monetary donations to purchase materials. A gift policy allows the library to control its own resources (size of collection, cost of maintaining the collection, staff time) while expanding community support. Be especially cautious about accepting gifts that have any conditions attached.

Issues

- Does your library have a collection development policy? This should be in place before developing a policy on gifts since acceptance or rejection of gifts must be based on the current and future needs of the collection.
- Some libraries choose to foster an atmosphere of support by "accepting" every donation, regardless of its lack of value. This encourages community support of the library but requires a great amount of staff time to handle materials, much of which will be immediately taken to the trash or recycling center. Some libraries maintain lists of other community agencies that use and welcome outdated issues of newsmagazines, condensed or abridged versions of books, etc., and refer donors to these agencies. Do you have staff and volunteers to sort and cull through and process large quantities of material? Have staff and volunteers been trained to know what items will support the library collection and which are worth adding to the collection? How can items that are not added to the collection be handled? Does the library have used book sales, or can materials be given to the Friends of the Library to sell? Free materials still cost time, money, and space! Do you know how much time it takes

to sort through and deal with gift items? If not, consider using the work forms provided through the Public Library Association's *Staffing for Results* to determine the amount of time and the cost for staff to do this.

- It is not appropriate for library staff to set values for donated materials. Library staff is not skilled at establishing fair-market values for tax purposes and must not do so. While a receipt should be provided that acknowledges the gift, indicating the number of items or number of bags or boxes donated, it is up to the person making the donation to set a value. It is also best that staff members not spend their time making lists of the books and other materials donated on the receipt; donors should itemize the materials if they wish to have a record.

- Small and medium sized public libraries are not equipped to serve as museums or archives, nor is it usually within their mission to collect archival materials other than, perhaps, local history. In the event that your library chooses to accept a gift of rare or valuable books, either for display or for sale, the donor should have the items appraised by a qualified appraiser as part of the donation process.

- It is preferable not to have to return unwanted items to the donor or to inform the donor as to the final disposition of the items. It is extremely cumbersome to do this and opens the library to ill will if someone must keep track of who donated every item and inform them when the item is being traded, sold, given to another agency, or otherwise discarded. Library policy should transfer to the library sole and complete ownership of donated items. Except in very rare instances, all items should be accepted only as outright gifts. It is generally not considered wise to accept items on "permanent loan" or to which the donor has attached conditions for use, display, care, or disposition.

- Groups, individual authors, legislators, and businesses may want to donate specific titles and magazines. These gifts should be subject to your collection development policy unless the library chooses to have a special collection for works of local authors. Remember that local authors want their books to be in their local library, and an individual representing various causes may want to donate titles that reflect their values. These can be important contributions to the collection, or they may simply fill already crowded shelves.

- Donor plates are a particularly effective way to acknowledge donations, but they can be time consuming. Many libraries use donor plates only for new books, memorial purchases, and other special recognitions. Before deciding that a donor plate will be inserted in every donated book, consider carefully the number of donated items you expect to add each year and the impact on your staff. A few minutes, multiplied a hundred times, will add up to many hours that could be spent on other duties.

- Decide what kinds of items and materials are acceptable and appropriate as donations. Does the library wish to accept as gifts materials in formats no longer acquired through the library budget? For example, few libraries purchase vinyl records or audiocassettes any longer, preferring compact discs, but may be willing to add to their collection through donations. In fact, some formats are no longer available for purchase, but donations can maintain the collection for many additional years.

- Will the library accept items such as 8mm film, filmstrips, or eight-track tapes if it does not have the equipment with which to use the items? Does the library have a special collection, such as a local history collection, where older formats might still be welcome because of the subject content?

- Does the library wish to accept donations of toys, tools, equipment, etc.? Remember that these special collections can require a great deal of work to maintain. Does the library wish to accept gifts of art? Who will recommend which pieces of art are accepted or rejected? Is space available to house and display these items so they will be used? How do these items fit with the service responses selected during the library's planning process?

- Donations of used equipment, especially computers, may cost the library for repairs, maintenance, and software upgrades, which can exceed the price of purchasing new equipment. However, in many cases, donations may be the only way for the library to replace outdated technology, such as microfilm or microfiche viewers, that may still be important to a part of the library's collection.

- Unless these items fit within the scope of one of the library's primary service responses, primary source documents or archival materials, such as private papers, manuscripts, and government records, are more appropriately placed in a large public library, archives, or an academic library. Special collections should be accepted with caution, even if the donor will provide funds to catalog, store, and secure the items, unless the library is already collecting similar items. Your policy may be able to deal with all categories of items that are not currently found in the library's collection through a general statement that is flexible.

MODEL POLICY: GIFTS

The (name of library) welcomes gifts of new and used books, audio recordings, videos and DVDs, and similar materials. Items will be added to the collection in accordance with the selection policy of the library. Once donated, items become the property of (name of library), and may be transferred to other libraries and nonprofit agencies, sold, traded, or discarded if they are not added to the collection. The donor may place no conditions on the donation. Donated items will not be returned to the donor, and the library will not accept any item that is not an outright gift.

The library will acknowledge receipt of donated items, but is unable to set fair-market or appraisal values. It is recommended that the donor make a list of items donated. If items are being donated to obtain a tax benefit, it is the donor's responsibility to establish fair-market value or obtain expert assistance in establishing any value. Once a donated item has been added to the library collection, it is subject to all other library policies and may be discarded according to the policy on withdrawal and disposition of library materials.

Monetary gifts, bequests, and memorial or honorary contributions are particularly welcome. Funds donated will be used to purchase items in accordance with the selection policy of the library. Books and other materials purchased with bequests and memorial or honorary contributions will be identified with special donor plates whenever possible. If requested at the time the donation is made, notification of memorial or honorary contributions will be sent to the family of the person being recognized. Suggestions for subject areas or other areas of interest are welcome and will be followed to the extent that such items meet the library's selection policy and collection needs.

Acceptance of donations of equipment, real estate, stock, artifacts, works of art, collections, etc., will be determined by the library board based on their suitability to the purposes and needs of the library, laws and regulations that govern the ownership of the gift, and the library's ability to cover insurance and maintenance costs associated with the donation.

Approved by (governing body) on (insert date)

_____

Signature of responsible representative

- Donations of money usually serve the library better, allowing the library to purchase items that are most needed. Does the library have a foundation, friends group, or other venue to accept financial donations? Does the library want to encourage bequests by having brochures and information available for people who might want to leave funds in their will? A brochure can also address what items the library will and will not accept through bequest and offer guidelines as to what level of bequest is required before the library will place the donor's name on the building, a room, equipment, or furniture.

MATERIALS IN LANGUAGES OTHER THAN ENGLISH

Background

In most communities, languages other than English are spoken and read by a significant number of citizens. Library patrons or potential patrons who are more comfortable reading for pleasure and information in a language other than English might reasonably expect to find some materials for their use in the public library. Community analysis will help determine the languages other than English in which materials should be available. Consider also whether partnerships with other area libraries would allow better coverage of materials in a variety of world languages. Although your library will want to have a collection that includes materials in any language spoken by a significant segment of your community, patrons may be better served by being able to borrow materials in other less-represented languages from a nearby library.

While it is not necessary to have a specific policy permitting the library to collect non-English language materials, some libraries find it useful to have one in order to validate spending tax money on items that may appear to serve a limited segment of the population. Libraries in communities with strong anti-immigration forces have faced criticism for collecting materials in non-English languages. Selecting, acquiring, and cataloging materials in other languages may also present a challenge to the library staff who do not speak the language, and a policy can help set forth parameters for obtaining help with this area of the collection.

Issues

- Does the library have a general collection development policy? Does this policy fully address serving specific segments of the community? Is this service likely to raise questions or complaints from citizens who do not understand the need for materials in languages other than English? If necessary, can you clearly explain why the library needs materials in other languages? If not, consider "Ten Reasons Why We Buy Spanish Books" developed by Albert Milo, director of Fullerton (CA) Public Library.[1] Although it was written in 1995, Milo's list of reasons is still valid and can be applied to any language that is spoken by a significant segment of your community.

- Consider adopting the "Declaración de los Derechos de las Bibliotecas" (The Library Bill of Rights translated into Spanish) in support of the library's mission.
- Official figures often underestimate populations of persons who prefer to speak or read languages other than English. People who speak English for daily work may still prefer to read in their first language. Do you have census and other figures for non-English or non-native English-speaking citizens in the service area of your library? Do you know how many current and potential library users would benefit from materials in the language(s) the library will collect?
- Does the library have one or more staff members who are informed, trained, and capable of meeting the needs of the non-English-speaking community? If not, who in the community could offer input in the selection of materials for the non-English collection?
- Many books produced in other countries will never be reviewed in

---

MODEL POLICY: MATERIALS IN LANGUAGES OTHER THAN ENGLISH

The (name of library) strives to have a collection that reflects the diversity of the population it serves. To that end, part of the collection development budget will be allocated to purchase materials in the preferred language of residents who are not native speakers of English. Materials considered for purchase will be evaluated as much as possible under the same guidelines and policies used for English-language materials. When necessary, staff will seek assistance in the selection of materials from appropriate community members. Citizen recommendations are always welcome and appreciated.

Approved by (governing body) on (insert date)

Signature of responsible representative

the standard library review sources. Many have weak bindings and will have to be rebound or treated as ephemeral. The library's policy may need to exempt non-English language materials from strict selection criteria, and selectors may need to depend more on personal examination, patron suggestions, and non-standard selection tools. Selectors should still strive to provide the best quality materials and the highest caliber of writing available. Consider sending a staff person to major book fairs, such as the Guadalajara International Book Fair, to gain firsthand access to a wide range of publications in Spanish. The American Library Association partners with this book fair to provide free passes and travel support.

REQUEST FOR RECONSIDERATION OF MATERIALS

Background

Individuals or groups may question an item or items in the collection of the library. Legitimate concern about the accuracy or fairness of information must be balanced with intellectual freedom issues and the mission of the library. Complaints about material should be welcomed and handled in a dignified manner. Prompt, courteous, and proper handling of complaints can help avoid disastrous public relations problems.

At the same time, no one person or group of individuals has the right to tell others what they should read or view. A public library should have a diverse collection that includes materials that promote ideas and viewpoints that are contradictory, and perhaps even offensive, to the beliefs of members of some segments of any community. Keep in mind that while libraries should offer a diverse collection that reflects the major viewpoints on a variety of subjects, not every subject will have an equal amount of information available on all viewpoints. Challenges to materials in the library should be used to promote the library as a place where information about many ideas is available.

While the library director, and ultimately the library's governing authority, has final responsibility for handling patron complaints or concerns about library material, generally the head librarian for the department (children, teens, adults, media) is the first person to review and respond to a request for reconsideration of material. In larger libraries a committee may review material and make a recommendation for disposition. In every instance, the library director should provide a written response to the patron in all instances where a specific title has been evaluated following a written complaint. In addition to providing good customer service, and potentially developing a better relationship between the patron and the library, this

132

written document concludes the process and serves as a record of the incident's disposition.

Issues

- Do you have a selection policy and a collection development plan? These documents explain how the library determines what is placed in the collection and how items are removed when no longer useful. Is the collection weeded regularly to remove outdated materials? It is important to have these documents and a policy on reconsideration of materials in place and supported by the library's governing authority before a complaint us filed. It is more difficult to determine procedures for handling complaints and to get support after a challenge has been made, when emotions are high.
- Has the library endorsed the Library Bill of Rights and its interpretations and are copies displayed around the library? Do you have a copy of the *Intellectual Freedom Manual?* Are there other state or local statements on intellectual freedom? Do you know which local, state, and national organizations are available to assist you if groups advocating the wholesale removal of library materials target the library?
- Are you familiar with any laws in the jurisdiction of your library that define obscenity? Are there any applicable laws that relate to the use of adult materials by minors? Do you know how the courts have defined local community standards for your area? In at least one case, the local community was defined by the courts to be the entire state, and specifically excluded the immediate city, which was more liberal than the rest of the state. However, "The authorities are not in agreement as to the geographical area determining "community standards' of obscenity. The question has not yet been decided by the United States Supreme Court. The answer may depend upon the nature—federal or state—of the statute under which the issue of obscenity arises. The view has been taken [in cases in Indiana, Michigan, Ohio, Oregon, and Rhode Island that have not been overturned] that the question of obscenity must be determined on the basis of a national standard."[2]
- How frequently will the library evaluate an item for removal from the collection? Some individuals and groups have tried to overwhelm the library by repeatedly resubmitting requests for reconsideration. Does the complaint have to be submitted by a resident of the library's governing jurisdiction? Must the complainant have a library card? These issues should be considered carefully. The library serves the

MODEL POLICY: REQUEST FOR RECONSIDERATION OF MATERIALS

The (name of library) welcomes comments and suggestions regarding the continued appropriateness of materials in the collection, especially with regard to outdated materials. Suggestions and recommendations will be considered and utilized by the library in the ongoing process of collection development.

Individuals may take issue with library materials that do not support their own views or values on a subject or that is not compatible with their beliefs. Staff is available to discuss concerns and to identify alternate materials that may be available. If a patron's concern is not satisfied through discussion with staff, a formal, written request for reconsideration of materials may be submitted to the library director. Copies of this form are available at the reference desk or from the director's office.

The (name of library) is not a judicial body. Laws governing obscenity, subversive materials, and other questionable matters are subject to interpretation by the courts. Therefore, no challenged material will be removed solely based on a complaint of obscenity or any other category covered by law until a local court of competent jurisdiction has ruled against the material. No material will be knowingly added to the library collection that has been previously determined to be in noncompliance with local laws.

For a request for reconsideration to be considered, the form must be completed in full. The patron submitting the request must be a resident of the (library's jurisdiction) and hold a valid borrower's card. The library staff and the director consider each request in terms of the criteria outlined in the library's materials selection policy and the principles of the ALA Library Bill Of Rights and related statements, printed reviews, and other appropriate sources. The director will respond, in writing within 30 days of receipt, to the patron's request for reconsideration. The response will indicate the action to be taken and reasons for or against the request. An item will be evaluated for reconsideration only once in a 12-month period.

Approved by (governing body) on (insert date)

_____
Signature of responsible representative

EXHIBIT 7–1
REQUEST FOR RECONSIDERATION OF LIBRARY MATERIALS

Many libraries provide a form, similar to this sample, that focuses a patron's attention on specific issues to be addressed if they feel that a book or other item should be removed from the library shelves. The form also serves as a record of the complaint.

Author _____ Date _____

Title _____

What objections do you have to the material? Please cite specific pages and/or passages. Are your objections moral, political, religious, or aesthetic?

How was the item brought to your attention?

What have you heard or read about the material? What was the source of the information about this item?

What do you think is the theme or intent of the material?

Is there anything good or of value to this material?

What would you like the library to do with this item?

Name _____ Phone _____

Address _____ City _____

Are you speaking on behalf of an organization or group?
   ☐ Yes   ☐ No

If yes, what group or organization? _____

entire community, but the concerns of those who actually use the library may be perceived as more valid.

- Are procedures in place and staff trained to handle complaints about materials? Many complaints can be resolved by respectful interest in the patron's concern and a clear, levelheaded discussion about the role of the library to provide materials for many points of view. Many libraries use a standard form that guides the patron through the reconsideration process and ensures that information pertinent to the objection is provided to library staff. This form, or a simple listing of criteria that must be included in the complaint, usually asks for contact information and information about any organization the complainant represents. (See sample form in Exhibit 7-1.) Other questions might explore the nature of the objection, whether the complainant has read the entire book (or viewed the entire film), suggestions for alternative selections, and the perceived theme of the work.

DESELECTION OF MATERIALS

Background

The cycle of service requires that while materials are added to the collection, some must also be discarded. Outdated, inappropriate, shabby items that may camouflage useable items while making library shelves look full will hamper an otherwise good collection. A policy about deselection, or weeding, of library materials should detail criteria for deselecting, pinpoint decision-making responsibility, and establish proper methods for disposing of discarded items. When addressing the appropriate methods for disposing of discarded items, it is especially important to be sure that the library complies with local ordinances and takes steps to avoid negative publicity that may ensue if the public does not understand the deselection process. Deselection should not be used as a way to avoid dealing with a patron complaint about materials or to respond to censorship challenges (see also "Request for Reconsideration of Materials" policy). Many libraries include deselection within their selection policy, while others prefer to deal with this matter in a separate policy.

Issues

- Do you have a written collection development policy? This is the first step in understanding the direction that the library collection should be taking. Weeding can provide feedback on the collection's strengths and weaknesses and the information collected during the weeding process should be considered in revising a yearly plan for allocating collection development funds. Be sure to include nonprint and electronic resources in your weeding policy.

- Have you identified the primary service responses of the library? Significant changes in the service responses during a new cycle of planning may affect decisions about keeping or discarding certain items.
- Who will be responsible for weeding the collection? Although final responsibility for the collection rests with the library director, a good rule of thumb is to have the same people who select the materials also be responsible for its removal.
- Mistakes and indecision are inevitable in any process based on judgment. Standard evaluation tools and specialized bibliographic aids can also help determine potential future usefulness and identify classic titles in a particular field of study. *The CREW Method: Expanded Guidelines for Collection Evaluation and Weeding for Small and*

MODEL POLICY: DESELECTION OF MATERIALS

Materials that no longer fit the stated mission and service priorities of the library will be withdrawn from the collection. This may include materials that are damaged, that include obsolete information, or that have not been used within a reasonable period of time. Decisions will be based on accepted professional practice, such as those described in *The CREW Method*, and the professional judgment of the library director or designated staff. When necessary, local specialists will be consulted to determine the continued relevance and reliability of materials. Items withdrawn from the collection will be disposed of in accordance with local law, which permits discarding worn, dirty, or dangerously outdated material into the trash, recycling of paper, or transfer to the Friends of (name of library) for sale. No withdrawn items may be sold or given directly to individuals or groups; however, items that do not sell in the Friends sale may be transferred to other nonprofit organizations or placed in a "free books" area for anyone to take. Discarded magazines and newspapers may be given to other area libraries or social service agencies or recycled at the discretion of the library director.

Approved by (governing body) on (insert date)

Signature of responsible representative

Medium-Sized Public Libraries published online by the Texas State Library and Archives Commission offers formulas based on the age of the book (last copyright), maximum permissible time without usage (circulation), and various negative factors (inaccuracy, beyond repair, trivial, etc.). Libraries use the CREW guidelines to assist in making weeding decisions, but the SUNLINK Weed of the Month Club, www.sunlink.ucf.edu/weed, and *A Practical Guide to Weeding School Library Collections* by Donna J. Baumbach and Linda L. Miller, a book based on the SUNLINK information, also offer detailed guidelines, including examples of specific titles, to weed. Do you know who in the community can be called on to help with areas of the collection that are tougher to evaluate? Final decisions always rest with the library director, but experts can often help staff understand specialized fields.

- Does the library's governing authority have laws, ordinances, or policies governing how property can be disposed? Sometimes all items removed from the library collection must be sold at public auction. Since this is a very unsatisfactory way to dispose of library materials, try to get authority to give the items to a Friends of the Library group, offer materials to other libraries, literacy groups, or social service agencies, or sell discarded items directly in the library. Avoid giving items to specific individuals, even if local regulations do not prohibit this, because doing so can lead to charges of favoritism or the appearance of misuse of funds. A number of libraries have recently found themselves the subjects of negative publicity because the public did not understand that discarded books were of little or no value. In other cases, books that appeared to be in good condition but were surplus copies were discarded even though community members wanted to put them to use elsewhere. Be sure to check with legal counsel, but many libraries have engendered goodwill by putting some gently used discards out for the public to take, recycling reading. If you do this, be sure to clearly mark the books as discards or they may find their way back to the shelves.

LINKING TO EXTERNAL RESOURCES

Background

The explosion of information available on the Internet has allowed libraries to gather and share resources that are widely and freely available. Web sites are a logical extension of the library and provide patrons with access to timely and, hopefully, accurate sources of information. Some Web sites are produced and maintained by organizations, businesses, research centers, academic institutions, and associations that create documents or other information related to their mission or areas of interest. Even Web sites created by an individual may demonstrate accuracy and authority when it was created for a topic about which they are passionate. The library's virtual collection can be greatly enhanced by linking to these sources. Patrons often feel more comfortable accessing Web sites that they know the library has selected for their use.

Apply the same kinds of decision-making processes to the Web sites that your library will link to from the library's reference, resources, or other Web pages. Be sure that someone is responsible for regularly checking that the sites are still valid. Having a policy in place also helps the library staff respond to requests from eager entrepreneurs who want the library to provide reciprocal linking—that is, the business will link to the library's Web site in exchange for the library linking to theirs.

Libraries are not required to obtain permission in order to link to other Web sites; however, be careful that your link does not imply any endorsement or affiliation with the third party unless an agreement to such is in place. For example, the library might link to a medical association's Web site in order to provide medical information to patrons. However, the library cannot imply that the association endorses the library's reference services or is a supporter of the library. Many libraries provide a redirection page to remind patrons' that they are leaving the library Web site and that no endorsement or guarantees are provided with regard to the information that will be found through external links. This type of link also serves to separate the library from other organizations.

There is some discussion within legal circles about the practice of "deep linking" whereby the link is to an internal page rather than to the site's home page or introductory information. Some Web sites use technology to make it difficult to link directly to an internal page, but many do not. Commercial sites, in particular, object to deep linking because referred visitors bypass advertisements. It is not considered to be a copyright violation simply to link to another Web page, and it is certainly more convenient for patrons to be able to get directly to the information you want them to see. However, some commercial and licensed products attempt to require that you get permission before deep linking. As with many issues related to technology, it is unclear what the outcome of this debate will be.

More likely than hearing from a business or organization for linking to their site, the library may receive complaints for *not* linking to a site. In at least one case, a company sued a city for not linking to their site. The suit claimed that by allowing links to other sites, the city created a nonpublic forum and, therefore, was violating the First Amendment by denying the company's request to be included on the Web site. "The significant issue that was appealed was that the policy permitting links on the city's Web site was vague, overbroad, and violated First Amendment rights by giving local officials unfettered discretion to deny a link to the publication based on its content."[3] The American Library Association offers information, as well as links to articles, about this issue online at www.ala.org/ala/oif/ifissues/. A well-written policy that specifies what criteria the library will use in approving external links will go a long way toward avoiding problems.

Issues

- Do you agree that it is the library's responsibility to provide patrons with access to authoritative sources from the Internet?
- Consider whether it is appropriate for the library to link to commercial Web sites. Under what conditions will the library link to a document or resource provided by a for-profit business? Are there categories of Web sites that the library will *not* link to?
- Who will be responsible for selection and deselection of Web sites? Many libraries assign this responsibility to the same person who would select other materials in a given subject area. Others prefer that a Webmaster or electronic resources librarian be responsible for all Web content. To whom will unsolicited requests for reciprocal linking be directed?
- Will the library link to fee-based sites if some of the content is available at no charge? What if the fee-based site provides the most authoritative source of information? For example, many people want to check their credit history to ensure that they are not vulnerable to identify theft. While there are circumstances under which a person can receive this report at no charge, the three major credit reporting agencies charge for their services.
- Some sites require additional software, such as Adobe Acrobat, Shockwave, or RealAudio, in order to access the resources. Are these software programs available on library computers?
- Do staff and volunteers know how to evaluate a Web site to determine who produced it, its authority, its scope, and its currency? Are you familiar with review sources such as Librarians' Index to the Internet (www.lii.org), Scout Report (www.scout.cs.wisc.edu/scout/report), and Library Journal's Web Watch that can provide help in selecting appropriate Web sites?
- Care must be taken to ensure that the library does not infringe on trademarks when adding logos or trademarked symbols to the Web

MODEL POLICY: LINKING TO EXTERNAL RESOURCES

The Web site of the (name of library) serves as a logical extension of the library's information resources and supports its mission to connect patrons with timely, accurate sources of information. In order to strengthen the library's print and nonprint collection, effort will be made to find valuable sites that are unique and that supplement the existing print and electronic collection available in the library.

The library's Web site is not intended to be open as a full or partial public forum. Library staff, under the direction of the library director, will select Web sites to link to from the online reference resources and other subject areas on the library's Web site. Whenever possible, priority will be given to links to other governmental and community Web sites that provide legal, noncommercial, public service information. The library may link to commercial sites when the director has determined that sufficient free content is available to make it a worthwhile resource or when the resource is the most authoritative and no free resource is available. Requests for Web sites to be placed on the (name of library) Web site must be reviewed and approved by the library director. Staff will write a short annotation that describes the content of the linked Web site.

Library staff will run link-checking software monthly to ensure that the links remain active and viable. At least annually, all links will be checked to ensure that the content remains accurate, reliable, and timely. Sites that no longer meet the needs of library patrons or that no longer meet the selection criteria will be removed. Patron complaints or concerns about site content will be handled under the library's "Request for Reconsideration of Materials" policy.

Approved by (governing body) on (insert date)

_____
Signature of responsible representative

site. Minow and Lipinski offer an example in *The Library's Legal Answer Book* where a library uses the Public Broadcast Service's logo to direct library patrons to all of the PBS DVDs in the collection.[4] If you plan to use trademarked logos on the library Web site, do a little research to learn more about what is fair use and what might be considered infringement. Most companies provide guidelines for using their logos and symbols when providing hotlinks to their services. Do staff and volunteers understand the use of trade-marked material and where to find related information if logos and symbols will be used for links?

- Are you familiar with link-checking programs such as Link Runner that ensure that links remain active and viable? For smaller Web sites, free link checkers or the link checker that comes with your Web development software might suffice, but most libraries will need to purchase a more robust software program. Keep in mind that these software programs will not check to see that the content is still relevant to your patrons' needs and that the site has not been "highjacked" and now features unsavory content. Staff or volunteers will still need to cull the links on a regular basis.
- Will staff annotate the links in order to help patrons understand the content and potential use of the Web sites?

NOTES

1. Milo, Albert. Ten Reasons Why We Buy Spanish Books. Available: www.reforma.org/refogold.htm. Accessed February 21, 2008.
2. WestLaw. www.westlaw.com. Eagan, MN: Thomson-West. Accessed February 22, 2008.
3. Torrans, Lee Ann. 2003. *Law for K-12 Libraries and Librarians*. Westport, CT: Libraries Unlimited, p. 123.
4. Minow, Mary and Tomas A. Lipinski. 2003. *The Library's Legal Answer Book*. Chicago: American Library Association, p. 99–100.

Chapter 8

Reference and Information Services

The services that the library provides, including reference services, reader's advisory, access to information, and programs, can play a role that is even more vital to the community than the library's collection. Without the services provided by trained and educated staff, the library would be nothing but a building full of materials. In fact, recent surveys and research indicate that one of the most important roles of the public library is as a place for people to gather, meet, get help with information needs, and attend programs.

Keep in mind that no library can possibly be all things to all people. The service priorities that the public library selects will influence the types, level, and extent of reference and information services provided. A public library that has selected Know Your Community as a primary service response will offer a different type of reference collection and a specific array of reference services than will a library that has selected Satisfy Curiosity as its primary service priority. The Internet and remote access to services, along with social networking services, have substantially changed the types of services and the delivery methods for the services libraries can provide. Patrons can search the library catalog after hours, print full-text copies of articles through electronic databases, and download information from the Internet. They can also chat online with a reference librarian or obtain homework help from a librarian thousands of miles away in the middle of the night. Policies about services support the library's selected service priorities and enable the community to know what the library staff can do to help them with their educational, informational, and recreational needs.

REFERENCE AND INFORMATION SERVICES

Background

Reference and information services continue to be an integral part of public service, especially for those libraries that have selected service priorities such as Stimulate Imagination, Build Successful Enterprises, and Get Facts Fast. Regardless of the service responses that have been selected, every public library provides some level of reference service.

In the past, reference service was primarily provided in person for patrons in the library. Today, increasingly, reference services are provided by telephone, live chat or instant messaging, mail, e-mail, and fax. Staff should endeavor to serve patrons uniformly and fairly, usually providing service first to the person who has taken the time to come into the library. All questions should be considered legitimate, and no preference should be given, nor should service be withheld based on age, type of question, status of the requester, etc.

Staff time and workload may require that some levels of service be established. For example, staff workload might limit the amount of time staff can spend researching quiz or contest questions, although caution must be taken to avoid probing too deeply into a patron's reasons for wanting the information. Genealogical research can also take a great deal of time, and some libraries limit the amount of time staff can spend searching old city directories, local newspapers, and other sources. Some libraries may want a separate policy dealing with homework assistance (see policy in this chapter). Consider carefully what services will be restricted, and keep in mind that reference service may be the most visible service that the library provides.

The Internet has also greatly changed the nature of reference services for many libraries. Routine questions about local population or history, links to online dictionaries and almanacs, and "frequently asked questions" on library Web sites may mean that the questions that are actually asked of the reference librarian are more in-depth and require more research to answer. Questions can also be received from nonpatrons living in any part of the world. Develop policies that support the library's primary service responses and that maximize the available resources while still assuring equitable access to assistance. Above all, policies should not be based on age or other discriminatory factors.

Reference staff also needs to exercise caution when providing legal, medical, or consumer information. Information should be supplied, but advice or interpretation of the information must be avoided. When appropriate, staff should make referrals to other community groups or organizations that may be able to serve the patron more completely.

Issues

- What are the primary service responses that the library has selected? What is the workload at the reference desk? How many staff members work on the reference desk? Are all questions, including directional and general information, handled through one service desk? Does the library have an active telephone reference service, or is most of the work done in person? How are reference questions received? Priority is usually given to those patrons who come into the library before those who call, but staff will still need to be assigned to handle questions received through other channels. Do you want to establish guidelines that limit how much time will be spent helping a patron over the telephone or through live chat sessions?
- Have staff members been trained to do reference and research work? Is training available for those staff members who do not have a degree in library science or who have not taken formal reference classes? Are procedures in place so that less skilled staff or volunteers know when to refer the question on to another staff member?
- What level of research is performed at the reference desk? Has the library selected a service response, such as Be an Informed Citizen, which may require a substantial collection of government documents and information resources and may require specialized tools and skills? Does the library have a system for referring questions that cannot be answered locally to another library or to a regional or state reference backup service? Online networks using instant messaging and chat programs have allowed libraries to create referral networks for patrons. Good customer service requires that the staff member verify that the patron is satisfied with the information located and make referrals or offer suggestions for further research, if necessary.
- Will reference questions be accepted by electronic means, such as e-mail and fax? Some simple questions of a factual nature (e.g., population of a city, definition of a word) may be understandable without a reference interview, but often questions that appear to be simple become more complex. Does the library want to offer reference assistance via chat, instant messaging, or e-mail? If questions are accepted electronically, will they be answered in the same manner? It can take more staff time when responses must be typed into a computer, but e-mail can be an effective way to respond to patrons quickly and efficiently. Chat or instant messaging can also provide a more satisfactory reference interview because it can be dealt with in real time with electronic conversation. Given the rapidly chang-

MODEL POLICY: REFERENCE AND INFORMATION SERVICES

The reference staff at (name of library) endeavors to provide accurate information and materials in response to requests from library users in an efficient, courteous, and timely manner. In order to ensure that quality service is provided, only staff trained in providing reference service will work at the reference desk. Questions are generally answered in the order received, with priority given to questions asked by patrons who are in the library.

Services available through the reference desk include information services (answers to specific questions, call number and ownership of a specific book, recommendations on subject materials); instruction on the use of the library and library materials (indexes, online services, catalog, reference tools); bibliographic verification of items requested (title, author, publisher, ISBN, price); reader's advisory (suggestions on books to read, videos and DVDs to view, recordings to hear); referral to community services; and assistance in locating materials.

Before responding to a reference request, staff must understand the question completely. When answering specific information questions, staff will always cite the source of the answer. Personal beliefs, opinions, and experience are generally not acceptable sources of answers to reference questions but, if given, will be appropriately identified as such. Staff will accompany the patron to the location of the desired materials in the library and confirm that the information meets the patron's need. If a patron's question cannot be completely met through the library's resources, staff will refer the patron to a more appropriate resource to obtain the desired information whenever possible. Staff will attempt to provide accurate contact information for other agencies when referring a patron but cannot make the actual phone call on behalf of the patron.

Telephone reference service and service provided through technologies, such as online chat sessions, are usually limited to supplying readily available information that does not require extensive research and that can be accurately imparted over the telephone or in brief written passages. The patron best performs extensive research that requires selection of appropriate material, interpretation of data and sources, or analysis of information, although library staff is available to offer guidance. Detailed information, especially that which is subject to analysis or interpretation, will not be relayed over the telephone. Samples of available materials can be gathered and held for patron pickup. Staff cannot photocopy material to be mailed except under circumstances authorized by the library director (such as for disabled patrons who cannot come to the library, for other libraries, etc.).

Telephone reference questions that can be answered quickly (within two or three minutes) without affecting service to patrons in the library should be handled while the patron waits on the phone. Questions that require more time to answer, or that are received while other patrons are waiting in the library, will be handled as callbacks. All callbacks will be cleared by the end of the day or the patron will be notified of the delay. Privacy and concern for accuracy of information will be considered when leaving messages on answering machines or with another household member.

Additional care and caution will be exercised when providing legal, medical, or consumer information. To avoid misunderstandings, it is preferred that patrons visit the library to review this type of information, rather than receiving the information over the telephone, or that patrons be directed to reliable online resources to view and interpret the information for themselves. Reference staff will provide definitions, quote material verbatim, and direct patrons to information sources but will not offer advice or opinions, condense or abstract information, or suggest a course of action or diagnosis. Staff will provide the source and copyright date for legal and medical information.

All requests for reference information are confidential. Reference staff may consult with one another when necessary to serve the patron or consult with staff at other libraries, agencies, and organizations. Questions are tallied for statistical purposes and may be compiled to assist in staff training. In all cases, patron confidentiality and privacy will be maintained.

Approved by (governing body) on (insert date)

_____
Signature of responsible representative

ing nature of technology, you might write the policy broadly enough to encompass new methods for receiving questions and delivering responses.

- Will questions be accepted electronically from nonresidents or those who don't hold a library card? Library Web pages that invite local residents to send reference questions via e-mail may also appear to invite questions from around the world. Providing worldwide reference assistance may not be feasible, but many libraries have established cooperative programs with other libraries to allow access to varied collections and expertise and to expand hours of service. Will materials be copied and faxed or scanned for e-mailing to patrons? Does the library have a policy on faxing and scanning materials?

- Can reference staff make long-distance calls to obtain information needed to answer a reference question? Is a community information file maintained for referrals, especially when questions involve legal, medical, or psychological information?
- If searching online databases incurs costs to the library beyond flat-rate licensing fees, the library may want to have a separate policy on database searching to ensure that all patrons have equitable access to limited resources. Similarly, many libraries that offer patron access to the Internet want to have a separate policy that establishes appropriate use of the Internet connection.
- Will reference and information transactions be recorded for statistical use, collection development, training, or other purposes? Be careful not to compromise patron confidentiality and privacy while assisting patrons in the library, when seeking assistance from other staff, specialists, and organizations, and when staff must call a patron back with answers and information.

HOMEWORK ASSISTANCE

Background

While many of us automatically associate homework with school-age children, it is important to recognize that homework assistance can be requested by anyone of any age. Many adults take college classes, and homework assignments are not limited to children and teens. The policy regarding homework assistance should treat all requests similarly for any student, including adult learners.

Each library must examine its own mission and service priorities and determine the extent of assistance reference staff can provide with homework. Depending on the library's philosophy and the service priorities selected, the library can answer the questions asked, help patrons find the answers, or teach patrons how to use library resources to find the answers on their own. In reality, most librarians try to find a balance based, in part, on the particulars of the immediate situation. For example, a child who is fact-checking a paper may call in with a quick question about the population of a country. That child doesn't want, and probably doesn't need, a lesson on how to use an almanac. On the other hand, many school assign-

---

MODEL POLICY: HOMEWORK ASSISTANCE

Homework questions and assistance with school assignments received from students, regardless of age or grade level, will be answered in the same manner as any other reference question (see also the policy on "Reference and Information Services"). Priority will be given to questions asked by patrons in the library. Telephone and online chat assistance will be limited to short, factual questions that can be answered without interpretation of materials. Materials may be pulled from the shelves and held for patron pickup.

If a teacher informs the reference desk staff that the search process and use of research materials are part of the assignment, staff will defer to the teacher's request and limit assistance to helping students locate appropriate materials without supplying answers.

Elementary grade students needing intensive assistance with their homework (e.g., interpretation of assignments, tutoring, explanation of math problems, etc.) will be referred to the school district's homework assistance program and the library's online homework help program.

Approved by (governing body) on (insert date)

Signature of responsible representative

---

ments are designed to provide a specific learning experience and staff is circumventing the process if they do the work.

Many libraries contract with an online service to provide homework help for school-age students, organize homework tools in a specific quiet study area, or gather Web resources in a specific spot on the library's home page. The library may also have paid or volunteer staff who provide homework help or tutoring. Many school districts also provide homework help phone lines. While these services are helpful and supplement staff time limitations, they generally don't fulfill the needs of every patron.

Issues

- Discussion should include a look at the ways in which homework assistance differs from other reference questions. Has the library selected Succeed in School or Understand How to Find, Evaluate, and Use Information as service priorities? Should reference assistance be provided to help the patron find the answer or to teach the patron how to use library resources? Will the level of service or the extent of assistance with homework be different for in-library patrons versus telephone or chat questions?

- How will staff determine if the question is related to a homework assignment? Contact and cooperation with area schools is helpful but often hard to establish. It may be difficult to discern homework questions from other reference requests until the same question is heard several times. Does the library have a relationship with the school district that encourages teachers to provide alerts regarding specific assignments? Does the library own any of the standard textbooks used by the district?
- Have you discussed homework assignments and assistance with the schools in your service area? Does the school district offer after-school homework help? Are there other groups or organizations in the community offering intensive homework help? Could another community group offer this service in the library? Does the library have funds to provide a commercial homework help service? This would free up library staff while still making the service available to students.

FAXING

Background

Fax machines have been around for some time and are now available in even the smallest communities. While they may seem to be ubiquitous, available even in many homes, fax services may be needed or desired in some communities. A policy will establish the scope and limitations of the service and, if necessary, determine how fees will be applied.

Libraries may look at faxing information as a way of sharing resources with other libraries. It may also provide a way to extend reference services, especially to those who cannot come into the library or who need information more quickly than it can be delivered by other means. Faxing material costs the library staff time and usually requires that documents be photocopied before they can be faxed. Telephone charges may also be an issue if calls are long distance. Acting as a fax service, where patrons request that the library fax or receive items that are not library related, can be more time-consuming and place a burden on staff that may be beyond the scope of the library's mission.

Issues

- Can staff handle the anticipated workload associated with fax service? Does your budget include funds to cover costs of this added service? What level of service will the budget allow?
- Is your fax telephone number published and available to patrons who might want to fax questions or correspondence to the library? Publishing a fax number in directories may result in the receipt of many junk faxes, which cost paper and toner and tie up the fax machine. Should the library fax number be included on library promotional materials distributed to patrons?

MODEL POLICY: FAXING

Fax service is provided by the (name of library) when the information requested is brief and readily available in printed form. Staff cannot conduct extensive research, compile information, or gather data from a variety of sources to be faxed. Fax service will be limited to information provided as part of the reference services of the library.

Materials and information may be requested by incoming fax and requests so received will be treated in the same manner as telephone reference questions.

Staff will adhere to copyright restrictions when faxing materials and a copyright violation warning will be affixed to the front page of copyrighted materials being faxed. Staff may refuse to fax materials that would violate copyright laws.

Outgoing fax calls will be made only within the local dialing area except for those made to other libraries. Requests for outgoing or incoming fax services that are not related to library business will be referred to local fax businesses listed in the telephone directory. Library staff and trustees may send outgoing faxes on a self-service basis but may not incur long-distance charges.

Incoming faxes will not be accepted on behalf of patrons except for those originating from another library. No charges will made for photocopies associated with fax service, however photocopies made to facilitate faxing will be destroyed after use.

Approved by (governing body) on (insert date)

Signature of responsible representative

- Will your staff accept faxed reference questions from patrons or from other libraries? Simple, factual questions may be handled via fax, but longer, more involved questions usually require that a reference interview be conducted.
- Does the library's service area include places for which the library is a long-distance telephone call? If it does, patrons may prefer to fax requests rather than incur extensive long-distance charges from lengthy telephone calls. Can the library budget support long-distance calls to fax information to patrons?
- Are other businesses available in your community that will send and receive non-library-related faxes for patrons for a fee? Many libraries choose not to compete unnecessarily with local businesses, but in very small communities the library may be the only business with a publicly available fax machine. Will staff and trustees be able to use outgoing fax services that do not incur any costs or if they reimburse the costs (such as long-distance charges) even if that service is not available to the public?
- Do you have a policy on copyright and are staff familiar with copyright law? Faxing usually involves making a photocopy first. Copyright principles require that this photocopy be destroyed once the fax has been sent; it may not be kept for future use.[1]
- Will the library try to collect fees for photocopies that were made in order to fax information to the patron? This could create more work than warranted if the library must prepare and fax an invoice with the document. However, if fax requests will take more of the library's budget than can be afforded, a method for collecting fees might be needed.

PHOTOCOPYING

Background

Photocopiers are now standard equipment in most public libraries. They offer patrons a convenient way to copy information from reference books, magazines, and other noncirculating materials. Photocopiers also may reduce mutilation of library materials because they offer patrons a way to get a copy without cutting up periodicals and reference materials. The library photocopier will generally be older and less sophisticated than those found in a copy center or print shop and, except in rare cases where the library has established a for-profit copy shop, should not be expected to substitute for professional copying services.

Issues

- How will the fee for photocopies be established? Fees should be low enough (cost recovery) to encourage patrons to copy materials rather than mutilate books and periodicals. Some libraries offer a small amount of free copying to discourage theft and mutilation of materials. Children, who rarely have money for photocopies and may not have considered the need to copy information, are often also offered a few free copies for school needs.
- Are you familiar with copyright restrictions and do you have them

---

MODEL POLICY: PHOTOCOPYING

The (name of library) provides a photocopier for public use, primarily to facilitate patron use of noncirculating materials such as reference books, magazines, newspapers, and local history materials. Fees for the copier are established by the library board and are approved by the city council. Fees are reviewed annually. As a deterrent against mutilation and theft of library materials, any patron may request up to five free copies per day from noncirculating materials.

Photocopiers are self-service and, with the exception of assisting disabled patrons and patrons who request free copies as stipulated in this policy, staff is not available to make copies. When assisting with the copier, staff will not knowingly violate copyright law. Patrons using the photocopier must adhere to the U.S. Copyright Law when copying materials subject to copyright.

The library attempts to maintain its equipment in good working order; however, the library is not a retail print or copy shop. Copies are for convenience only and those seeking high quality printing or copies (such as for resumes, business correspondence, etc.) are directed to local printing businesses. The library will reimburse only for the first copier malfunction or poor quality copy. At the discretion of the staff, patrons may be permitted to take materials to a nearby copy center if the copier is out of order. Decisions will be made based on the immediacy of need, the type of material, and anticipated length of time that the copier will be out of service.

Approved by (governing body) on (insert date)

Signature of responsible representative

posted by the photocopier? Does the library have a policy on copyright?

- How will staff handle requests for copies when the equipment is not working? If a business with a photocopier is nearby, patrons might be permitted to take items there to be copied. Will refunds be given for poor copies? Is the copier to be self-service (except for patrons with disabilities that prevent their making their own copies) or will staff make copies, collate, and double-side print? Keep in mind that liability for copyright violations may increase if staff performs or closely supervises copying.
- Will library staff and trustees be able to make copies for their personal use at a lower fee, or do they pay the same fee as the public?

DATABASE SEARCHING

Background

Access to information in electronic format is a standard service in most libraries today. This may include online or CD-ROM products that supplement or replace print indexes and CD-ROM products that include full-text copies of magazine articles, online searching tools, and access to Internet resources. Cooperative networks may provide access, at no or low cost to the local library, to databases as part of regional or statewide licenses. Some licenses offer unlimited access to some databases but charge the consortia or sponsoring agency per search or for additional simultaneous users for other databases. Licensing agreements may restrict or limit remote access or require authentication of users to ensure that use is limited to library patrons.

Even products that do not have an associated cost for the search may have costs to the library for paper and toner to print out search results. Policies regarding the use of electronic resources and databases should allow as much flexibility as possible while maintaining control of costs and avoiding unreasonably massive printing. Fees, if any are charged, should be fair and related to cost recovery and should be structured so that they do not prevent access to information that is not available from another source. All patrons, including children, should have equal access to online and electronic services under the same conditions. Depending on the types of databases the library has available, this policy might best be combined with a policy on Internet access or use of public computers. However, the following issues must still be considered.

Issues

- Has the library endorsed the American Library Association's Interpretation of the Library Bill of Rights on "Access to Electronic Information, Services, and Networks"?
- Does the library own, lease, or have access to databases or electronic information resources? What are the costs associated with these resources? Are the resources purchased or leased at a flat rate or are charges made for metered use or simultaneous users? Can per-use charges be easily determined? Do you want to establish some fee-based services while allowing library staff to use database searching as a tool at no charge to the patron when doing so best meets the research needs? Are there licensing restrictions that limit or regulate remote access to electronic resources?
- Are staff available to conduct online searches on behalf of patrons or are the searches self-service? Mediated searches take up staff time but may result in more efficient, and therefore less expensive, searching. Is similar information available through other library resources? In other words, does the electronic resource simply make searching quicker and more current, or is it the only source of similar information available in the library? Some libraries absorb search costs if it is the only source of information, but may pass along costs for searches conducted at the patron's request for expediency.
- How many search stations are available? Is remote access available from home or office for patrons who have a valid library card? Do you want to set a time limit on searching because patrons queue up to use the searching tool(s)? Can patrons schedule time to conduct their database searches? Are staff or volunteers available and trained to provide instruction on how to formulate search strategies, use electronic resources, and navigate the Internet?
- Can patrons print out search results? Do you want to or need to charge for paper for printouts? Can patrons download search results to their own storage device, such as a flash drive, or can they e-mail search results to themselves? Is the USB port on the public access computers readily accessible to patrons who want to use a flash drive? Older PCs may not have a USB port or it may be at the back of the computer and require a lot of moving of equipment to reach. Be sure that computer security issues are addressed as flash drives can download viruses and other executable files to library computers. Additionally, some flash drives do not work with some computers for a variety of, often incomprehensible, reasons.

MODEL POLICY: DATABASE SEARCHING

In accordance with the (name of library's) policy on collection development, information may be acquired in a variety of available electronic
formats. Whenever possible, and if doing so is economically viable, the
library will acquire electronic information that allows the least restrictive
use of electronic resources. Whenever possible, remote access to electronic resources will be made available to library cardholders.

Access to basic electronic resources will generally be available free
of charge to all library patrons. When it is not possible to provide electronic resources without charge, charges will be established by (governing authority) on a cost-recovery basis. Charges will also be
established for printing search results.

Search results may be saved to a flash drive or forwarded electronically to a patron's e-mail address if these functions are supported by
the electronic resource. The library does not and cannot guarantee com-
patibility between programs and peripheral devices.

Search time on unmediated electronic resources may be limited to
15 minutes per patron when others are waiting to use the equipment.
Electronic resources are generally only one of the available sources of
information, and reference staff will help patrons locate other library
resources that will meet their information needs. Staff is also available
by appointment to discuss search strategies, provide instruction on how
to use the electronic resources, and offer suggestions for other resources
that may be useful.

Approved by (governing body) on (insert date)

_____
Signature of responsible representative

INTERNET USE POLICY

Background

The Internet has become a ubiquitous part of public library service and is
now considered a basic service for most libraries. In fact, 99 percent of all
public libraries now provide free Internet access.[2] While it has dramatically
changed the way people can access information, the Internet is both another research tool and another service that the library may offer to the
public. The Internet is also the source of some of the staff's greatest frustra-

tions as most libraries lack sufficient work stations, must limit time each patron can spend online, and deal with complaints about uses that some people consider to be inappropriate or less important (for example, playing games).

With a computer and an Internet account it is possible to search millions of computers and retrieve thousands of pieces of information. Some of the information retrieved is accurate and valid; some is erroneous, inflammatory, or offensive; and, yes, some of it may be pornographic, racist, disgusting, or dangerous. In 1997, it was calculated that "one percent or less of all materials on the Internet is obscene and much of it requires a credit card to access."[3] While that number has most likely increased, and inappropriate and offensive content is certainly out there, it is important to remember that a lot of useful information is available via the Internet.

Staff, patrons, parents, the community, and governing authorities will be more comfortable if policies are in place to establish appropriate and acceptable use of the Internet in the library. Policies may or may not result in limitations on service, but the results of conscious and deliberate decisions, arrived at after research, input, thought, and consideration will benefit all who are involved in providing or using library resources. Because of the changing nature of the issues, the highly charged emotions that may be connected with the topic, and the rapidly changing environment, this section is longer than most of the others provided in this book. Keep in mind that technology, federal laws, and court cases continue to change rapidly; Internet policies may need to be reviewed more frequently than others.

Access to the Internet is now a basic service, and few libraries now question the need to provide it. With almost universal basic connectivity in the United States, some of the issues now relate to the quality of service, speed of access,[4] and appropriate or equitable use of the service. Even if most people in your community have Internet access at home or via a cell phone or other portable device, there are many good reasons for providing access in the library, not the least of which is the vast resources available to help when answering reference questions. For those who cannot afford personal access, who require only infrequent access, are temporary visitors in your community, or the homeless, the library may provide the only free and readily available point of access. More and more government agencies and other organizations have discontinued publication of information in paper formats, many companies are only accepting employment applications online, and more services, such as registration for jury service and paying bills, are available via the Internet, compounding problems for those without Internet access. Even when paper copies are made available, electronically delivered information is almost always more timely and more current, and increasingly the "official" version of documents are those that are available online. An excellent discussion for trustees and library board members about Internet connections is "Do You Dare?"[5] Although it was written more than a decade ago, this document succinctly offers guidance for board members and raises questions to consider. For more detailed information and guidance, refer to *Managing the Internet Controversy* edited by Mark Smith.

Librarians are information specialists, trained to formulate search strategies that ensure retrieval of a manageable amount of relevant information. Quantity means nothing if the information is not valid. Librarians also help patrons evaluate the source of information, its accuracy and reliability, and suggest alternate resources. We do this with print resources and we do it with electronic resources, including the Internet. Internet services continue to change at lightning speed. As difficult as it may be for library staff to keep up with changes, it is even more difficult for the average patron who uses information resources only occasionally.

There are no right or wrong answers, and few questions you, your staff, or your board have are unanswerable. It is unlikely that your library will face any situation that others have not also had to deal with. Examine the other policies your library has already established. Decisions that have already been made about charging for services, age restrictions, and assisting patrons will influence many aspects of your Internet policies. Decisions about limits on printing or charges for paper probably have already been established in other library policies (see policies on database searching and public use of computers). Consider also the impact of changing federal regulations on access, use, and retrieval of personal information. Documents like "Access to Electronic Information, Services, and Networks: An Interpretation of the Library Bill Of Rights" can provide insight into issues to be discussed and information on case law and other background related to intellectual freedom and Internet use. Privacy and security issues also must be considered with regard to wireless connections. An excellent resource is the "Steal This Wireless Policy Checklist," provided by Louise Alcorn on her blog http://maintainitproject.org/node/219.

Issues

- Do you and your staff, the library board, and governing authorities understand the Internet, how it has evolved, and the continuing changes? Are you familiar with the range and multitude of information available? Before establishing policies on patron use of the Internet, staff and the library's governing body should clearly understand the Internet's potential and the inability of any organization to fully monitor or control access to the information provided through this network of computers. Early in the process, provide demonstrations of the Internet for decision makers; don't assume that just because they use e-mail, for example, they understand what information is available through searches or how social networking tools benefit library users. An excellent resource for basic information about issues related to libraries and the Internet is ALA's "Libraries and the Internet Toolkit" available online at www.ala.org/ala/oif/iftoolkits/litoolkit/.

- Many misconceptions exist about the seemingly infinite capabilities and functions of the Internet. Be certain that all who are involved in the development of policy understand terminology, concepts, and capabilities (chat rooms, social networking, instant messages, blogs, wikis, etc.). (Social Networking Libraries, http://socialnetlibraries.wordpress.com/, provides a primer for those new to the subjects mentioned.) What Internet functions will be available to patrons?

- How will you deal with issues on pornography, sexually explicit sites, and other objectionable materials that are available over the Internet? Are you familiar with federal, state, county, and local ordinances that might affect your policies? Legislation and court actions have affected libraries and the Internet for more than a decade. The Supreme Court ruled on June 26, 1997, that the Communications Decency Act (CDA) is unconstitutional because it violated the First Amendment protections of free speech. Obscene speech, as determined by *Miller v. California* 413 U.S. 15 (1973), which established a three-pronged obscenity test, and child pornography are not protected by the First Amendment. However, keep in mind that material that might be offensive or indecent is not de facto also obscene. State laws or local ordinances may restrict materials that might otherwise be protected. Patrons or staff who display pornography to others, distribute child pornography, etc., may be committing criminal acts or acts of sexual harassment and should be dealt with through the legal system. Some libraries include a statement advising patrons about laws dealing with obscenity and child pornography, and before they can access the Internet the patron must take action indicating that he or she has at least seen the warning. The American Library Association offers question-and-answer information about CDA at its Web site (www.ala.org) with links to other associations and organizations that have an interest in the Internet. It is important that library staff and board members keep up with changes in cyberspace law and consult with legal counsel before making decisions.

- In December 2000, Congress passed the Children's Internet Protection Act (CIPA) and the Neighborhood Children's Internet Protection Act (NCIPA). For public libraries, this legislation places restrictions on the use of funding that is available through the Library Services and Technology Act (LSTA) and on the Universal Service discount program (referred to as e-rate) in the form of requirements for filtering or blocking access to certain types of Internet material. NCIPA focuses on the elements that are required in a library's Internet safety policy and applies only to libraries that receive e-rate discounts. Although the American Library Association and other groups objected to the requirements, in part because filters and blocking software are ineffective and overly restrictive, the U.S. Supreme Court upheld the legislation. Do you know whether your library is required to comply with CIPA or NCIPA? Libraries that receive LSTA funds for computer-related services or that accept telecommunications discounts for Internet access or internal computer connections under the federal E-rate program must filter. Some libraries chose to forgo these programs rather than filter Internet access, but most are now filtering.
- If the library does filter, NCIPA requires that specific information be included in the library's Internet safety policy, and requires that some kind of public hearing be held before adopting the policy. The general language of the law has led some libraries to interpret the requirement for a public hearing to include discussion of the policy at a regular board meeting if the public is notified of such meetings. Check with your state library or refer to the Texas State Library's Web site www.tsl.state.tx.us/ld/consulting/tech/cipa.html# (More Information) for details that would be applicable nationally to ensure that your policy includes all features required by NCIPA.
- Have the staff and the library's governing authority read and discussed "Access to Electronic Information, Services, and Networks: An Interpretation of the Library Bill of Rights"? Are you and the library's board or other governing authority familiar with various filtering software packages? Carefully consider any decision to use filters. In 1997, the American Library Association adopted a resolution opposing the use of filtering software as a violation of the Library Bill of Rights. On January 17, 2001, the American Library Association went further, adopted a resolution that opposes federally mandated filtering. A copy of both resolutions is provided in Resource D of this book. While every library is free to develop

its own policies, the ALA has taken the position that filters are ineffective and violate the Constitutional rights of Americans.

- Access to the Internet via filtered or unfiltered computers is a constantly evolving discussion, and the library manager must keep up to date about the issues.[6] Libraries may face as many complaints and threats of lawsuits for filtering as they are of facing legal difficulties for not filtering. "The Internet has been held to be a 'public forum' which means that expression communicated through it enjoys the highest level of protection from government Interference."[7] The use of filtering software by the library may impede free speech. Even if you have decided not to filter, an understanding of how each software package works and comparison of capabilities and limitations will aid in explaining your decision. If you decide to filter, knowledge of the software allows you to choose the least restrictive filtering mechanism. Some researchers have calculated that filters restrict access to one out of five legitimate sites while failing to block about 20 percent of material that would be considered objectionable. Filtering devices can provide a false sense of security for concerned parents and, in the opinion of some, could open the library to liability when the "protection" fails. Within children's departments, most libraries have elected to filter based, in part, on federal law and regulations that make it mandatory. Some libraries have elected to offer levels of filtering, allowing the user or the user's guardian to select the level of filtering when accessing computers that are outside the children's department.

- While the Internet has the capability to support a variety of uses, the library should select those uses that fit the service priorities selected to fulfill the library's mission and meet community needs. Some uses and some users may be accorded priority, while the library may elect to restrict or eliminate other uses. Will access to chat rooms and MUDs (multiuser domains, or other multiuser simulation environments, virtual reality sites, or interactive games) be permitted? Do these functions or protocols further the mission of the library or fulfill one of the library's service priorities? Can patrons download files to portable storage devices? Permitting patrons to download files may reduce the demand for printing, and more and more libraries are allowing this. Again, if you do not understand these functions and their capabilities, find someone who can explain and demonstrate them for you. (Often your state, regional, or system library has staff that can assist you; if not, contact local colleges and high schools or community business partners.) Use for

MODEL POLICY: INTERNET USE

As part of its mission to provide a broad range of information in a variety of formats, the (name of library) provides access to the Internet. Staff will conduct Internet searches on behalf of patrons when warranted as part of the library's reference and information services. Computers are also available for patrons who wish to conduct their own searches or use other Internet resources.

The library is responsible only for the information provided on its own Web site. Access points and links to information resources on the library's home page are selected by library staff and are checked regularly to ensure that they remain valid and consistent with the roles of the library. The library cannot monitor or control information accessed via the Internet. The library cannot guarantee that information on the Internet is accurate. If requested, staff will assist patrons in conducting searches and offer guidance on evaluating sources and verifying information.

Library staff will assist patrons with searches and suggest search strategies, but can provide limited assistance in teaching patrons how to use the Internet. The library will occasionally offer short introductory classes to familiarize patrons with the basics of Internet searching. Videotapes, DVDs, books, and other learning resources are also available for patron use.

The library director will determine the Internet functions that are enabled, but generally they will be limited to those that assist patrons in locating and obtaining information. When it is technically possible to do so, files may be downloaded to portable storage devices or printed to designated printers. Patrons who download files are responsible for verifying that the files are free of computer viruses. Charges for printing will be established on a cost-recovery basis by (governing authority). By logging on to the Internet, patrons agree to abide by the library policy on public use of computers.

Parents or guardians are responsible for Internet use by their children. The library will make available to parents information related to safe Internet practices and computers in the children's room point to age-appropriate Web sites. Staff is available to assist children who are conducting searches. In accordance with federal CIPA regulations, all library public workstations use filtering software. Adults who need unfiltered access for any lawful purpose may use workstations that are labeled as unfiltered or may request access from a staff member, which will be granted on a per-search basis. Parents are reminded that filtering software can be circumvented by experienced computer users; therefore, they should monitor their child's use of the Internet.

Patrons, including minors, who access the Internet in the library, may not display text or graphics defined by federal or state law as obscenity or pornography. In addition, minors are prohibited from accessing materials considered to be "harmful to minors." Library employees are authorized to take appropriate actions to enforce the rules of conduct and to prohibit use of computers by individuals who fail to comply with the Internet Safety Policy as stated or implied herein.

Deliberate and continued display of some materials that are not obscene or pornographic may still constitute sexual harassment. Actions that violate federal, state, or local laws will be referred to the appropriate law enforcement agencies. Repeated actions that create a disturbance or that may be considered sexual harassment may result in the loss of some or all library privileges. U.S. copyright law governs unauthorized use or distribution of copyrighted materials. Users may not copy or distribute electronic materials, except as permitted by the fair-use regulation without permission of the copyright owner.

While the use of chat rooms, social networking sites, wikis, blogs, and other Internet functions are not prohibited, the Library neither encourages nor offers technical support for their use. Patrons should be aware that the anonymity of some functions might also provide cover for individuals with criminal intentions. Users, including minors, are warned that other individuals may obtain unauthorized access to personal information and/or may misrepresent themselves. Users, including minors, are advised not to share personal identification information to unknown or otherwise unverified sources via electronic communication.

Approved by (governing body) on (insert date)

Signature of responsible representative

research and homework purposes may take precedence over playing games on the Internet. Visits to chat rooms may not be permitted at all. Social networking sites, such as MySpace and virtual worlds, have come under federal scrutiny. If passed, legislation like the Deleting Online Predators Act (DOPA) would require public libraries to block access to wide array of content and technologies such as instant messaging, online e-mail, wikis, and blogs. Consider how these functions further the library's mission and service priorities and pay attention to legislation that is introduced and debated.

- Will the library limit access by metering use? How will this be handled? Will patrons be required to have a library card or register for use? Especially where there are not sufficient computers to completely fulfill demand, library cardholders may want to be able to reserve searching time or make appointments to use the terminals. Does the library have the staff to monitor Internet use closely? An elaborate system to "qualify" users, reserve time, assign specific computers to patrons, and clear or reset terminal preferences will not be easy to handle if staffing levels are low. Without sufficient staff, you may need to limit the variety of uses and invest in more security devices to protect the integrity of the computer or its network. Day-to-day maintenance and regular checks on the system will take staff time. Add to this the time needed to reset computers; scan for computer viruses; work with patrons; handle time slots or mediate disputes about waiting times; disperse headphones, sell diskettes or flash drives, paper, or other supplies; and unlock and lock disk drives. Is staff time available to handle each function? If not, look for alternatives that permit the most access for patrons within the limitations of the budget of the library. Volunteers can certainly help, but remember that once a service level is set, it can be difficult to pull back. Start conservatively and expand services as resources permit.
- Will staff conduct formal or informal Internet training for patrons? As savvy as we think all people are, many still need help learning to establish an e-mail account and understanding various functions. Can printed and electronic resources be purchased or developed to address basic skills and answer routine questions about searching? Are staff or volunteers available to offer training classes or to "train on the fly" as users need help? Despite the prevalence of computers and the availability of the Internet, many public libraries find that the demand for training classes and one-on-one assistance outpaces the supply of staff and volunteers.
- Will library staff establish specific starting points for searches on a homepage or front-end menu? These can help by pointing to frequently used sites and can reduce searching time and misuse by leading inexperienced or casual users to sites that fit with the library's mission and roles, including kid's pages and other age-appropriate sites. Many libraries also place disclaimers that patrons must read on the opening screen and click through before proceeding into the Internet. Disclaimers remind patrons that policies have been estab-

lished, reinforce the library's purposes in providing the level of access available, and may provide some degree of protection from liability if a patron encounters offensive material or retrieves erroneous information. Disclaimers may also alert patrons to the need to protect their home computers from viruses if files are downloaded from the Internet through library workstations. It's always a good idea to have disclaimers checked by legal counsel.

- Have you determined where Internet computers will be located? For example, can computers be placed in several locations around the building, or will they be consolidated into one area such as a computer room? Decisions about location may impact decisions about monitoring use, training and staff assistance, or the need for volunteers, as well as decisions about filtering sites, restricting use by minors, or rationing supplies. Location may also affect the privacy of patrons who are using the computers.

- Will children be permitted to use the Internet on an equal basis with adults? The Library Bill of Rights and its interpretation on "Free Access to Libraries for Minors" endorse the right of youth to have unrestricted access to information and library resources. Has the library's governing authority endorsed or adopted these statements? Will parental permission be required for children to use the Internet? Before establishing a separate process for Internet use, consider revising the application for a library card to include a statement of parental responsibility for all library materials and services selected or used by their child. What impact would restricting access to minors have on the ability of children to get information they need or want? What impact will monitoring approved use by children have on staff time and the staff's ability to help other patrons? Do you have information available for parents on child safety on the Internet? As The National Center for Missing and Exploited Children says in their excellent resource *Keeping Kids Safer on the Internet*, "Allowing kids to go online without supervision or ground rules is like allowing them to explore a major metropolitan area by themselves."[8] Few parents would do that, nor would they expect the library to guard their child in the city. The aforementioned publication can be purchased (first 50 copies are free) or downloaded from the Internet. Many libraries link to this document from their homepage to help parents understand how the Internet works, the value of resources available, and ways to help their child stay safe. Remember that the library staff cannot act in loco parentis; parents can restrict the materials and services accessible to their child, but only for their child. Keep in mind that the library may have to comply with federal or state laws that mandate certain elements be included in Internet safety policies or filtering access.

PROCTORING EXAMS

Background

In an era of distance education and self-paced learning, more and more students don't visit a campus or educational facility for their studies. Especially in small and medium sized communities, the library may be the only place where students can find a quiet (or relatively quiet) place to study. Increasingly they are also looking to the library as a place where they can take exams. Proctoring is a process whereby a student takes an exam under the supervision of a person or persons who are not connected with their learning institution or place of business.

Many libraries offer proctoring services as a means to support their mission as a place for lifelong learning or as part of the service response Succeed in School. Keep in mind that proctoring exams can take a lot of time. Proctoring can include overseeing an exam for a person who is seeking to advance in his or her field or who needs to pass continuing education tests to maintain a license. It can also include monitoring a midterm or final exam for a student in a university course.

Issues

- Does the library have space to provide a quiet area for exams and test taking? Is it easy for staff to monitor the area? Some schools require continual observation to ensure that no cheating occurs. Others are more liberal and ask only that the student be in an area that is observable by staff.
- How much demand is there for the service? An occasional request may not pose much of an impact on other library services, but if the community supports a lot of distance education students, demand may quickly increase. The burden is on the student to know the rules for his or her institution and to ensure that they match what the library can provide.
- Can the student bring the exam to you, or does it have to be mailed directly to the librarian? Who is responsible for returning the exam? Some schools require that the exam be under the control of the librarian at all times. Will you accept exams that require special handling, such as faxing or receipt and delivery through overnight shipping services?

- How far in advance can the exam be sent to the library? You don't want to be in the position of holding onto an exam for months or even weeks before the student is ready to take the exam. Are you willing or able to handle exams that are not on paper? Some exams require audio recording equipment or must be taken online, requiring a computer that can be monitored by library staff.
- Will proctoring be available during all hours that the library is open? You may want to restrict proctoring to less busy times or avoid heavy time periods, such as Sunday afternoons, when it may not be possible to provide even minimal oversight.
- Will a fee be charged for proctoring? The attention takes time and may require that space, such as a quiet conference room, be reserved. Exams may also require that the same person monitor the student over the course of several hours, tying up the librarian's time.
- How far in advance will you receive exams, and how far in advance must the student schedule time to take the exam? Most libraries, regardless of size of staff, are not in a position to drop everything in order to proctor an exam. Some libraries offer minimal oversight by

---

MODEL POLICY: PROCTORING EXAMS

As part of its mission to support lifelong learning and the selected service response, Succeed in School, the (name of library) provides proctoring services for students enrolled in distance education courses and for testing required for career advancement. Exams may be on paper or online. The library will provide monitoring but cannot provide one-on-one proctoring or continuous, uninterrupted monitoring of exams. Librarians and library assistants will conduct the proctoring. Several staff members may be involved in proctoring, and the library cannot guarantee that the same staff member will be available during the entire test period. Students are responsible for determining whether the library's level of supervision matches the requirements of his or her institution.

Exam proctoring must be scheduled a minimum of one week in advance and is subject to the availability of staff and appropriate space. Proctoring is available during regular library hours, Monday through Saturday. Due to reduced staff and heavy use, the library cannot schedule proctoring on Sundays. All proctoring must be completed no later than 30 minutes prior to library closing. The library will make every attempt to meet the needs of the student, but proctoring may be cancelled if the library is closed due to inclement weather or other emergencies, including computer malfunctions or severe staffing shortages.

Exams must be mailed to the attention of the library director and should arrive no earlier than a month before the exam will be taken. Faxed or e-mailed exams cannot be accepted. Exams that have been left for more than 45 days will be discarded. It is the student's responsibility to ensure that the exam has arrived in time. The student is responsible for providing supplies, such as pencils, paper, Scantron forms, or blue books, which are not provided by the educational institution. The library cannot provide these items. Photo identification, such as a driver's license or school ID card, must be presented at the time that the exam is taken and must match the name on the exam materials.

A fee for proctoring is set by the (name of governing authority) and is payable at the time the exam is scheduled. The school or the student is responsible for providing a properly addressed envelope with sufficient postage for returning the exam to the school. The library is unable to provide overnight delivery service. Testing materials will be handled in the same manner as all other library mail. Staff is not able to make special trips to the post office or arrange for pickup by delivery or mailing services. The library cannot assume responsibility for completed exams that are not received by the educational institution.

Approved by (governing body) on (insert date)

—————————————————————————

Signature of responsible representative

having the test taker sit near the reference desk, with monitoring being done by anyone who is working the desk.

- Where else in the community might proctoring be available? Some libraries will not proctor some tests, such as the GED, because of their length or the degree of supervision required. It is helpful to be able to refer patrons to other resources.

NOTES

1. Simpson, Carol Mann. 2005. *Copyright for School Libraries: A Practical Guide*. Worthington, OH: Linworth, p. 65.
2. Bertot, John Carlo et al. 2006. *Public Libraries and the Internet 2006*. Tallahassee, FL: Florida State University.
3. Symons, Ann. 1997. Kids, Sex and the Internet. *Texas Library Journal* 73, no. 2 (Summer): 69.
4. ALA Office for Information Technology Policy. Internet Access Principles

(June 2007). Available: www.ala.org/ala/washoff/woissues/techinttele/Internet_Access_Prin.pdf. Accessed November 12, 2007.

5.   Weissman, Sara K. Do You Dare? (June 1, 1997). Available: http://members.aol.com/saraweiss/access/index.html.

6.   For a discussion about one library's decision to require written requests before filters will be disabled, read: Oder, Norman. 2007. Monroe County Adopts Tough Net Policy. *Library Journal* 132, no. 11 (June 15): 16–17.

7.   One Lawyer's Opinion. *Texas Library Journal* 73, no. 2 (Summer): 71.

8.   National Center for Missing and Exploited Children. 2006. *Keeping Kids Safer on the Internet: Tips for Parents and Guardians*. Alexandria, VA: The National Center for Missing and Exploited Children. Available: www.missingkids.com/en_US/publications/NC168.pdf.

Chapter 9

Access and Use of Facilities

The First Amendment to the Constitution of the United States guarantees the right to free speech. As a public institution, the library is considered to be a limited public forum for the expression of ideas. Libraries are not required to make their bulletin boards, meeting rooms, and display cases available to anyone else, but once these areas are opened to outside groups, rules and policies must be applied fairly and equitably. This can be easier said than done when the group wanting to use the meeting room has views that may be abhorrent to a major segment of the community; however, avoidance of controversy is not a valid reason for restricting free speech. Written policies are particularly important when dealing with free speech issues because the courts have found that the lack of a written policy and reliance solely on the discretion of the library director may constitute leaving "too much discretion to government officials without specific guidance."[1] Policies can establish guidelines that allow the library to meet its priorities and serve the community without interference or disruption while still providing a public forum for diverse ideas. Keep in mind that the courts continue to rule on issues related to First Amendment rights, and it is always a good idea to have legal counsel review the library's policies, especially if the policies restrict access to some groups or provide broad authority to the director in deciding on the appropriateness of content.

The policies presented in this chapter deal with access to and use of library spaces and facilities, including exhibit cases and decorations. Interestingly, additional policies dealing with intellectual freedom can be found in Chapter 7, "Collection Development," and Chapter 8, "Reference and Information Services."

USE OF MEETING ROOMS

Background

Many communities have come to recognize that the library is a public forum, a commons that encourages people to gather for discussion, socializing, and learning. Frequently, the library offers the only meeting space readily available for free or at a low cost. As part of its planning process, some libraries determine that one of their primary service responses will be to provide public spaces and common gathering areas, Visit a Comfortable Place in the latest version of the Public Library Association's service responses. This service response emphasizes use of the facility as a place for community activities and meetings to occur, and also emphasizes use of virtual spaces, such as the library's Web site, to provide opportunities for social networking and discourse.

Not all government buildings, or spaces within those buildings, are open to the public. Libraries are under no obligation to make space available for meetings and gatherings. But once the door to the meeting room is open to outside groups, a "public forum" has been established. Especially in publicly funded libraries, once a public forum has been established, there are many factors to consider. Policies can limit times and days that the meeting room is available, frequency of use, minimum and maximum size of group, charging of fees, and the types of events that are acceptable. Policies can even define the community it will allow to use the meeting room, such as limiting use to noncommercial organizations. But as a public building, the library may not, and should not be able to, limit meeting content, even when the views expressed in the meeting may create conflicts within the community.

Additionally, the courts have found that libraries cannot restrict religious groups from using public spaces simply because they are a religious organization.[2] Interestingly, the Supreme Court recently declined to hear an appeal from a circuit court that ruled in favor of excluding religious services from being held in a library's meeting room. The original circuit court decision "held that the library had a legitimate interest in screening and excluding meeting room activities that could interfere with the library's primary mission of providing a quiet place for reading, and that the library could reasonably conclude that a worship service could undermine the library's purpose of making itself available to the whole community by disrupting the library and alienating other users."[3] The court cautioned that the library could not prohibit religious groups from engaging in other religious activities and acknowledged that it might be difficult for a library to distinguish between these kinds of activities and worship services. However, since the religious group had self-identified its activity as a religious worship service the library could apply its policy and exclude the group from using the meeting rooms for the stated purpose. Although this decision applies only in the region covered by the court, it may set a precedent.

Keep in mind that in addition to meeting rooms, the sidewalk in front of the library may also be considered as a public forum, and the library would not be able to restrict petitioners from gathering outside the building.

Issues

- Has the library adopted the American Library Association's Interpretation of the Library Bill of Rights that pertains to meeting rooms? Does the library want to make its meeting room available to outside groups and organizations? If not, the policy should state that the meeting room is for library use only.
- Has the library selected a service priority, such as Visit a Comfortable Place, that emphasizes public space and opportunities for gathering? If the library wants to make its meeting room available to the public, the policy should consider access issues to ensure fair and equitable availability of meeting space.
- How frequently can a particular group schedule the meeting room? Groups meeting weekly or monthly may quickly overbook the meeting room, making it difficult for those needing space on an occasional basis to find any time available. This can also make it difficult to schedule library programs. Limiting the frequency of use also makes the library an unsuitable location for regular church services, ongoing club meetings, and such. Knowing what other meeting facilities are available in the community (recreation centers, community halls, churches) will help when making decisions and provide information about alternatives for those groups that the library cannot accommodate. Examine the policies for using other community meeting room space, especially those operated by the same or related governing authority as the library.
- How far in advance can groups reserve the meeting room? Allowing bookings to be made too far in advance may make it difficult to schedule library functions. On the other hand, permitting the room to be booked only a week or two in advance does not allow groups time to publicize their meetings. When does the booking period begin? Some libraries require all organizations and clubs to sign up for the year but may start the year in September (when school starts

MODEL POLICY: USE OF MEETING ROOMS, 1

A meeting room is available in the (name of library) primarily to support library programs and functions that further the work of the library. When not being used by the library, the room is available for use by established not-for-profit organizations and noncommercial groups based in (city, county). In accordance with the American Library Association's Library Bill of Rights and its interpretation pertaining to meeting rooms, the library does not limit use of the meeting room based on the subject matter or content of the meeting or on the beliefs or affiliations of the meeting's sponsors. However, all meetings must adhere to the rules established by the (governing authority). Failure to comply with the established rules may result in loss of future use.

Except for library and library-related programs, groups and organizations may reserve the meeting room no more than one time each month. A limited series of weekly or daily meetings may be scheduled at the discretion of the library director. The meeting room may be reserved up to 90 days in advance. Fees, rules, and procedures for use of the meeting room are established by (governing authority) and are reviewed annually. A copy of the fee schedule, rules, and procedures will be provided with the application for meeting room use. A completed and signed application must be returned to the library director within two business days or the reservation may be subject to cancellation. The library director may waive fees under exceptional circumstances.

Groups and organizations using the meeting room are required to set up for their meeting, return furniture and equipment to its original location, and leave the room clean and in good condition. The library will attempt to supply standard, nonconsumable meeting equipment and supplies, such as an easel for flip chart pads, a chalkboard, and a speaker's podium if these items are requested when the reservation is made. However, availability of equipment cannot be guaranteed, and meeting planners are encouraged to provide their own equipment. The library cannot provide consumable supplies (pens, paper).

Use of the meeting room does not imply endorsement, support, or cosponsorship by (name of library) of the activities that take place in the meeting room or of the beliefs of the group using the meeting room. Groups or individuals using the meeting room may not imply that the event or program is sponsored, cosponsored, or endorsed by the library in any advertising or publicity.

All meetings and programs held in the library meeting rooms must be open to the public. No selling, solicitation, or taking of orders for future purchases may occur without written permission from the library director. No admission fees may be charged for programs held in the meeting room. Groups and organizations failing to comply with any part of this policy or the established procedures will be denied further use of the meeting room. A library staff member may be present at any time during the meeting.

Approved by (governing body) on (insert date)

_____

Signature of responsible representative

or when the library's fiscal year begins), which can cause confusion unless it is widely publicized.

- Does the person booking the meeting room have to be a registered library user (have a library card)? Must the person booking the room be a resident of the service area of the library?
- Will use be limited to formalized groups, or can individuals and informal groups use the room? Is use limited to groups and individuals in the immediate community? Do you want to set a minimum size for the group in order to avoid booking the meeting room for small conferences or discussions? Does the library have small group workspace elsewhere in the building? The maximum size is generally established by fire codes.
- Must meetings be open to the public or can private, closed meetings be held? Can admission or registration fees be charged to those attending functions held in the meeting room? Can club dues be collected? Can items be sold or displayed for orders to be taken? Are there any circumstances under which items or services can be sold (for example, for library or charity fund-raisers)? Will for-profit groups or commercial enterprises be permitted to use the meeting room even if direct sales will not occur during the meeting?
- If the meeting or program will be advertised, it may appear that the library is cosponsoring the event since it is being held at the library. Does library administration want to regulate wording used by organizations in their advertising or require that organizations include a statement that indicates the library does not endorse the activities?
- Will library functions or meetings that further the goals of the library receive priority or special privileges in scheduling?

MODEL POLICY: USE OF MEETING ROOMS, 2

The library's meeting room is for the use by library staff for library-related and library-sponsored functions, such as children's story time programs, Friends of the Library meetings, and library programs. When not in use, the meeting room may be used as a quiet study room by individual patrons. Groups needing regular or occasional meeting space will be referred to other meeting facilities in the community.

Approved by (governing body) on (insert date)

_____
Signature of responsible representative

- Will a fee be charged for use of the meeting room? Who establishes the fees, and will they be different for profit and nonprofit groups? Under what circumstances, and by whose authority, can fees be waived?
- Can refreshments be served? If refreshments are permitted, how elaborate may they be? For example, will wedding receptions or birthday parties, which usually have very elaborate refreshments, be appropriate uses of the meeting room?
- What equipment will the library provide, if any, for meetings? Can equipment be rented or borrowed from the library? If the library has erasable dry marker boards, consider providing the marker pens to ensure that the proper ones, which do erase, are the only ones used. Is equipment available when the library is closed, and will staff be available to run the equipment or assist with problems? Are there limits on the type of equipment that can be brought in by those using the meeting room? (For example, can a piano be delivered for use during a program?)
- Does the library have staff to arrange tables and chairs, or will those using the room be responsible for moving furniture? Who is responsible for cleaning up? What happens if anything in the room is damaged or if items are missing after use? Do you want to hold a deposit that is returned after the room has been inspected?

EXHIBITS AND DISPLAY CASES

Background

Exhibits and display cases offer members of the community the opportunity to share information, learn about hobbies, crafts, and local art, and express ideas about many things. They can provide a wonderful venue for promoting local talent, skills, and materials, and can be used to generate good public relations and increase visits to the library. Nothing brings parents into the library faster than having their child's art on display! Displays and exhibits can also be used to promote library resources and services. Libraries do not have to make their exhibit space available to anyone else, but doing so may further the library's role as a center for community activities. While the library staff and administration do not have to endorse or advocate every viewpoint expressed in exhibits and displays, once these areas are opened up as public forums, the library may not exclude entire categories of speech. A carefully written policy will protect the library from charges of favoritism as well as from public outrage or dismay when displays or exhibits offend some segment of the community. As with other forums, the library is not required to make its exhibit space or display cases available to the public. Therefore, we have provided two model policies related to this topic.

Issues

- Have you read and adopted ALA's Library Bill of Rights and "Exhibit Spaces and Bulletin Boards, An Interpretation of the Library Bill of Rights"?
- What are the limitations and strengths of the library exhibit space? Some spaces are suited for small items only. Valuable or irreplaceable items should not be displayed in a case that cannot be locked. Sculpture and three-dimensional items may not fit into shallow cases. Consider the kinds of displays that are not appropriate for your library's display case.
- What function will exhibits and displays serve in meeting the overall mission of the library? Has the library selected Know Your Community as one of its primary service priorities?
- Will library staff create all displays, or will members of the public be able to create and set up their own displays? Must individuals or groups sponsoring an exhibit identify themselves in the exhibit? How much information must they provide (name only, or contact information also)? Will information be limited so as not to overwhelm the display case and appear to be a commercial for the organization?

MODEL POLICY: EXHIBITS AND DISPLAY CASES, 1

Display and exhibit space is available within the (name of library) for sharing educational, artistic, and cultural materials that promote interest in the use of books, library resources, and information, or that share information about local art and cultural organizations. The library staff has the primary responsibility for developing displays and exhibits using library resources. However, exhibits that are related to public events and timely topics may be scheduled. Preference for exhibit and display space is given to local nonprofit organizations. Exhibits that are solely for commercial purposes, including the sale of goods and services, will not be considered.

Displays are generally changed monthly, and no exhibit that will be relevant for less than two weeks will be considered. Groups desiring to provide a display or exhibit should contact the library director at least two months in advance. A group or organization may not exhibit items or display materials more frequently than once in a 12-month cycle.

Exhibits and displays may not contain dangerous or hazardous materials, including but not limited to explosives, biological, or chemical material, any device that creates noise while on display, firearms, or perishable materials. Although the library supports free speech and the First Amendment, exhibits may not include speech that is not constitutionally protected or material that would violate election laws if the library is being used as a polling site. The library director may also exclude other items if they are determined to be illegal or would pose a health hazard to library patrons. The library director will consult with appropriate public agencies as part of the decision process.

Displays should be arranged in a neat and attractive manner with printed labels that are legible. No prices may be display on items that are available for purchase, although a card (not to exceed 3" x 5" in size) may provide contact information for sales after the exhibit or display has been dismantled. For security and inventory reasons, staff cannot open display cases to show items to potential buyers or to permit items to be removed for sale.

The library will take reasonable care to ensure the safety and security of items displayed, however the library has no insurance to cover loss, damage, or theft. Exhibitors are encouraged to obtain insurance for items of value and will be required to sign a form releasing the library from liability. Items must be removed from the display cases or exhibit areas as scheduled. Items not removed as scheduled will be removed by staff and secured for 30 days. After 30 days, unclaimed items will be disposed of in accordance with local ordinance.

Display or exhibit of items in the library does not indicate endorsement of the issues, events, items, or services promoted by the displayed materials. Organizations that are denied the use of exhibit areas or display cases or that disagree with the director's decision regarding items to be displayed may appeal the decision to the library board.

Approved by (governing body) on (insert date)

_____

Signature of responsible representative

- Are you prepared to deal with displays that may offend some members of the community or that deal with one side of a controversial issue? Under the concepts of free speech, libraries that permit outside groups to use display cases or set up exhibits cannot compel the inclusion of opposing viewpoints. In general, libraries can establish content-neutral prohibitions related to the time, place, and manner of content but must tread very carefully in writing policies that prohibit specific types of content. In most cases, the library cannot restrict point of view even if the views upset some patrons.
- How frequently can one individual or organization display items or create exhibits? Do you want to establish a minimum and maximum length of time each display can remain on exhibit? Too many changes

MODEL POLICY: EXHIBITS AND DISPLAY CASES, 2

The (name of library) limits the use of its exhibit spaces to library-produced exhibits. Exhibits will be prepared by library staff to reflect topics of interest or potential interest to library visitors and will present a variety of ideas on issues of contemporary interest. Library staff may borrow items from local organizations, groups, or businesses to use in the display and may credit the lender. No library space is available for unsolicited exhibits or displays.

Approved by (governing body) on (insert date)

_____

Signature of responsible representative

will require a lot of staff time coordinating displays; too few changes make display cases stagnant and boring.

- Can display and exhibit areas be secured? What types of materials can be displayed based on security needs? For example, an exhibit of sculpture might not work if the display area is out of sight from staff that could monitor the area for vandalism. Posters and other art that is not behind glass can be easily altered or vandalized.
- Does the library's insurance policy cover items displayed, or does the library wish to state that no liability will be accepted for items displayed? Check with your legal counsel and give the information to anyone interested in exhibiting.
- Will the library permit exhibits of items that are for sale? If items that are for sale (such as art, crafts, and collectibles) are displayed, will sales be permitted from the display? Alternatively, will arrangements have to be made to purchase items outside of the library after the display has been dismantled?

DISTRIBUTION OF FREE MATERIALS

Background

Public libraries are one of the best sources of centralized local information in the community. Many other organizations, groups, and businesses want to use the library as a distribution point for their brochures, flyers, newspapers, notices, and posters. Especially if the library has determined that one of its primary or secondary service roles will be that of Know Your Community or Be an Informed Citizen, the library should encourage the display and distribution of free materials related to community events, activities, and organizations. A clear policy will help the library avoid being overwhelmed by materials and control the duration of distribution, types, formats, size of materials distributed. A well-written policy will also maintain order in the display rack, bulletin board, or information distribution area without impeding free speech.

The library may choose to permit only nonprofit or community groups to distribute information, excluding commercial items such as sales flyers and advertisements for products and services. As a limited public forum, the library is not endorsing the content of the material displayed or distributed and should not exclude materials from groups with differing viewpoints if they meet the criteria for access to bulletin boards and information distribution areas.

Issues

- Does distributing free informational materials further the library's role as a place where residents can find information about the community and local events? Has the library board endorsed the American Library Association's interpretation of the Library Bill of Rights regarding exhibit space and bulletin boards?
- Is the library a single building or are there branches? If all buildings in the library system are not suited for bulletin boards and distribution racks, the policy should indicate that space may be unavailable or limited to library resources because of space limitations.
- Does the library have more than one bulletin board or area for displaying information? In some cases, one bulletin board will be reserved solely for library information, while another area may be provided for public postings. This serves to separate library-endorsed information from self-posted materials that represent free speech. Bulletin boards are usually intended for single-copy posting, while distribution racks or tables may hold multiple copies for patrons to take.
- How much information can your bulletin board or other display area(s) hold? Do you have space for flyers, brochures, newspapers, etc., to be distributed?
- Does staff have time to monitor and maintain bulletin board and display areas? Will staff post items or will patron's self-post? Presenting items to staff ensures that all items meet the policy but can be time-consuming.
- Will the library limit the types of material or the types of organizations that can post items or distribute literature? Although the policy may limit the types of organizations (nonprofit, local arts, etc.), the library may not practice viewpoint discrimination. In other words, the library cannot allow pro-choice literature to be distributed but ban pro-life materials, although the library can apply a policy that limits materials to groups that have offices or provide services in the local community.
- How do you want to limit what is distributed? Size may be a factor for bulletin boards. Also consider how long items may be posted or distributed. Will items that generally promote an organization, rather than a specific event sponsored by that organization, be distributed? Will items that promote for-profit companies, individuals, and organizations be accepted? How will political campaign materials be handled?

MODEL POLICY: DISTRIBUTION OF FREE MATERIALS

Items that publicize or promote community organizations and local events further the role of the library as the central source for civic, cultural, educational, and recreational information.

Display space is available in most branches of (name of library system) for community organizations engaged in educational, cultural, intellectual, or charitable activities to disseminate information. Bulletin boards may not be used for personal or commercial advertisements. Posters and flyers displayed on the bulletin board may be no larger than 8 1/2 inches by 14 inches. Items may be displayed for a maximum period of one month. The person posting the item must write the posting date on the lower right-hand corner of the item. Library staff will remove items that are no longer current or that have been posted for one month. Items removed will be discarded; library staff cannot return posters and flyers that have been displayed.

Community organizations engaged in educational, cultural, intellectual, or charitable activities may distribute informational brochures through information racks or on public information distribution tables provided in branches that have space for them. Items that may be distributed in the information racks and distribution areas include flyers, brochures, leaflets, newspapers, and pamphlets that provide information about nonprofit civic, educational, cultural, or recreational organizations and events. Materials that promote programs or projects of a personal or commercial nature may not be distributed in the library. Items may be distributed for as long as they are valid. If space becomes limited, preference will be given to items of a timely nature and to organizations or groups that have not recently distributed items. Literature related to political campaigns, including issues, referenda, or candidates will be distributed for thirty days preceding an election unless the library is being used as a polling place, in which case election laws will take precedence.

Distribution or posting of items by the library does not indicate endorsement of the issues, events, or services promoted by those materials. Items left or posted that do not meet the criteria outlined in this policy will be removed and discarded. Questions about the policy and its application can be addressed to the library director.

Approved by (governing body) on (insert date)

_____
Signature of responsible representative

- Will the distribution of petitions, solicitation of signatures, canvass-ing, or surveying of patrons be permitted on library property? Does your governing jurisdiction have laws, rules, or guidelines concern-ing these activities on governed property? Again, the area outside the library may be considered public space that is available for the purpose of First Amendment rights as long as the petitioners do not interfere with the ability of others to use the library.

RELIGIOUS PROGRAMMING AND DECORATIONS

Background

Unless handled fairly and consistently, religious celebration of holidays, deco-rations, and programs on religion can create controversy and bad public relations. Although these issues tie in very closely with intellectual freedom, use of meeting rooms, and display of materials in the library, it may be use-ful to have a separate policy that addresses what is acceptable. What is ac-ceptable and encouraged in one community may be the direct opposite of what is supported in another, so it is critical to know what the community wants.

Issues

- Are you aware of the religious and cultural makeup of the commu-nity served by the library? Does the library collection mirror that makeup and include information on various religious and cultural beliefs?
- Does the community welcome the exploration, discussion, and cel-ebration of diverse beliefs, and do community members see the library as playing a role in encouraging diversity? Decorations and programming that reflects a wide range of beliefs may be accepted, while focusing on only one religion may not be welcome. The com-munity may be comfortable with traditional religions but not have considered the inclusion of less commonly known beliefs held by some members of the community (for example, Wiccan celebra-tions). In some communities, it is prudent to limit decorations and library-sponsored programs to seasonal celebrations that reflect secu-lar ideas (e.g., snowflakes, winter greenery, and snow characters rather than Santa Claus, Christmas trees, and crèches) and leave religious programming to community organizations who may use the library's meeting rooms.
- Are stories and activities presented in children's programs adver-tised in advance? It may be acceptable to use religious stories and

---

MODEL POLICY: RELIGIOUS PROGRAMMING AND DECORATIONS

As part of the library's service priority, Celebrate Diversity, the library may sponsor or present programs on a variety of topics, including holiday celebrations representing the diversity of world religions and cultures. Whenever possible, publicity will include details about the program so that parents may make decisions about attendance for themselves and their children. Decorations in the library, except at nonpublic staff desks, will be limited to secular seasonal or patriotic items, such as winter greenery, spring flowers, autumn harvest, and American flags. The library does not determine the content of programs presented by persons using the meeting room (see also the policy on "Use of Meeting Rooms"), and information presented or opinions expressed by outside speakers do not necessarily represent the views of the library.

Approved by (governing body) on (insert date)

———————————————————————————————
Signature of responsible representative

---

holiday activities if parents know about them ahead of time so they can make decisions for their own children. Some parents may want their children to attend a story time on Christmas but would avoid a program involving Halloween. Problems can often be prevented through advance publicity.

- Does the meeting room policy state that activities conducted in the room and statements made by presenters do not necessarily indicate endorsement by the library? Remember that as a public forum, policies may restrict the time, manner, and type of programming in the meeting room but must be content neutral as far as point of view.

PARTNERSHIPS WITH OTHER GROUPS AND ORGANIZATIONS

Background

Libraries are natural partners for many other community organizations. We have always collaborated with some groups, but partnerships have become more critical in past years. Funders want to know with whom we are working, how we are avoiding unnecessary duplication of services, and how we are reaching out to new audiences. Partners provide programming support, funding, public relations, materials, and access to potential library users. Collaborations help to stretch precious dollars, pool resources, and increase the library's exposure in the community. Libraries find that their role in the fabric of the community is enhanced and strengthened through partnerships.

Any partnership or collaboration involves a quid pro quo arrangement. It's not a one-way street with the library getting all of the benefit. Organizations, businesses, and groups look to partner with libraries for the same reasons we look to them but also because the library can provide legitimacy—people tend to trust libraries—and offers access to a wide patron base. A policy that addresses how potential partnerships and collaborative projects will be handled protects the library from having to work with every group that offers help and clearly outlines how partnerships are approved.

Partnerships are long-term relationships, usually expected to last a year or more. Some libraries also look for sponsorship for specific programs, such as sponsors to provide support for the children's summer reading program. While sponsors may return year after year, the benefit is for an immediate project, event, or program. Many libraries choose to address both partnerships and sponsorship in a single policy.

Issues

- What are the library's primary and secondary service responses? Most of the 18 service responses outlined by the Public Library Association's planning process include potential partnerships to some degree. Be sure that you are familiar with the types of partnerships and the partnering opportunities that are available.
- Will the library partner with for-profit or commercial entities? Are there types of businesses that are incompatible with the library's mission? For example, will you partner with a company that distributes alcoholic beverages? Does the library board take issue with the profit motive or with specific types of businesses? For example, most libraries have no problem partnering with child care centers, even those that are part of national chains, but may balk at partnering with a fast food restaurant chain.
- Does the potential partner's mission mesh well with the library's mission? Will the partner organization support the library's commitment to intellectual freedom and open access to information? Partners, even those who are contributing funds, cannot influence or control selection of materials for the collection. Many partners

MODEL POLICY: PARTNERSHIPS/SPONSORSHIPS

The (name of library) welcomes the opportunity to partner with private and public agencies and organizations when doing so benefits the library and the community we serve. Partnerships are considered to be long-term relationships with specific responsibilities and outcomes assigned to each partner. Sponsorships are considered as a means for agencies and organizations to support specific library projects, services, or programs and are short-term.

Each opportunity will be evaluated by the library director to determine the short- and long-term costs (including staff time) and benefits. Based on the scope of the partnership or sponsorship, the director will determine whether a formal agreement or contract is required. The library director may enter into formal agreements or memos of understanding. Contracts for more elaborate partnerships or sponsorships require approval of the board of trustees.

The mission and policies of potential partners and sponsors must be compatible with the policies, vision, mission, and goals of the library. Partners and sponsors agree to act in ways that are mutually beneficial and adhere to oral or written agreements. Priority will be given to organizations, agencies, and businesses that help the library extend or enhance services to the community.

The library will develop each partnership individually, documenting the terms and conditions. If deemed appropriate by the library director, these terms will be formalized in a written agreement or contract. The director will assign a staff member to be the primary liaison for the partnership and expects the partner to do the same. The library may cancel a partnership agreement at any time if the partner uses the library's name without prior consent or if the nature of the partner's mission changes substantially or in a manner that becomes inappropriate with the library's mission and image.

Approved by (governing body) on (insert date)

Signature of responsible representative

or sponsors enjoy a tax benefit from working with the library; however, the library must not set valuations on gifts or services. That is the responsibility of the donor.

- Partnerships take work. Does the staff have the time, or can they

make the time, to establish a strong relationship with partner groups? Will the long-term benefits of the partnership outweigh costs, both actual dollars and staff time?
- How will publicity about the partnership be handled? Care must be taken to ensure that the library's name and reputation are not inappropriately used.
- Will all partnerships or sponsorships require a written agreement? Who has the authority to agree to partnerships or sponsorships?

NAMING OF LIBRARY FACILITIES AND INTERIOR SPACES

Background

The opportunity to name all or part of a public library building is a great honor. However, it is also not an opportunity that should be offered lightly. Naming the entire library building after an individual is not a simple process and, especially if the person to be honored is still living, may come with strings attached or responsibilities that were not anticipated.

Some libraries choose to honor important or influential people in the community by naming the building for that person. Others look at naming as a fund-raising opportunity and a way to leverage public resources by requiring a substantial contribution of land or money before the donor can determine the name. Common also is the provision for naming opportunities within the building. For example, when a library building is undergoing remodeling, donors may contribute funds for specific features, such as chairs and tables, or areas, such as the children's room, the café, or a new wing. Their contribution is recognized by having that interior space named for them. It's best to have a naming policy in place before undergoing a building project, expansion, or renovation to avoid having to make decisions under pressure from the community or a special interest group.

Issues

- Does the parent governing authority, such as the city or county, have a naming policy? Does the policy cover the library or can it be modified to meet library needs?
- Who will have the authority to determine naming opportunities and to establish criteria for naming?
- Do you want to consider establishing a policy that limits naming of buildings to geographic areas, such as North Branch or Chinatown Branch? This eliminates a lot of potential problems and may provide a sense of "ownership" to the community served, but may also be perceived as boring or restrictive.

MODEL POLICY: NAMING OF LIBRARY FACILITIES AND INTERIOR SPACES

The naming of all new library buildings, including new buildings and buildings undergoing renovation, expansion, or remodeling, is the responsibility of the library board with the approval of the (name of governing authority).

Preference is given to naming facilities with geographic or functional designations. The library board may decide to honor an individual for his or her significant and outstanding contribution to the community, in keeping with the nature and mission of the library. When this option is pursued, input from the community will be solicited. Persons currently holding political office or serving in any official capacity on the library board or staff will not be considered for naming opportunities.

The board may also choose to name the building in honor of a donor or donors who request naming rights and who contribute a minimum of 51 percent of the total project costs, including construction, equipment, furnishings, and collections for the building as part of the acceptance of such gift. Buildings will not be named for corporations or religious organizations, regardless of the size of the gift.

When a new building is planned or an existing building is undergoing extensive renovations, the library board, with the approval of the (name of governing authority), may designate specific interior naming opportunities. Interior naming opportunities may be made available to individuals, families, foundations, and corporations making a significant contribution to the project, as determined by the square-footage costs of the specific area of interest, plus the cost of new equipment or collections for that area. The library director, in consultation with the library board and the library design team, will determine the manner by which interior naming opportunities will be recognized, e.g., signage and plaques.

Approved by (governing body) on (insert date)

——————————————————————————

Signature of responsible representative

- Will you prohibit specific categories of naming opportunities? For example, some libraries will not name a building after a corporation or a religious organization, although they will allow interior naming opportunities. When naming the building for a living person, consider the impact on that person. Will he or she feel obligated to attend all celebratory functions? Also consider that the reputation of public figures, especially celebrities, may change over time. Be cautious of setting precedence for naming buildings, or features of the building, in honor of fallen heroes, young people who have died tragically, etc. While it is tempting to honor the first local soldier who died in a war, will feelings be hurt when there is no naming opportunity for future honorees?

- If the building or other area is to be named for an individual, must that individual be a current or former resident of the community? Must the individual have had some connection to the roles and mission of the library, such as a pioneer librarian, an advocate for literacy, or a local writer? How can the community suggest names and what information is needed for a name to be considered?
- Can naming rights be "bought" through major contributions to the library? If so, do you want to establish specific funding targets for different naming opportunities? For example, it might be possible to name a bench in the atrium for $3,000 but require a contribution of $30,000 to have the children's wing named for the donor.
- Under what conditions might a building, or part of a building, be renamed? While it is wonderful when we can leverage public funds with private dollars, be careful about having every area of the library labeled with what may be perceived as price tags.

NOTES

1. Minow, Mary. Who's In and Who's Out? Library Meeting Room and Exhibit Space Policies. Infopeople Project (May 9, 2004). Available: www.librarylaw.com/MeetingRoomHandout.htm. Accessed November 14, 2007.
2. Minow. 2004.
3. Supreme Court Won't Hear Meeting Room Appeal. *American Libraries Online* (October 5, 2007). Available: www.ala.org/ala/alonline/currentnews/newsarchive/2007/october2007/meetingroom.cfm. Accessed December 3, 2007.

Chapter 10

Patron Conduct

Whether we refer to them as patrons, customers, library users, citizens, or something else, libraries exist to serve the needs of the people who visit, call, or in some other way contact the library. Staff are in the library primarily to assist patrons, but while serving the public is generally very rewarding, it can also be aggravating, trying, and frustrating. In 1991, when a court ruled in favor of Richard Kreimer, a homeless man who had been expelled from the Morristown (NJ) Public Library, librarians panicked. They were concerned that they would no longer be able to set rules for library use or guidelines for patron behavior. An appeals court found that, as limited public forums, libraries could set rules necessary to ensure the orderly use of the place. The court of appeals further found that persons using the library for other than its recognized purposes could be expelled,[1] reaffirming the ability of public libraries to develop guidelines related to appropriate conduct and use of the library.

Well thought out and clearly written policies that let patrons know the specific behaviors that are inappropriate and let staff know what actions will not be tolerated are more likely to hold up on review. Policies also ensure that rules are reasonable and are applied consistently and fairly. If you need additional information about how to handle a variety of potential problems and situations, refer to *It Comes with the Territory: Handling Problem Situations in Libraries* by Anne M. Turner.

LIBRARY BEHAVIOR

Background

Everyone who uses the library has the right to facilities that are safe and comfortable to use. Safety rules and policies that expect courteous behavior and responsible actions should be enacted and uniformly enforced. While some policies may need to be directed specifically to the special situations faced by children, young people should not be held to a higher standard than adults. Appropriate conduct should be expected from people of all ages. Some libraries prefer to separate the issue of unattended children who are left in the library without appropriate supervision from issues of behavior through separate policies that address child safety. Library policy should set a tone that supports behavior that is appropriate to the services provided by the library. It's also important that all staff receive training so that the library staff cultivates an atmosphere that fosters respect and appropriate behavior.

Issues

- Those using the library have the right to work in an environment that is conducive to its legitimate use. Are there physical factors that might interfere with having an environment that is conducive for studying, reading, and research? Are you able to provide quiet study areas or areas where teens can be a little louder?
- Rules of conduct should be made with the interests of patrons foremost in mind. Consider the library layout before imposing unnecessarily restrictive rules. For example, cellular phones, personal pagers, laptop computers, and portable audio devices, even the quietest of which make some noise, may be permitted in a general reading area, but not in quiet study areas. Personal audio devices with headphones may be used almost anywhere without disturbing others. Will cell phone conversations be louder than general conversation? If quiet study carrels are readily available, low-toned conversations may be permissible in general use areas.
- Will the library's electrical system and layout permit the use of personal appliances? Older buildings and buildings with inadequate power supplies may not be able to handle additional appliances. In addition, patrons might unplug library appliances in order to plug in their own devices, creating problems.
- All patrons, regardless of age, should be expected to follow the same rules of conduct. Children may require additional consideration because of their youth and vulnerability, but should not be held to a

higher standard of conduct than is expected of adults. Staff should not be expected to be babysitters for children left unattended. If this is a particular problem in your community, consider having a separate policy that deals with unattended children or children who are left in the library at closing that focuses on child safety issues (see policy on unattended children).

- Staff should not be subjected to abusive language and inappropriate behavior from patrons. Has staff been trained to respond coolly to anger? Have procedures been established so that staff may remove themselves from abusive situations?

- Do you understand the issues related to First Amendments rights and regulating behavior? Policies can address behavior and set conditions for use of the library but should be content neutral. For example, the policy can address behavior that disrupts others who are using the library but probably can't dictate that patrons not view adult Web sites on library computers, especially if the computers have privacy screens, unless the person viewing the Web site is being boisterous about the content.

- Policy should address general areas of behavior and be broad enough to include actions or behaviors not mentioned. Do not attempt to list every conceivable negative action or inappropriate behavior. A determined patron can always find something to do that you will not have considered! Your policy also does not have to itemize behaviors that are already against the law (for example, breaking and entering or engaging in acts of lewd conduct are already covered by laws in most jurisdictions). If you feel that these acts should be covered, include them in a general statement that cites the laws or indicates that criminal behavior will be reported to the authorities.

- The judge in the case of *Kreimer v. Morristown* has stated publicly that he did not rule against the library because he wanted to protect the rights of a "smelly, homeless man" to annoy patrons and drive them out of the library. Rather, he "declared a regulation invalid on the grounds that it was too vague and broad in giving librarians the discretion to oust or forever bar patrons."[2] Be sure that your policy is specific, addresses behaviors that pertain to the library's mission, and provides a process for an appeal and a way to regain admittance to the library.

- Do you know which local law enforcement agency will respond to calls for assistance? Have you discussed the parameters of legal enforcement? Do you have a commitment for support from that agency?

MODEL POLICY: LIBRARY BEHAVIOR

The (name of library) encourages people of all ages to visit the library. Those using the library and its resources have the right to expect a safe, comfortable environment that supports appropriate library services. The (name of library) seeks to foster a quiet and orderly environment that is conducive to reading, acquiring information, and study.

People entering the library are expected to respect the rights of other patrons to use the library. No person shall harass or annoy others by being noisy or boisterous, by playing audio equipment so that others can hear it, or by behaving in a manner that reasonably can be expected to disturb other persons.

People demonstrating disruptive behavior will be required to leave the library after one warning from library staff. Disruptive behavior includes, but is not limited to, noisy, boisterous actions; inappropriate behavior, including eating, smoking, running, or loud talking; misuse of library property; uncooperative attitude; or actions that deliberately annoy others or prevent the legitimate use of the library and its resources. Abusive language and behavior toward staff will not be tolerated.

Personal appliances, such as computers, audio devices, and calculators, may be used if the noise level is low and use does not interfere with others. Because of the lack of outlets and concern for electrical overload, all appliances must be battery-powered and may not be plugged into library outlets without staff approval. Staff will attempt to locate a suitable workstation in the public areas but cannot guarantee that an electrical outlet will be available. Cellular telephones and pagers should be turned off or switched to a nonaudible signal and should be answered outside the library.

Young children may not be safe when left unattended in the library. Staff will not know if children are leaving with a parent, a friend, or a stranger. Library staff will not deliberately seek out unattended children; however, unattended children frequently become disruptive when they become bored. Parents are responsible for ensuring the appropriate behavior of their children while in the library. If a parent or other responsible adult cannot be located, unattended children who are disruptive will be placed in the care of (specify local law enforcement officials). Under no circumstances will library staff take a child out of the building or transport children to another location.

Approved by (governing body) on (insert date)

_____

Signature of responsible representative

VIOLENCE AND WEAPONS

Background

Although these issues are included in the policy on patron conduct, some small and medium sized libraries find the need to have a separate, more specific policy that deals with issues related to carrying weapons and violent encounters. State and local laws may come into play regarding carrying of handguns and may also define what constitutes a weapon.

Issues

- Does state code define dangerous weapons or deal with an individual's right to carry a handgun? Does state law allow firearms to be carried in personal vehicles? If there are state laws or local ordinances, these should be cited in the policy.
- Does state law allow libraries or local jurisdictions to prohibit carrying concealed weapons in the library building even if carrying a concealed weapon would otherwise be legal?
- Does the library have security guards? Is it likely that security guards will carry weapons? With the exception of security guards, the policy should apply to staff and volunteers as well as patrons.
- How will the library define weapons, and will it distinguish between any item that could be used as a weapon (such as a Swiss Army knife) and items created specifically for use in protection or as weapons (such as explosives, fighting stars, switchblades, mace, or brass knuckles)? How will you handle heavy walking sticks, box cutters, and other items that might be used as a weapon? Remember that some patrons may have a physical need for a walking stick or cane.
- Keep in mind that staff should never get into a confrontation with anyone who is holding a weapon. If the library does not have security guards, be sure that staff is trained to understand conflict avoidance and has access to numbers for local police and public safety officials.

MODEL POLICY: WEAPONS IN THE LIBRARY

Library staff and patrons visiting the (name of library) have the right to work in a safe environment. This policy, along with the policy of patron conduct, intends to ensure the safety, security, and comfort of those who are in the library. Any behavior that is disruptive or that prevents the library from ensuring a safe environment or from fulfilling its mission will result in an appropriate response including denial of access to facilities and services.

Weapons of any kind are prohibited in the (name of library). Possession, use, or threat of use of a dangerous weapon will result in eviction from the library. Weapons are defined as any dangerous item designed for use in harming a person or animal, including but not limited to firearms, such as rifles, handguns, BB guns, etc., switchblades, martial arts weapons, and explosives. No open flames, incendiary devices, or explosive devices, including fireworks, are permitted in the library. Lighters, matches, and candles may not be used in the library.

This policy does not prevent legally licensed weapons from being stored in a vehicle that is parked on library property as long as the weapon is stored in accordance with applicable state laws. This policy does not apply to law enforcement officers and library or city security officials who are carrying weapons while on duty.

Violence or threats of violence will not be tolerated. If a patron is violent or makes violent threats, the library staff will call the local police and evict the patron from the library. Items that are commonly used for nonthreatening purposes, such as canes, knitting needles, and box cutters are permitted. However, patrons who threaten to or appear to be threatening to use such items as weapons will be dealt with in the same manner as those carrying dangerous weapons.

Patrons who are in possession of a dangerous weapon will be asked to remove the item from the building and will be provided with a copy of this policy. If the patron does not comply with the request, the library staff will call the local police.

Approved by (governing body) on (insert date)

Signature of responsible representative

UNATTENDED CHILDREN/CHILD SAFETY

Background

The primary concern regarding underage children who are left unattended in the library is for their safety. Secondary concerns are related to the impact of the behavior of unattended children, who may be bored or resentful, on the ability of other patrons to use the library and the amount of time staff must devote to addressing inappropriate behavior.

Preschool children should never be unsupervised. Many librarians believe that leaving children unsupervised constitutes child neglect. Children who are old enough to be in the library on their own are often referred to as "latchkey" children. These are children of school age who may be sent to the library after school until a working parent can pick them up, or the children may prefer being in the library to being home alone. These children should be subject to the same guidelines for patron behavior as adults and not be treated differently just because of their age.

An additional problem may occur with children who are old enough to be in the library alone but are unable to get home on their own and are still at the library at closing time. Although legally the library has no responsibility for children who are left unattended, most of us are concerned about their welfare. In small towns and close-knit communities, we may even feel more responsibility because we know the families (or at least know of the families).

Library managers must be concerned about potential liability for problems that may occur either because of library staff trying to help a child or because actions or policies establish an expectation of responsibility. Although library staff has no legal duty to help a child who has been left at closing, any library staff who do help have a responsibility to see the situation through to its conclusion. If, for example, the librarian waits with a child for a short period of time after closing but then decides to go ahead and leave, he or she may be held responsible for any problems that occur after his or her departure. "By taking on the responsibility of waiting with unattended children, the library has assumed a duty of due care."[3] Liability depends, in part, on what the library's policy says about unattended children.

Issues

- Any policy must address concern for the safety and well-being of children. Additional concerns are for maintaining an orderly place where all patrons can make appropriate use of the library.
- What is the age in your community under which children may not be left without adult supervision? The age under which a child can be considered abandoned if left without parental or other adult supervision is generally established by the legal system. In most

communities, there is not a hard and fast rule about when children can be left without parental supervision or under the care of a legal guardian. Many libraries consider the age at which children in their community might reasonably walk to and from school alone when developing guidelines. Keep in mind that maturity may be as much a factor as age. Above a reasonable age, maturity and the ability to self-regulate behavior must be considered.

- What other facilities are there for child care in the community? Problems with unattended children are better resolved by offering solutions for parents who may feel they have no other choices for their children. The Public Library Association's Service to Children Committee implores libraries to be involved in finding solutions to a community-wide problem and suggests that the library serve as a catalyst for change. At the very least, being able to offer parents alternatives may help alleviate the problem of unattended children being left in the library.

- Have you discussed concerns about the safety of children and appropriate actions with the local law enforcement authorities? Support from law enforcement authorities will allow the library to establish policies and write procedures that will be enforceable. Without support, the library runs the risk of receiving no response or getting an inappropriate response from law enforcement agents who may feel that the library is unnecessarily calling on them. In many locations, child protective service agencies will help library staff understand what constitutes child neglect and provide information on resources for parents.

- Have you discussed liability for unattended children with your legal counsel? Although the public library does not have the same provision of care responsibilities that schools and child care centers have, local laws may set stricter standards. Under no circumstances is it advisable for library staff to transport children in a personal vehicle. Especially in small, close-knit communities, this can be an uncomfortable, but necessary part of the policy. If the library's policy directs staff to stay with unattended children after closing, the library is establishing the duty of due care, and staff are taking care of the child as part of their library duties. If there is not a policy directing staff to stay with unattended children after closing or to take other action such as taking the child somewhere else, the library staff who do take action faces personal liability if problems arise. Keep in mind that if staff are directed to stay with a child after closing, this is considered work time and the staff members should be compen-

MODEL POLICY: UNATTENDED CHILDREN/CHILD SAFETY

The (name of library) is a public facility that offers services to a wide range of citizens, and children are especially welcome. The library has the responsibility to provide an environment that is safe and comfortable for every patron who is appropriately using its services and facilities. Children and young people are expected to adhere to the same standards of patron conduct expected of adults. Parents, guardians, or assigned chaperones are responsible for the behavior of their children while in the library.

Children under the age of seven should never be left unsupervised in any area of the library. If a parent cannot be located within five minutes, the unattended child will be taken to the security office and staff will call the (proper authorities) to report an abandoned child.

Older children who are disruptive or misbehaving will be asked to leave the library; see policy on "Library Behavior". If the child cannot safely leave the library to return home on his or her own, staff will either allow the child to remain at the library under close supervision until a parent can be contacted or will contact the (proper authorities), depending on the severity of the situation.

Children who are old enough to be in the library on their own will be asked about transportation approximately 15 minutes prior to the library's closing. Children who have not been picked up at closing time will be given the opportunity to call a parent or other responsible adult. Children who have not been picked up within fifteen minutes after closing will be left in the care of (proper authorities). Under no circumstances will staff transport children in a vehicle or accompany them home.

Approved by (governing body) on (insert date)

Signature of responsible representative

sated appropriately. It's probably good practice, and provides an added measure of security, to have two staff members stay with a child.

- Are parents leaving young children in the library while they run other errands? Some parents assume that the library is a safe place for their children and will drop young children off for programs while they leave for a short time. Are signs posted warning parents not to leave the building while their children are in library-sponsored programs? Are brochures available that explain concern for the safety of children left unattended? If possible, brochures should also offer suggestions for alternatives to leaving a child alone in the library.

- Is the library within walking distance of most households in the community or near public transportation? Are library hours clearly posted and kept as consistent as possible so that parents know when the library closes? It may be necessary to contact the police if children are left waiting outside alone after all staff members have left the building.

HARASSMENT AND LEWD BEHAVIOR

Background

It is understood that patrons and staff should be able to work in an environment that is free from sexual harassment, lewd behavior, bullying, or other forms of harassment. It is important that the library respond to any allegations of harassment, especially sexual harassment, including those involving two or more patrons or a patron and a staff member. A policy on harassment, and immediate action in response to complaints of inappropriate behavior, will reduce the likelihood of a lawsuit against the library and its governing authority. Keep in mind that the best defense against liability is to provide an atmosphere that discourages any type of harassment and avoids creating a potentially hostile environment.

Issues

- Does your state have any laws or regulations dealing with harassment? If so, consult those laws and be prepared to provide the legal citation.
- Has staff received training to recognize and respond to sexual harassment? Have staff been instructed on how to respond to complaints from patrons about lewd behavior or other types of harassment? All complaints should be taken seriously and staff should thank library users, especially children, for reporting all incidents.
- Do you know what law enforcement agency to contact to report serious incidents of lewd conduct? Serious incidents include any incidents involving an unwilling person, inappropriate or indecent behavior with a child, and continued behavior that makes another person unable to continue using the library. Minor incidents, such as teenagers making out in the library or name-calling may be handled as inappropriate behavior unless problems persist. Be aware

---

MODEL POLICY: HARASSMENT AND LEWD BEHAVIOR

Patrons and staff have the right to enjoy an environment free from harassment or lewd conduct. Harassment is defined as persistent and unwelcome conduct or actions. Sexual harassment includes unwelcome sexual advances, unwelcome requests for sexual favors, unwelcome physical contact of a sexual nature, or unwelcome verbal, nonverbal, or physical conduct of a sexual nature.

Anyone, including patrons, who harasses staff or another patron will be asked to leave the library and a report will be filed with the director. Repeated acts of harassment or acts that appear to have the potential to escalate into violent or illegal actions will also be reported to (proper authorities).

Lewd acts, sexual misconduct, and sexual harassment are not acceptable actions. Those who commit minor acts, such as teenagers who "make out" in the library will be given one warning and then asked to leave. Serious acts involving minors will be reported to (proper authorities). All acts of sexual harassment will be also reported to the director for investigation.

Approved by (governing body) on (insert date)

_____

Signature of responsible representative

---

of the line between consenting behavior between teenagers and sexual bullying.
- Bullying is a type of harassment. Even without immediate harm or threat of harm, bullying often escalates into violent behavior.
- Does the library's governing authority have a policy prohibiting sexual harassment? To what office or agency are incidents to be reported? Do staff know the process for reporting incidents of harassment?
- Must a staff member have observed the incident in order to call law enforcement? Some jurisdictions require that the person involved or a witness file the complaint. Check with your legal counsel.
- Any incident involving a child should be reported to the child's parent, who should also be informed of any action taken by the library.

PATRON USE OF LIBRARY SUPPLIES

Background

Patrons are expected to bring their own common office supplies (e.g., paper, pens, paper clips, index cards) if they need them for use in the library. Supply budgets are limited, and these materials are generally consumable or, if they are borrowed for use, may not ever be returned. However, in the interest of customer service, libraries frequently provide scratch paper (usually recycled from the photocopier or left over from other projects) and pencils for use at the card or online catalog. Libraries may also provide paper cutters, scissors, staplers, or other materials for use at the photocopier.

Consider the public relations value of supplying some items versus the nuisance factor of having to justify not loaning a pencil or providing a paper clip to a patron. It is helpful to have some pencils available for loan if the library serves students and children, especially if the library has selected Succeed in School as one of its primary or secondary roles. Some libraries choose to have small quantities of paper, envelopes, pens, correction fluid, diskettes or thumb drives, etc., available for purchase at cost or to generate small amounts of revenue for the library.

Issues

- What supplies can be provided without cost, at low cost, or without affecting the library supply budget? Would a stapler and similar equipment aid those who use the photocopier?
- Does the library wish to resell small quantities of common supplies?

MODEL POLICY: PATRON USE OF LIBRARY SUPPLIES

The (name of library) supplies scratch paper, recycled from the photocopier and other sources, for note taking but cannot provide other office or school supplies. Office supplies purchased with library budget funds are for use by the library staff in the completion of their work. Because they are purchased with public tax funds, these items cannot be sold or given away. Small quantities of typing paper, pens, index cards, computer diskettes and thumb drives, etc., are available for purchase at the circulation desk priced on a cost-recovery basis.

Approved by (governing body) on (insert date)

Signature of responsible representative

Does the library's governing authority permit revolving accounts to allow the purchase of additional items for sale from the funds collected? Who will collect the money? How will supplies be replenished? Is there a library store or gift shop that could sell office supplies?

- Are stores located nearby that sell paper, pens, and other office supplies? How inconvenient will it be for someone to have to run out to purchase index cards, paper, correction fluid, etc.?

FOOD AND DRINK IN THE LIBRARY

Background

Many libraries, especially those that have selected roles or service priorities that encourage use of the library as a place or destination (such as the Public Library Association's role Visit a Comfortable Place) recognize that many patrons want to enjoy a cup of coffee or snack while using the library. Bookstores allow (and even sell) coffee, and coffee shops sell books and magazines. Internet cafés flourish and somehow manage to deal with issues related to liquids and computers.

While these for-profit entities may consider a few ruined items to be a cost of doing business, libraries should weigh the customer service benefits of meeting current expectations against the real (rather than perceived) problems of space, spills, and cleaning. Creating a welcoming environment, especially for teens (who are incessantly hungry) and for adults who may spend hours working in the library, is vital to the future of public libraries. Many libraries already permit food to be served in the meeting rooms. If there have been few problems in those locations, it's not likely there will be vast problems in other library areas. A library that does not have the capacity to provide space for food and drink may want to include this prohibition in the policy of behavior and conduct rather than in a separate policy.

Issues

- Does the library have space for people to enjoy a snack or beverage? Many libraries prefer to provide a specific space where vending machines, a coffee cart, trash cans, etc., can be located along with easy to clean tables and chairs.
- Does the library have a friends group or other organization that is willing to sell coffee and snacks? Does the library have space that will meet local health codes for providing food and beverages? Is there a coffee shop close to the library that would compete with library sales? Stephanie Gerding's article "Fund-Raising Perks of

> ### MODEL POLICY: FOOD AND DRINK IN THE LIBRARY
>
> The (name of library) strives to provide a clean and comfortable environment where people can enjoy the materials and services provided by the library. Food and beverages may be consumed in meeting and conference rooms and in the designated "coffee corner." Beverages in lidded containers can be consumed in any part of the public area and include covered coffee, soda, and juice containers and plastic beverage bottles with caps. Please immediately report spills to a staff member to avoid damage to library property.
>
> Approved by (governing body) on (insert date)
>
> _____
> Signature of responsible representative

Library Cafés" in *Public Libraries* outlines the issues related to running a food service business in the library and includes examples from small and rural libraries.

- Will having food and drinks create an unwarranted amount of work for staff? Often the anticipated problems are unfounded. Much of the initial concern raised in the 1990s when the first libraries opened their doors to coffee and cafés has died down.
- What level of service will meet the needs and expectations of library patrons in your community? Generally, service can range from minimal, such as a self-service coffee pot or simply permitting patrons to bring coffee and other beverages and snacks into the library, to something in between, such as providing vending machines or coffee cart and an area for consuming snacks, all the way up to a full-service café that is within the library but is run by a private business under contract.

THEFT OF MATERIALS

Background

Libraries lose items to theft; it is a part of doing business, and a clever and determined thief will overcome any security or theft detection system. The challenge is to reduce theft without creating the feeling of an armed camp where legitimate library users are under constant surveillance and considered guilty unless proven innocent. Policies should be written so that everyone is subject to the same inconvenience or questioning. Remember that this type of policy must be reasonable and must be applied fairly and consistently to avoid any allegations of prejudicial treatment. Even the appearance that only some people are subject to the policy could result in adverse legal action. If personal items are to be examined, signs should be posted alerting patrons that items brought into the library are subject to search. It is probably better to err on the side of losing a few items rather than to become the "library police."

Issues

- Do you know what percentage of the library collection is lost to theft each year? Do you have a theft detection system? How reliable is it? What is the frequency of false alarms? Has staff been adequately trained in the methods of desensitizing tags?

MODEL POLICY: THEFT OF MATERIALS

All items removed from the (name of library) must be charged out through the circulation desk. It is a violation of (cite local ordinance) to deliberately remove an item from the library unless the item has been properly charged out in accordance with established library procedures.

To protect the investment in library materials made by taxpayers, as patrons leave the library, security staff may conduct random examinations of book bags, backpacks, briefcases, and other large containers brought into the library. Any uncharged items will be returned to the circulation desk to be charged out. If staff believes that, due to the large volume of materials and/or value of materials, theft was intended, the police will be immediately notified.

Signs indicating that personal items may be examined will be posted at the entrance and inside the library. Storage lockers are provided at no charge for library patrons not wishing to have their personal items subject to search. Bedrolls, duffel bags, suitcases, and other large tote bags must be stored in the lockers or checked at the front desk, but may not be brought into the library. Library staff will exercise caution with items stored at the desk but cannot assume responsibility for loss or theft.

Approved by (governing body) on (insert date)

Signature of responsible representative

- Do you want to examine books, book bags, briefcases, backpacks, and other containers as they leave the library? Do you have staff to handle this function? Are signs posted to inform people that their belongings may be searched as they leave the library?
- Does the library have security staff that can monitor patrons coming in and exiting the library? If not, is staff comfortable with this responsibility? Staff should not confront aggressive or agitated persons and should receive training on how to deal with people who are angry, emotionally disturbed, or threatening.
- Do you want to exclude suitcases, bedrolls, duffel bags, and other large bags from being brought into the library? Is there a place where these items can be safely stored while the owner is using the library? Take care that excluding some items from the library does not act also to exclude the owner from using the library. Caution is especially important if items will be stored at the circulation desk. Staff should not be subjected to charges of pilfering or held responsible for monitoring personal items.
- Have you discussed your plans with your legal counsel? Are you familiar with any laws or local ordinances that deal with the search of an individual's property? Are there local ordinances that address the unlawful removal of materials from the library? If so, be sure to cite the law.

NOTES

1. Bielefield, Arlene and Lawrence Cheeseman. 1995. *Library Patrons and the Law*. New York: Neal-Schuman, pp. 93–94.
2. Sarokin, H. Lee. Haters' Speech (December 15, 2006). Available: http://x-judge.blogspot.com/2006/12/haters-speech.html. Accessed November 28, 2007.
3. Minow, Mary and Tomas A. Lipinsky. 2003. *The Library's Legal Answer Book*. Chicago: American Library Association, p. 270.

Part III

Essential Professional Resources Needed for Good Policy

Resource A

Codes of Ethics

AMERICAN LIBRARY ASSOCIATION CODE OF ETHICS

As members of the American Library Association, we recognize the importance of codifying and making known to the profession and to the general public the ethical principles that guide the work of librarians, other professionals providing information services, library trustees, and library staffs.

Ethical dilemmas occur when values are in conflict. The American Library Association Code of Ethics states the values to which we are committed and embodies the ethical responsibilities of the profession in this changing information environment.

We significantly influence or control the selection, organization, preservation, and dissemination of information. In a political system grounded in an informed citizenry, we are members of a profession explicitly committed to intellectual freedom and the freedom of access to information. We have a special obligation to ensure the free flow of information and ideas to present and future generations.

The principles of this Code are expressed in broad statements to guide ethical decision making. These statements provide a framework; they cannot and do not dictate conduct to cover particular situations.

I. We provide the highest level of service to all library users through appropriate and usefully organized resources; equitable service policies; equitable access; and accurate, unbiased, and courteous responses to all requests.

II. We uphold the principles of intellectual freedom and resist all efforts to censor library resources.
III. We protect each library user's right to privacy and confidentiality with respect to information sought or received and resources consulted, borrowed, acquired, or transmitted.
IV. We respect intellectual property rights and advocate balance between the interests of information users and rights holders.
V. We treat coworkers and other colleagues with respect, fairness, and good faith, and advocate conditions of employment that safeguard the rights and welfare of all employees of our institutions.
VI. We do not advance private interests at the expense of library users, colleagues, or our employing institutions.
VII. We distinguish between our personal convictions and professional duties and do not allow our personal beliefs to interfere with fair representation of the aims of our institutions or the provision of access to their information resources.
VIII. We strive for excellence in the profession by maintaining and enhancing our own knowledge and skills, by encouraging the professional development of coworkers, and by fostering the aspirations of potential members of the profession.

Adopted January 22, 2008, by the ALA Council.

ETHICS STATEMENT FOR PUBLIC LIBRARY TRUSTEES

Trustees in the capacity of trust upon them shall observe ethical standards with absolute truth, integrity, and honor.

Trustees must avoid situations in which personal interests might be served or financial benefits gained at the expense of library users, colleagues, or the situation.

It is incumbent upon any trustee to disqualify himself/herself immediately whenever the appearance or a conflict of interest exists.

Trustees must distinguish clearly in their actions and statements between their personal philosophies and attitudes and those of the institution, acknowledging the formal position of the board even if they personally disagree.

A trustee must respect the confidential nature of library business while being aware of and in compliance with applicable laws governing freedom of information.

Trustees must be prepared to support to the fullest the efforts of librarians in resisting censorship of library materials by groups or individuals.

Trustees who accept library board responsibilities are expected to perform all of the functions of library trustees.

Adopted by the Board of Directors of the American Library Trustee Association, July 1985.

Adopted by the Board of Directors of the Public Library Association, July 1985.

Amended by the Board of Directors of the American Library Trustee Association, July 1988. Approval of the amendment by the Board of Directors of the Public Library Association, January 1989.

Resource B

Guidelines for the Development and Implementation of Policies, Regulations, and Procedures Affecting Access to Library Materials, Services, and Facilities

The American Library Association has adopted the *Library Bill of Rights* and Interpretations of the *Library Bill of Rights* to provide library governing authorities, librarians, and other library staff and library users with guidelines on how constitutional principles apply to libraries in the United States of America.

Publicly supported libraries exist within the context of a body of law derived from the United States Constitution and appropriate state constitutions, defined by statute, and implemented by regulations, policies, and procedures established by their governing bodies and administrations. These regulations, policies, and procedures establish the mission of the library; define its functions, services, and operations; and ascertain the rights and responsibilities of the individuals served by the library.

Publicly supported library service is based upon the First Amendment right of free expression. The publicly supported library is a governmental entity that provides free, equal, and equitable access to information for all people of the community it serves. When this purpose is confirmed in policies and practices, the library is a designated limited public forum for access to information. When library policies or practices make meeting rooms, exhibit spaces, and/or bulletin boards available for public use, these spaces are designated as limited public forums for the exchange of information.

Since the *Library Bill of Rights* "affirms that all libraries are forums for information and ideas," libraries that are not publicly supported are encouraged to observe these guidelines as they develop policies, regulations, and procedures.

Libraries adopt administrative policies and procedures regulating the organization and use of library materials, services, and facilities. These policies and procedures affect access and may have the effect of restricting, denying, or creating barriers to access to the library as a public forum, including the library's resources, facilities, and services. Library policies and procedures that impinge upon First Amendment rights are subject to a higher standard of review than may be required in the policies of other public services and facilities.

Policies, procedures, or regulations that may result in denying, restricting, or creating physical or economic barriers to access to the library's public forum must be based on a compelling government interest. However, library governing authorities may place reasonable and narrowly drawn restrictions on the time, place, or manner of access to library resources, services, or facilities, provided that such restrictions are not based upon arbitrary distinctions between individuals or classes of individuals.

GUIDELINES

The American Library Association's Intellectual Freedom Committee recommends that publicly supported libraries use the following guidelines, based on constitutional principles, to develop policies, regulations, and procedures:

All library policies, regulations, and procedures should be carefully examined to determine if they may result in denying, restricting, or creating barriers to access. If they may result in such restrictions, they:

1. should be developed and implemented within the legal framework that applies to the library. This includes: the United States Constitution, including the First and Fourteenth Amendments, due process, and equal and equitable treatment under the law; the applicable state constitution; federal and state civil rights legislation; all other applicable federal, state and local legislation; and applicable case law;

2. should cite statutes or ordinances upon which the authority to make that policy is based, when appropriate;

3. should be developed and implemented within the framework of the Library Bill of Rights and its Interpretations;

4. should be based upon the library's mission and objectives;

5. should impose restrictions on the access to, or use of library resources, services or facilities only when those restrictions are necessary to achieve the library's mission and objectives;

6. should narrowly tailor prohibitions or restrictions, in the rare instances when they are required, so they are not more restrictive than needed to serve their objectives;

7. should attempt to balance competing interests and avoid favoring the majority at the expense of individual rights, or allowing individual users' rights to interfere materially with the majority's rights to free, equal, and equitable access to library resources, services, and facilities;

8. should avoid arbitrary distinctions between individuals or classes of users, and should not have the effect of denying or abridging a person's right to use library resources, services, or facilities based upon arbitrary distinctions such as origin, age, background, or views;

In the *Library Bill of Rights* and all of its Interpretations, it is intended that "origin" encompasses all the characteristics of individuals that are inherent in the circumstances of their birth; "age" encompasses all the characteristics of individuals that are inherent in their levels of development and maturity; "background" encompasses all the characteristics of individuals that are a result of their life experiences; and "views" encompasses all the opinions and beliefs held and expressed by individuals;

9. should not target specific users or groups of users based upon an assumption or expectation that such users might engage in behavior that will materially interfere with the achievement of substantial library objectives;

10. must be clearly stated so that a reasonably intelligent person will have fair warning of what is expected;

11. must provide a means of appeal;

12. must be reviewed regularly by the library's governing authority and by its legal counsel;

13. must be communicated clearly and made available in an effective manner to all library users;

14. must be enforced evenhandedly and not in a manner intended to benefit or disfavor any person or group in an arbitrary or capricious manner;

Libraries should develop an ongoing staff training program designed to foster the understanding of the legal framework and principles underlying library policies and to assist staff in gaining the skill and ability to respond to potentially difficult circumstances in a timely, direct, and open manner. This program should include training to develop empathy and understanding of the social and economic problems of some library users;

15. should, if reasonably possible, provide adequate alternative means of access to information for those whose behavior results in the denial or restriction of access to any library resource, service, or facility.

Adopted by the ALA Intellectual Freedom Committee June 28, 1994; revised January 19, 2005.

Resource C

Library Bill of Rights and Interpretations

THE LIBRARY BILL OF RIGHTS

The American Library Association affirms that all libraries are forums for information and ideas, and that the following basic policies should guide their services.

I. Books and other library resources should be provided for the interest, information, and enlightenment of all people of the community the library serves. Materials should not be excluded because of the origin, background, or views of those contributing to their creation.

II. Libraries should provide materials and information presenting all points of view on current and historical issues. Materials should not be proscribed or removed because of partisan or doctrinal disapproval.

III. Libraries should challenge censorship in the fulfillment of their responsibility to provide information and enlightenment.

IV. Libraries should cooperate with all persons and groups concerned with resisting abridgment of free expression and free access to ideas.

V. A person's right to use a library should not be denied or abridged because of origin, age, background, or views.

VI. Libraries which make exhibit spaces and meeting rooms available to the public they serve should make such facilities available on an equitable basis, regardless of the beliefs or affiliations of individuals or groups requesting their use.

Adopted June 18, 1948. Amended February 2, 1961, and January 23, 1980; inclusion of "age" reaffirmed January 23, 1996, by the ALA Council.

EVALUATING LIBRARY COLLECTIONS: AN INTERPRETATION OF THE LIBRARY BILL OF RIGHTS

The continuous review of library materials is necessary as a means of maintaining an active library collection of current interest to users. In the process, materials may be added and physically deteriorated or obsolete materials may be replaced or removed in accordance with the collection maintenance policy of a given library and the needs of the community it serves. Continued evaluation is closely related to the goals and responsibilities of all libraries and is a valuable tool of collection development. This procedure is not to be used as a convenient means to remove materials presumed to be controversial or disapproved of by segments of the community. Such abuse of the evaluation function violates the principles of intellectual freedom and is in opposition to the Preamble and Articles I and II of the *Library Bill of Rights*, which state:

> The American Library Association affirms that all libraries are forums for information and ideas, and that the following basic policies should guide their services.
> I. Books and other library resources should be provided for the interest, information, and enlightenment of all people of the community the library serves. Materials should not be excluded because of the origin, background, or views of those contributing to their creation.
> II. Libraries should provide materials and information presenting all points of view on current and historical issues. Materials should not be proscribed or removed because of partisan or doctrinal disapproval.

The American Library Association opposes such "silent censorship" and strongly urges that libraries adopt guidelines setting forth the positive purposes and principles of evaluation of materials in library collections.

Adopted February 2, 1973; amended July 1, 1981, by the ALA Council.

DIVERSITY IN COLLECTION DEVELOPMENT: AN INTERPRETATION OF THE LIBRARY BILL OF RIGHTS

Throughout history, the focus of censorship has fluctuated from generation to generation. Books and other materials have not been selected or have been removed from library collections for many reasons, among which are prejudicial language and ideas, political content, economic theory, social philosophies, religious beliefs, sexual forms of expression, and other potentially controversial topics.

Some examples of censorship may include removing or not selecting materials because they are considered by some as racist or sexist; not purchasing conservative religious materials; not selecting materials about or by minorities because it is thought these groups or interests are not represented in a community; or not providing information on or materials from non-mainstream political entities.

Librarians may seek to increase user awareness of materials on various social concerns by many means including, but not limited to, issuing bibliographies and presenting exhibits and programs. Librarians have a professional responsibility to be inclusive, not exclusive, in collection development and in the provision of interlibrary loan. Access to all materials legally obtainable should be assured to the user, and policies should not unjustly exclude materials even if they are offensive to the librarian or the user. Collection development should reflect the philosophy inherent in Article II of the *Library Bill of Rights*: "Libraries should provide materials and information presenting all points of view on current and historical issues. Materials should not be proscribed or removed because of partisan or doctrinal disapproval." A balanced collection reflects a diversity of materials, not an equality of numbers. Collection development responsibilities include selecting materials in the languages in common use in the community the library serves. Collection development and the selection of materials should be done according to professional standards and established selection and review procedures.

There are many complex facets to any issue, and variations of context in which issues may be expressed, discussed, or interpreted. Librarians have a professional responsibility to be fair, just, and equitable and to give all library users equal protection in guarding against violation of the library patron's right to read, view, or listen to materials and resources protected by the First Amendment, no matter what the viewpoint of the author, creator, or selector. Librarians have an obligation to protect library collections from removal of materials based on personal bias or prejudice and to select and support the access to materials on all subjects that meet, as closely as possible, the needs, interests, and abilities of all persons in the community the library serves. This includes materials that reflect political, economic, religious, social, minority, and sexual issues.

Intellectual freedom, the essence of equitable library services, provides for free access to all expressions of ideas through which any and all sides of a question, cause, or movement may be explored. Toleration is meaningless without tolerance for what some may consider detestable. Librarians cannot justly permit their own preferences to limit their degree of tolerance in collection development, because freedom is indivisible.

Adopted July 14, 1982; amended January 10, 1990, by the ALA Council.

LABELS AND RATING SYSTEMS: AN INTERPRETATION OF THE LIBRARY BILL OF RIGHTS

Libraries do not advocate the ideas found in their collections or in resources accessible through the library. The presence of books and other resources in a library does not indicate endorsement of their contents by the library. Likewise, the ability for library users to access electronic information using library computers does not indicate endorsement or approval of that information by the library.

Labels

Labels on library materials may be viewpoint-neutral directional aids that save the time of users, or they may be attempts to prejudice or discourage users or restrict their access to materials. When labeling is an attempt to prejudice attitudes, it is a censor's tool. The American Library Association opposes labeling as a means of predisposing people's attitudes toward library materials.

Prejudicial labels are designed to *restrict access*, based on a *value judgment* that the content, language or themes of the material, or the background or views of the creator(s) of the material, render it inappropriate or offensive for all or certain groups of users. The prejudicial label is used to warn, discourage, or prohibit users or certain groups of users from accessing the material. Such labels may be used to remove materials from open shelves to restricted locations where access depends on staff intervention.

Viewpoint-neutral directional aids facilitate access by making it easier for users to locate materials. The materials are housed on open shelves and are equally accessible to all users, who may choose to consult or ignore the directional aids at their own discretion.

Directional aids can have the effect of prejudicial labels when their implementation becomes *proscriptive* rather than *descriptive*. When directional aids are used to forbid access or to suggest moral or doctrinal endorsement, the effect is the same as prejudicial labeling.

Rating Systems

A variety of organizations promulgate *rating systems* as a means of advising either their members or the general public concerning their opinions of the contents and suitability or appropriate age for use of certain books, films, recordings, Web sites, or other materials. The adoption, enforcement, or endorsement of any of these rating systems by the library violates the *Library Bill of Rights*. Adopting such systems into law may be unconstitutional. If such legislation is passed, the library should seek legal advice regarding the law's applicability to library operations.

Publishers, industry groups, and distributors sometimes add ratings to material or include them as part of their packaging. Librarians should not endorse such practices. However, removing or destroying such ratings—if placed there by, or with permission of, the copyright holder—could constitute expurgation (see *Expurgation of Library Materials: An Interpretation of the Library Bill of Rights*).

Some find it easy and even proper, according to their ethics, to establish criteria for judging materials as objectionable. However, injustice and ignorance, rather than justice and enlightenment, result from such practices. The American Library Association opposes any efforts that result in closing any path to knowledge.

Adopted July 13, 1951; amended June 25, 1971; July 1, 1981; June 26, 1990; January 19, 2005, by the ALA Council.

CHALLENGED MATERIALS: AN INTERPRETATION OF THE LIBRARY BILL OF RIGHTS

The American Library Association declares as a matter of firm principle that it is the responsibility of every library to have a clearly defined materials selection policy in written form that reflects the *Library Bill of Rights*, and that is approved by the appropriate governing authority.

Challenged materials that meet the criteria for selection in the materials selection policy of the library should not be removed under any legal or extra-legal pressure. The *Library Bill of Rights* states in Article I that "Materials should not be excluded because of the origin, background, or views of those contributing to their creation," and in Article II, that "Materials should not be proscribed or removed because of partisan or doctrinal disapproval." Freedom of expression is protected by the Constitution of the United

States, but constitutionally protected expression is often separated from unprotected expression only by a dim and uncertain line. The Constitution requires a procedure designed to focus searchingly on challenged expression before it can be suppressed. An adversary hearing is a part of this procedure.

Therefore, any attempt, be it legal or extra-legal, to regulate or suppress materials in libraries must be closely scrutinized to the end that protected expression is not abridged.

Adopted June 25, 1971; amended July 1, 1981; amended January 10, 1990, by the ALA Council.

EXPURGATION OF LIBRARY MATERIALS: AN INTERPRETATION OF THE LIBRARY BILL OF RIGHTS

Expurgating library materials is a violation of the *Library Bill of Rights*. Expurgation as defined by this interpretation includes any deletion, excision, alteration, editing, or obliteration of any part(s) of books or other library resources by the library, its agent, or its parent institution (if any). By such expurgation, the library is in effect denying access to the complete work and the entire spectrum of ideas that the work intended to express. Such action stands in violation of Articles I, II, and III of the *Library Bill of Rights*, which state that "Materials should not be excluded because of the origin, background, or views of those contributing to their creation," that "Materials should not be proscribed or removed because of partisan or doctrinal disapproval," and that "Libraries should challenge censorship in the fulfillment of their responsibility to provide information and enlightenment." The act of expurgation has serious implications. It involves a determination that it is necessary to restrict access to the complete work. This is censorship. When a work is expurgated, under the assumption that certain portions of that work would be harmful to minors, the situation is no less serious. Expurgation of any books or other library resources imposes a restriction, without regard to the rights and desires of all library users, by limiting access to ideas and information. (See also other Interpretations to the Library Bill of Rights, including Access to Electronic Information, Services, and Networks and Free Access to Libraries for Minors.)

Further, expurgation without written permission from the holder of the copyright on the material may violate the copyright provisions of the United States Code.

Adopted February 2, 1973, by the ALA Council; amended July 1, 1981; January 10, 1990.

FREE ACCESS TO LIBRARIES FOR MINORS: AN INTERPRETATION OF THE LIBRARY BILL OF RIGHTS

Library policies and procedures that effectively deny minors equal and equitable access to all library resources available to other users violate the *Library Bill of Rights*. The American Library Association opposes all attempts to restrict access to library services, materials, and facilities based on the age of library users.

Article V of the *Library Bill of Rights* states, "A person's right to use a library should not be denied or abridged because of origin, age, background, or views." The "right to use a library" includes free access to, and unrestricted use of, all the services, materials, and facilities the library has to offer. Every restriction on access to, and use of, library resources, based solely on the chronological age, educational level, literacy skills, or legal emancipation of users, violates Article V.

Libraries are charged with the mission of developing resources to meet the diverse information needs and interests of the communities they serve. Services, materials, and facilities that fulfill the needs and interests of library users at different stages in their personal development are a necessary part of library resources. The needs and interests of each library user, and resources appropriate to meet those needs and interests, must be determined on an individual basis. Librarians cannot predict what resources will best fulfill the needs and interests of any individual user based on a single criterion such as chronological age, educational level, literacy skills, or legal emancipation.

Libraries should not limit the selection and development of library resources simply because minors will have access to them. Institutional self-censorship diminishes the credibility of the library in the community, and restricts access for all library users.

Children and young adults unquestionably possess First Amendment rights, including the right to receive information in the library. Constitutionally protected speech cannot be suppressed solely to protect children or young adults from ideas or images a legislative body believes to be unsuitable for them.[1] Librarians and library governing bodies should not resort to age restrictions in an effort to avoid actual or anticipated objections, because only a court of law can determine whether material is not constitutionally protected.

The mission, goals, and objectives of libraries cannot authorize librarians or library governing bodies to assume, abrogate, or overrule the rights and responsibilities of parents. As "Libraries: An American Value" states, "We affirm the responsibility and the right of all parents and guardians to guide their own children's use of the library and its resources and services."

Librarians and governing bodies should maintain that parents—and only parents—have the right and the responsibility to restrict the access of their children—and only their children—to library resources. Parents who do not want their children to have access to certain library services, materials, or facilities should so advise their children. Librarians and library governing bodies cannot assume the role of parents or the functions of parental authority in the private relationship between parent and child.

Lack of access to information can be harmful to minors. Librarians and library governing bodies have a public and professional obligation to ensure that all members of the community they serve have free, equal, and equitable access to the entire range of library resources regardless of content, approach, format, or amount of detail. This principle of library service applies equally to all users, minors as well as adults. Librarians and library governing bodies must uphold this principle in order to provide adequate and effective service to minors.

Adopted June 30, 1972; amended July 1, 1981; July 3, 1991, June 30, 2004, by the ALA Council.

ACCESS FOR CHILDREN AND YOUNG ADULTS TO NONPRINT MATERIALS: AN INTERPRETATION OF THE LIBRARY BILL OF RIGHTS

Library collections of nonprint materials raise a number of intellectual freedom issues, especially regarding minors. Article V of the *Library Bill of Rights* states, "A person's right to use a library should not be denied or abridged because of origin, age, background, or views."

The American Library Association's principles protect minors' access to sound, images, data, games, software, and other content in all formats such as tapes, CDs, DVDs, music CDs, computer games, software, databases, and other emerging technologies. ALA's *Free Access to Libraries for Minors: An Interpretation of the Library Bill of Rights* states:

> . . . The "right to use a library" includes free access to, and unrestricted use of, all the services, materials, and facilities the library has to offer. Every restriction on access to, and use of, library resources, based solely on the chronological age, educational level, literacy skills, or legal emancipation of users violates Article V.
>
> . . . [P]arents—and only parents—have the right and responsibility to restrict access of their children—and only their children—to library resources. Parents who do not want their children to have access to

certain library services, materials, or facilities should so advise their children. Librarians and library governing bodies cannot assume the role of parents or the functions of parental authority in the private relationship between parent and child.

Lack of access to information can be harmful to minors. Librarians and library governing bodies have a public and professional obligation to ensure that all members of the community they serve have free, equal, and equitable access to the entire range of library resources regardless of content, approach, format, or amount of detail. This principle of library service applies equally to all users, minors as well as adults. Librarians and library governing bodies must uphold this principle in order to provide adequate and effective service to minors.

Policies that set minimum age limits for access to any nonprint materials or information technology, with or without parental permission, abridge library use for minors. Age limits based on the cost of the materials are also unacceptable. Librarians, when dealing with minors, should apply the same standards to circulation of nonprint materials as are applied to books and other print materials except when directly and specifically prohibited by law.

Recognizing that librarians cannot act in loco parentis, ALA acknowledges and supports the exercise by parents of their responsibility to guide their own children's reading and viewing. Libraries should provide published reviews and/or reference works that contain information about the content, subject matter, and recommended audiences for nonprint materials. These resources will assist parents in guiding their children without implicating the library in censorship.

In some cases, commercial content ratings, such as the Motion Picture Association of America (MPAA) movie ratings, might appear on the packaging or promotional materials provided by producers or distributors. However, marking out or removing this information from materials or packaging constitutes expurgation or censorship.

MPAA movie ratings, Entertainment Software Rating Board (ESRB) game ratings, and other rating services are private advisory codes and have no legal standing (*Expurgation of Library Materials*). For the library to add ratings to nonprint materials if they are not already there is unacceptable. It is also unacceptable to post a list of such ratings with a collection or to use them in circulation policies or other procedures. These uses constitute labeling, "an attempt to prejudice attitudes" (*Labels and Rating Systems*), and are forms of censorship. The application of locally generated ratings schemes intended to provide content warnings to library users is also inconsistent with the *Library Bill of Rights*.

The interests of young people, like those of adults, are not limited by subject, theme, or level of sophistication. Librarians have a responsibility to ensure young people's access to materials and services that reflect diversity of content and format sufficient to meet their needs.

Adopted June 28, 1989, amended June 30, 2004, by the ALA Council.

RESTRICTED ACCESS TO LIBRARY MATERIALS: AN INTERPRETATION OF THE LIBRARY BILL OF RIGHTS

Libraries are a traditional forum for the open exchange of information. Attempts to restrict access to library materials violate the basic tenets of the *Library Bill of Rights.*

Some libraries place materials in a "closed shelf," "locked case," "adults only," "restricted shelf," or "high-demand" collection. Some libraries have applied filtering software to their Internet stations to prevent users from finding targeted categories of information, much of which is constitutionally protected. Some libraries block access to certain materials by placing other barriers between the user and those materials.

Because restricted materials often deal with controversial, unusual, or sensitive subjects, having to ask a librarian or circulation clerk for access to them may be embarrassing or inhibiting for patrons desiring the materials. Requiring a user to ask for materials may create a service barrier or pose a language-skills barrier. Even when a title is listed in the catalog with a reference to its restricted status, a barrier is placed between the patron and the publication. (See also "Labels and Rating Systems.") Because restricted materials often feature information that some people consider objectionable, potential library users may be predisposed to think of the materials as objectionable and, therefore, be reluctant to ask for access to them.

Limiting access by relegating materials into physically or virtually restricted or segregated collections or restricting materials by creating age-related, linguistic, economic, psychological, or other barriers violates the *Library Bill of Rights.* However, some libraries have established restrictive policies to protect their materials from theft or mutilation or because of statutory authority or institutional mandate. Such policies must be carefully formulated and administered to ensure they do not violate established principles of intellectual freedom. This caution is reflected in ALA policies, such as "Evaluating Library Collections," "Free Access to Libraries for Minors," "Preservation Policy," and the ACRL "Code of Ethics for Special Collections Librarians."

In keeping with the "Joint Statement on Access" of the American Library Association and Society of American Archivists, libraries should avoid accepting donor agreements or entering into contracts that impose permanent restrictions on special collections. As stated in the "Joint Statement," it is the responsibility of libraries with such collections "to make available original research materials in its possession on equal terms of access."

All proposals for restricted access collections should be carefully scrutinized to ensure that the purpose is not to suppress a viewpoint or to place a barrier between certain patrons and particular content. A primary goal of the library profession is to facilitate access to all points of view on current and historical issues.

Adopted February 2, 1973, by the ALA Council; amended July 1, 1981; July 3, 1991; July 12, 2000; June 30, 2004.

LIBRARY-INITIATED PROGRAMS AS A RESOURCE: AN INTERPRETATION OF THE LIBRARY BILL OF RIGHTS

Library-initiated programs support the mission of the library by providing users with additional opportunities for information, education, and recreation. Article I of the *Library Bill of Rights* states: "Books and other library resources should be provided for the interest, information, and enlightenment of all people of the community the library serves."

Library-initiated programs take advantage of library staff expertise, collections, services, and facilities to increase access to information and information resources. Library-initiated programs introduce users and potential users to the resources of the library and to the library's primary function as a facilitator of information access. The library may participate in cooperative or joint programs with other agencies, organizations, institutions, or individuals as part of its own effort to address information needs and to facilitate information access in the community the library serves.

Library-initiated programs on site and in other locations include, but are not limited to, speeches, community forums, discussion groups, demonstrations, displays, and live or media presentations.

Libraries serving multilingual or multicultural communities should make efforts to accommodate the information needs of those for whom English is a second language. Library-initiated programs that cross language and cultural barriers introduce otherwise underserved populations to the resources of the library and provide access to information.

Library-initiated programs "should not be proscribed or removed [or canceled] because of partisan or doctrinal disapproval" of the contents of the program or the views expressed by the participants, as stated in Article

II of the *Library Bill of Rights*. Library sponsorship of a program does not constitute an endorsement of the content of the program or the views expressed by the participants any more than the purchase of material for the library collection constitutes an endorsement of the contents of the material or the views of its creator.

Library-initiated programs are a library resource, and, as such, are developed in accordance with written guidelines, as approved and adopted by the library's policymaking body. These guidelines should include an endorsement of the *Library Bill of Rights* and set forth the library's commitment to free and open access to information and ideas for all users.

Library staff select topics, speakers, and resource materials for library-initiated programs based on the interests and information needs of the community. Topics, speakers, and resource materials are not excluded from library-initiated programs because of possible controversy. Concerns, questions, or complaints about library-initiated programs are handled according to the same written policy and procedures that govern reconsiderations of other library resources.

Library-initiated programs are offered free of charge and are open to all. Article V of the *Library Bill of Rights* states: "A person's right to use a library should not be denied or abridged because of origin, age, background, or views."

The "right to use a library" encompasses all the resources the library offers, including the right to attend library-initiated programs. Libraries do not deny or abridge access to library resources, including library-initiated programs, based on an individual's economic background or ability to pay.

Adopted January 27, 1982; amended June 26, 1990; July 12, 2000, by the ALA Council.

MEETING ROOMS: AN INTERPRETATION OF THE LIBRARY BILL OF RIGHTS

Many libraries provide meeting rooms for individuals and groups as part of a program of service. Article VI of the *Library Bill of Rights* states that such facilities should be made available to the public served by the given library "on an equitable basis, regardless of the beliefs or affiliations of individuals or groups requesting their use."

Libraries maintaining meeting room facilities should develop and publish policy statements governing use. These statements can properly define time, place, or manner of use; such qualifications should not pertain to the content of a meeting or to the beliefs or affiliations of the sponsors. These statements should be made available in any commonly used language within the community served.

If meeting rooms in libraries supported by public funds are made available to the general public for non-library-sponsored events, the library may not exclude any group based on the subject matter to be discussed or based on the ideas that the group advocates. For example, if a library allows charities and sports clubs to discuss their activities in library meeting rooms, then the library should not exclude partisan political or religious groups from discussing their actives in the same facilities. If a library opens its meeting rooms to a wide variety of civic organizations, then the library may not deny access to a religious organization. Libraries may wish to post a permanent notice near the meeting room stating that the library does not advocate or endorse the viewpoints of meeting or meeting room users.

Written policies for meeting room use should be stated in inclusive rather than exclusive terms. For example, a policy that the library's facilities are open "to organizations engaged in educational, cultural, intellectual, or charitable actives" is an inclusive statement of the limited uses to which the facilities may be put. This defined limitation would permit religious groups to use the facilities because they engage in intellectual activities, but would exclude most commercial uses of the facility.

A publicly supported library may limit use of its meeting rooms to strictly "library-related" activities, provided that the limitation is clearly circumscribed and is viewpoint neutral.

Written policies may include limitations on frequency of use and whether or not meetings held in library meeting rooms must be open to the public. If state and local laws permit private as well as public sessions of meetings in library, libraries may choose to offer both options. The same standard should be applicable to all.

If meetings are open to the public, libraries should include in their meeting room policy statement a section that addresses admission fees. If admission fees are permitted, libraries shall seek to make it possible that these fees do not limit access to individuals who may be unable to pay but who wish to attend the meeting. Article V of the *Library Bill of Rights* states that "a person's right to use a library should not be denied or abridged because of origin, age, background, or views." It is inconsistent with Article V to restrict indirectly access to library meeting rooms based on an individual's or group's ability to pay for that access.

Adopted July 2, 1991, by the ALA Council.

EXHIBIT SPACES AND BULLETIN BOARDS: AN INTERPRETATION OF THE LIBRARY BILL OF RIGHTS

Libraries often provide exhibit spaces and bulletin boards. The uses made of these spaces should conform to the *Library Bill of Rights*. Article I states, "Materials should not be excluded because of the origin, background, or views of those contributing to their creation." Article II states, "Materials should not be proscribed or removed because of partisan or doctrinal disapproval." Article VI maintains that exhibit space should be made available "on an equitable basis, regardless of the beliefs or affiliations of individuals or groups requesting their use."

In developing library exhibits, staff members should endeavor to present a broad spectrum of opinion and a variety of viewpoints. Libraries should not shrink from developing exhibits because of controversial content or because of the beliefs or affiliations of those whose work is represented. Just as libraries do not endorse the viewpoints of those whose work is represented in their collections, libraries also do not endorse the beliefs or viewpoints of topics that may be the subject of library exhibits.

Exhibit areas often are made available for use by community groups. Libraries should formulate a written policy for the use of these exhibit areas to assure that space is provided on an equitable basis to all groups that request it.

Written policies for exhibit space use should be stated in inclusive rather than exclusive terms. For example, a policy that the library's exhibit space is open "to organizations engaged in educational, cultural, intellectual, or charitable activities" is an inclusive statement of the limited uses of the exhibit space. This defined limitation would permit religious groups to use the exhibit space because they engage in intellectual activities, but would exclude most commercial uses of the exhibit space.

A publicly supported library may designate use of exhibit space for strictly library-related activities, provided that this limitation is viewpoint neutral and clearly defined.

Libraries may include in this policy rules regarding the time, place, and manner of use of the exhibit space, so long as the rules are content neutral and are applied in the same manner to all groups wishing to use the space. A library may wish to limit access to exhibit space to groups within the community served by the library. This practice is acceptable provided that the same rules and regulations apply to everyone, and that exclusion is not made on the basis of the doctrinal, religious, or political beliefs of the potential users.

The library should not censor or remove an exhibit because some members of the community may disagree with its content. Those who object to the content of any exhibit held at the library should be able to submit their complaint and/or their own exhibit proposal to be judged according to the policies established by the library.

Libraries may wish to post a permanent notice near the exhibit area stating that the library does not advocate or endorse the viewpoints of exhibits or exhibitors.

Libraries that make bulletin boards available to public groups for posting notices of public interest should develop criteria for the use of these spaces based on the same considerations as those outlined above. Libraries may wish to develop criteria regarding the size of material to be displayed, the length of time materials may remain on the bulletin board, the frequency with which material may be posted for the same group, and the geographic area from which notices will be accepted.

Adopted July 2, 1991, by the ALA Council; amended June 30, 2004, by the ALA Council.

ECONOMIC BARRIERS TO INFORMATION ACCESS: AN INTERPRETATION OF THE LIBRARY BILL OF RIGHTS

A democracy presupposes an informed citizenry. The First Amendment mandates the right of all persons to free expression and the corollary right to receive the constitutionally protected expression of others. The publicly supported library provides free, equal, and equitable access to information for all people of the community the library serves. While the roles, goals, and objectives of publicly supported libraries may differ, they share this common mission.

The library's essential mission must remain the first consideration for librarians and governing bodies faced with economic pressures and competition for funding.

In support of this mission, the American Library Association has enumerated certain principles of library services in the *Library Bill of Rights*.

Principles Governing Fines, Fees, and User Charges

Article I of the *Library Bill of Rights* states:

> Books and other library resources should be provided for the interest, information, and enlightenment of all people of the community the library serves.

Article V of the *Library Bill of Rights* states:

> A person's right to use a library should not be denied or abridged because of origin, age, background, or views.

The American Library Association opposes the charging of user fees for the provision of information by all libraries and information services that receive their major support from public funds. All information resources that are provided directly or indirectly by the library, regardless of technology, format, or methods of delivery, should be readily, equally, and equitably accessible to all library users.

Libraries that adhere to these principles systematically monitor their programs of service for potential barriers to access and strive to eliminate such barriers when they occur. All library policies and procedures, particularly those involving fines, fees, or other user charges, should be scrutinized for potential barriers to access. All services should be designed and implemented with care so as not to infringe on or interfere with the provision or delivery of information and resources for all users. Services should be re-evaluated regularly to ensure that the library's basic mission remains uncompromised.

Librarians and governing bodies should look for alternative models and methods of library administration that minimize distinctions among users based on their economic status or financial condition. They should resist the temptation to impose user fees to alleviate financial pressures, at long-term cost to institutional integrity and public confidence in libraries.

Library services that involve the provision of information, regardless of format, technology, or method of delivery, should be made available to all library users on an equal and equitable basis. Charging fees for the use of library collections, services, programs, or facilities that were purchased with public funds raises barriers to access. Such fees effectively abridge or deny access for some members of the community because they reinforce distinctions among users based on their ability and willingness to pay.

Principles Governing Conditions of Funding

Article II of the *Library Bill of Rights* states:

> Materials should not be proscribed or removed because of partisan or doctrinal disapproval.

Article III of the *Library Bill of Rights* states:

> Libraries should challenge censorship in the fulfillment of their responsibility to provide information and enlightenment.

Article IV of the *Library Bill of Rights* states:

> Libraries should cooperate with all persons and groups concerned with resisting abridgment of free expression and free access to ideas.

The American Library Association opposes any legislative or regulatory attempt to impose content restrictions on library resources or to limit user access to information as a condition of funding for publicly supported libraries and information services.

The First Amendment guarantee of freedom of expression is violated when the right to receive that expression is subject to arbitrary restrictions based on content.

Librarians and governing bodies should examine carefully any terms or conditions attached to library funding and should oppose attempts to limit through such conditions full and equal access to information because of content. This principle applies equally to private gifts or bequests and to public funds. In particular, librarians and governing bodies have an obligation to reject such restrictions when the effect of the restriction is to limit equal and equitable access to information.

Librarians and governing bodies should cooperate with all efforts to create a community consensus that publicly supported libraries require funding unfettered by restrictions. Such a consensus supports the library mission to provide the free and unrestricted exchange of information and ideas necessary to a functioning democracy.

The Association's historic position in this regard is stated clearly in a number of Association policies:

> 50.4 "Free Access to Information," 50.8 "Financing of Libraries," 51.2 "Equal Access to Library Service," 51.3 "Intellectual Freedom," 53 "Intellectual Freedom Policies," 59.1 "Policy Objectives," and 60 "Library Services for the Poor."

Adopted by the ALA Council, June 30, 1993.

ACCESS TO ELECTRONIC INFORMATION, SERVICES, AND NETWORKS: AN INTERPRETATION OF THE LIBRARY BILL OF RIGHTS

Introduction

Freedom of expression is an inalienable human right and the foundation for self-government. Freedom of expression encompasses the freedom of speech and the corollary right to receive information.[2] Libraries and librarians protect and promote these rights by selecting, producing, providing access to, identifying, retrieving, organizing, providing instruction in the use of, and preserving recorded expression regardless of the format or technology.

The American Library Association expresses these basic principles of librarianship in its *Code of Ethics* and in the *Library Bill of Rights* and its Interpretations. These serve to guide librarians and library governing bodies in addressing issues of intellectual freedom that arise when the library provides access to electronic information, services, and networks.

Libraries empower users by providing access to the broadest range of information. Electronic resources, including information available via the Internet, allow libraries to fulfill this responsibility better than ever before.

Issues arising from digital generation, distribution, and retrieval of information need to be approached and regularly reviewed from a context of constitutional principles and ALA policies so that fundamental and traditional tenets of librarianship are not swept away.

Electronic information flows across boundaries and barriers despite attempts by individuals, governments, and private entities to channel or control it. Even so, many people lack access or capability to use electronic information effectively.

In making decisions about how to offer access to electronic information, each library should consider its mission, goals, objectives, cooperative agreements, and the needs of the entire community it serves.

The Rights of Users

All library system and network policies, procedures, or regulations relating to electronic information and services should be scrutinized for potential violation of user rights.

User policies should be developed according to the policies and guidelines established by the American Library Association, including *Guidelines for the Development and Implementation of Policies, Regulations and Procedures Affecting Access to Library Materials, Services and Facilities.*

Users' access should not be restricted or denied for expressing or receiving constitutionally protected speech. If access is restricted or denied for behavioral or other reasons, users should be provided due process, including, but not limited to, formal notice and a means of appeal.

Information retrieved or utilized electronically is constitutionally protected unless determined otherwise by a court of law with appropriate jurisdiction. These rights extend to minors as well as adults (*Free Access to Libraries for Minors; Access to Resources and Services in the School Library Media Program; Access for Children and Young People to Videotapes and Other Nonprint Formats*).[3]

Libraries should use technology to enhance, not deny, access to information. Users have the right to be free of unreasonable limitations or conditions set by libraries, librarians, system administrators, vendors, network service providers, or others. Contracts, agreements, and licenses entered into by libraries on behalf of their users should not violate this right. Libraries should provide library users the training and assistance necessary to find, evaluate, and use information effectively.

Users have both the right of confidentiality and the right of privacy. The library should uphold these rights by policy, procedure, and practice in accordance with *Privacy: An Interpretation of the Library Bill of Rights*.

Equity of Access

The Internet provides expanding opportunities for everyone to participate in the information society, but too many individuals face serious barriers to access. Libraries play a critical role in bridging information access gaps for these individuals. Libraries also ensure that the public can find content of interest and learn the necessary skills to use information successfully.

Electronic information, services, and networks provided directly or indirectly by the library should be equally, readily, and equitably accessible to all library users. American Library Association policies oppose the charging of user fees for the provision of information services by libraries that receive their major support from public funds (50.3 "Free Access to Information"; 53.1.14 "Economic Barriers to Information Access"; 60.1.1 "Minority Concerns Policy Objectives"; 61.1 "Library Services for the Poor Policy Objectives"). All libraries should develop policies concerning access to electronic information that are consistent with ALA's policy statements, including *Economic Barriers to Information Access: An Interpretation of the Library Bill of Rights; Guidelines for the Development and Implementation of Policies, Regulations and Procedures Affecting Access to Library Materials, Services and Facilities*; and *Resolution on Access to the Use of Libraries and Information by Individuals with Physical or Mental Impairment*.

Information Resources and Access

Providing connections to global information, services, and networks is not the same as selecting and purchasing materials for a library collection. Determining the accuracy or authenticity of electronic information may present special problems. Some information accessed electronically may not meet a library's selection or collection development policy. It is, therefore, left to each user to determine what is appropriate. Parents and legal guardians who are concerned about their children's use of electronic resources should provide guidance to their own children.

Libraries, acting within their mission and objectives, must support access to information on all subjects that serve the needs or interests of each user, regardless of the user's age or the content of the material. In order to preserve the cultural record and to prevent the loss of information, libraries may need to expand their selection or collection development policies to ensure preservation, in appropriate formats, of information obtained electronically. Libraries have an obligation to provide access to government information available in electronic format.

Libraries and librarians should not deny or limit access to electronic information because of its allegedly controversial content or because of the librarian's personal beliefs or fear of confrontation. Furthermore, libraries and librarians should not deny access to electronic information solely on the grounds that it is perceived to lack value.

Publicly funded libraries have a legal obligation to provide access to constitutionally protected information. Federal, state, county, municipal, local, or library governing bodies sometimes require the use of Internet filters or other technological measures that block access to constitutionally protected information, contrary to the *Library Bill of Rights* (ALA *Policy Manual*, 53.1.17, "Resolution on the Use of Filtering Software in Libraries"). If a library uses a technological measure that blocks access to information, it should be set at the least restrictive level in order to minimize the blocking of constitutionally protected speech. Adults retain the right to access all constitutionally protected information and to ask for the technological measure to be disabled in a timely manner. Minors also retain the right to access constitutionally protected information and, at the minimum, have the right to ask the library or librarian to provide access to erroneously blocked information in a timely manner. Libraries and librarians have an obligation to inform users of these rights and to provide the means to exercise these rights.[4]

Electronic resources provide unprecedented opportunities to expand the scope of information available to users. Libraries and librarians should provide access to information presenting all points of view. The provision of access does not imply sponsorship or endorsement. These principles pertain to electronic resources no less than they do to the more traditional sources of information in libraries (*Diversity in Collection Development*).

Adopted January 24, 1996; amended January 19, 2005, by the ALA Council.

ACCESS TO LIBRARY RESOURCES AND SERVICES REGARDLESS OF SEX, GENDER IDENTITY, OR SEXUAL ORIENTATION: AN INTERPRETATION OF THE LIBRARY BILL OF RIGHTS

American libraries exist and function within the context of a body of laws derived from the United States Constitution and the First Amendment. The *Library Bill of Rights* embodies the basic policies that guide libraries in the provision of services, materials, and programs.

In the preamble to its *Library Bill of Rights*, the American Library Association affirms that *all* [emphasis added] libraries are forums for information and ideas. This concept of *forum* and its accompanying principle of *inclusiveness* pervade all six Articles of the *Library Bill of Rights*.

The American Library Association stringently and unequivocally maintains that libraries and librarians have an obligation to resist efforts that systematically exclude materials dealing with any subject matter, including sex, gender identity, or sexual orientation:

- Article I of the *Library Bill of Rights* states that "Materials should not be excluded because of the origin, background, or views of those contributing to their creation." The Association affirms that books and other materials coming from gay, lesbian, bisexual, and/or transgendered presses, gay, lesbian, bisexual and/or transgendered authors or other creators, and materials regardless of format or services dealing with gay, lesbian, bisexual, and/or transgendered life are protected by the *Library Bill of Rights*. Librarians are obligated by the *Library Bill of Rights* to endeavor to select materials without regard to the sex, gender identity, or sexual orientation of their creators by using the criteria identified in their written, approved selection policies (ALA policy 53.1.5).
- Article II maintains that "Libraries should provide materials and information presenting all points of view on current and historical issues. Materials should not be proscribed or removed because of partisan or doctrinal disapproval." Library services, materials, and programs representing diverse points of view on sex, gender iden-

tity, or sexual orientation should be considered for purchase and inclusion in library collections and programs. (ALA policies 53.1.1, 53.1.9, and 53.1.11). The Association affirms that attempts to proscribe or remove materials dealing with gay, lesbian, bisexual, and/or transgendered life without regard to the written, approved selection policy violate this tenet and constitute censorship.

- Articles III and IV mandate that libraries "challenge censorship" and cooperate with those "resisting abridgement of free expression and free access to ideas."

- Article V holds that "A person's right to use a library should not be denied or abridged because of origin, age, background, or views." In the *Library Bill of Rights* and all its Interpretations, it is intended that: "origin" encompasses all the characteristics of individuals that are inherent in the circumstances of their birth; "age" encompasses all the characteristics of individuals that are inherent in their levels of development and maturity; "background" encompasses all the characteristics of individuals that are a result of their life experiences; and "views" encompasses all the opinions and beliefs held and expressed by individuals. Therefore, Article V of the *Library Bill of Rights* mandates that library services, materials, and programs be available to all members of the community the library serves, without regard to sex, gender identity, or sexual orientation. This includes providing youth with comprehensive sex education literature (ALA Policy 52.5.2).

- Article VI maintains that "Libraries that make exhibit spaces and meeting rooms available to the public they serve should make such facilities available on an equitable basis, regardless of the beliefs or affiliations of individuals or groups requesting their use." This protection extends to all groups and members of the community the library serves, without regard to sex, gender identity, or sexual orientation.

The American Library Association holds that any attempt, be it legal or extra-legal, to regulate or suppress library services, materials, or programs must be resisted in order that protected expression is not abridged. Librarians have a professional obligation to ensure that all library users have free and equal access to the entire range of library services, materials, and programs. Therefore, the Association strongly opposes any effort to limit access to information and ideas. The Association also encourages librarians to proactively support the First Amendment rights of all library users, regardless of sex, gender identity, or sexual orientation.

Adopted June 30, 1993, by the ALA Council; amended July 12, 2000; June 30, 2004.

PRIVACY: AN INTERPRETATION OF THE LIBRARY BILL OF RIGHTS

Introduction

Privacy is essential to the exercise of free speech, free thought, and free association. The courts have established a First Amendment right to receive information in a publicly funded library.[5] Further, the courts have upheld the right to privacy based on the Bill of Rights of the U.S. Constitution.[6] Many states provide guarantees of privacy in their constitutions and statute law.[7] Numerous decisions in case law have defined and extended rights to privacy.[8]

In a library (physical or virtual), the right to privacy is the right to open inquiry without having the subject of one's interest examined or scrutinized by others. Confidentiality exists when a library is in possession of personally identifiable information about users and keeps that information private on their behalf.[9]

Protecting user privacy and confidentiality has long been an integral part of the mission of libraries. The ALA has affirmed a right to privacy since 1939.[10] Existing ALA policies affirm that confidentiality is crucial to freedom of inquiry.[11] Rights to privacy and confidentiality also are implicit in the *Library Bill of Rights*[12] guarantee of free access to library resources for all users.

Rights of Library Users

The *Library Bill of Rights* affirms the ethical imperative to provide unrestricted access to information and to guard against impediments to open inquiry. Article IV states: "Libraries should cooperate with all persons and groups concerned with resisting abridgement of free expression and free access to ideas." When users recognize or fear that their privacy or confidentiality is compromised, true freedom of inquiry no longer exists.

In all areas of librarianship, best practice leaves the user in control of as many choices as possible. These include decisions about the selection of, access to, and use of information. Lack of privacy and confidentiality has a chilling effect on users' choices. All users have a right to be free from any unreasonable intrusion into or surveillance of their lawful library use.

Users have the right to be informed what policies and procedures govern the amount and retention of personally identifiable information, why that information is necessary for the library, and what the user can do to maintain his or her privacy. Library users expect and in many places have a legal right to have their information protected and kept private and confidential by anyone with direct or indirect access to that information. In addition, Article V of the *Library Bill of Rights* states: "A person's right to use a library should not be denied or abridged because of origin, age, background, or views." This article precludes the use of profiling as a basis for any breach of privacy rights. Users have the right to use a library without any abridgement of privacy that may result from equating the subject of their inquiry with behavior.[13]

Responsibilities in Libraries

The library profession has a long-standing commitment to an ethic of facilitating, not monitoring, access to information. This commitment is implemented locally through development, adoption, and adherence to privacy policies that are consistent with applicable federal, state, and local law. Everyone (paid or unpaid) who provides governance, administration, or service in libraries has a responsibility to maintain an environment respectful and protective of the privacy of all users. Users have the responsibility to respect each others' privacy.

For administrative purposes, librarians may establish appropriate time, place, and manner restrictions on the use of library resources.[14] In keeping with this principle, the collection of personally identifiable information should only be a matter of routine or policy when necessary for the fulfillment of the mission of the library. Regardless of the technology used, everyone who collects or accesses personally identifiable information in any format has a legal and ethical obligation to protect confidentiality.

Conclusion

The American Library Association affirms that rights of privacy are necessary for intellectual freedom and are fundamental to the ethics and practice of librarianship.

Adopted June 19, 2002, by the ALA Council.

NOTES

1. See *Erznoznik v. City of Jacksonville*, 422 U.S. 205 (1975): "Speech that is neither obscene as to youths nor subject to some other legitimate proscription cannot be suppressed solely to protect the young from ideas or images that a legislative body thinks unsuitable [422 U.S. 205, 214] for them. In most circumstances, the values protected by the First Amendment are no less applicable when government seeks to control the flow of

information to minors. See *Tinker v. Des Moines School Dist.*, supra. Cf. *West Virginia Bd. of Ed. v. Barnette*, 319 U.S. 624 (1943)."

2. *Martin v. Struthers*, 319 U.S. 141 (1943); *Lamont v. Postmaster General*, 381 U.S. 301 (1965); Susan Nevelow Mart. 2003. The Right to Receive Information. *Law Library Journal* 95, no. 2: 175–189.

3. *Tinker v. Des Moines Independent Community School District*, 393 U.S. 503 (1969); *Board of Education, Island Trees Union Free School District No. 26 v. Pico*, 457 U.S. 853, (1982); *American Amusement Machine Association v. Teri Kendrick*, 244 F.3d 954 (7th Cir. 2001); cert. denied, 534 U.S. 994 (2001).

4. "If some libraries do not have the capacity to unblock specific Web sites or to disable the filter or if it is shown that an adult user's election to view constitutionally protected Internet material is burdened in some other substantial way, that would be the subject for an as-applied challenge, not the facial challenge made in this case." *United States, et al. v. American Library Association*, 539 U.S. 194 (2003) (Justice Kennedy, concurring). See Also: *Questions and Answers on Access to Electronic Information, Services and Networks: An Interpretation of the Library Bill of Rights.*

5. Court opinions establishing a right to receive information in a public library include *Board of Education. v. Pico*, 457 U.S. 853 (1982); *Kreimer v. Bureau Of Police For The Town Of Morristown*, 958 F.2d 1242 (3d Cir. 1992); and *Reno v. American Civil Liberties Union*, 117 S. Ct. 2329, 138 L.Ed.2d 874 (1997).

6. See in particular the Fourth Amendment's guarantee of "[t]he right of the people to be secure in their persons, houses, papers, and effects, against unreasonable searches and seizures," the Fifth Amendment's guarantee against self-incrimination, and the Ninth Amendment's guarantee that "[t]he enumeration in the Constitution, of certain rights, shall not be construed to deny or disparage others retained by the people." This right is explicit in Article Twelve of the Universal Declaration of Human Rights: "No one shall be subjected to arbitrary interference with his privacy, family, home or correspondence, nor to attacks upon his honour and reputation. Everyone has the right to the protection of the law against such interference or attacks." See: www.un.org/Overview/rights.html. This right has further been explicitly codified as Article Seventeen of the "International Covenant on Civil and Political Rights," a legally binding international human rights agreement ratified by the United States on June 8, 1992. See: www.unhchr.ch/html/menu3/b/a_ccpr.htm.

7. Ten state constitutions guarantee a right of privacy or bar unreasonable intrusions into citizens' privacy. Forty-eight states protect the confidentiality of library users' records by law, and the attorneys general in the remaining two states have issued opinions recognizing the privacy of users' library records. See: State Privacy Laws.

8. Cases recognizing a right to privacy include: *NAACP v. Alabama*, 357 U.S. 449 (1958); *Griswold v. Connecticut*, 381 U.S. 479 (1965); *Katz v. United States*, 389 U.S. 347 (1967); and *Stanley v. Georgia*, 394 U.S. 557 (1969). Congress recognized the right to privacy in the Privacy Act of 1974 and Amendments (5 USC Sec. 552a), which addresses the potential for government's violation of privacy through its collection of personal infor-

mation. The Privacy Act's "Congressional Findings and Statement of Purpose" states in part: "the right to privacy is a personal and fundamental right protected by the Constitution of the United States." See: http://caselaw.lp.findlaw.com/scripts/ts_search.pl?title=5&sec=552a.

9. The phrase "personally identifiable information" was established in ALA policy in 1991. See: Policy Concerning Confidentiality of Personally Identifiable Information about Library Users. Personally identifiable information can include many types of library records, for instance, information that the library requires an individual to provide in order to be eligible to use library services or borrow materials, information that identifies an individual as having requested or obtained specific materials or materials on a particular subject, and information that is provided by an individual to assist a library staff member to answer a specific question or provide information on a particular subject. Personally identifiable information does not include information that does not identify any individual and that is retained only for the purpose of studying or evaluating the use of a library and its materials and services. Personally identifiable information does include any data that can link choices of taste, interest, or research with a specific individual.

10. Article Eleven of the *Code of Ethics for Librarians* (1939) asserted that "It is the librarian's obligation to treat as confidential any private information obtained through contact with library patrons." See: *Code of Ethics for Librarians* (1939). Article Three of the current Code (1995) states: "We protect each library user's right to privacy and confidentiality with respect to information sought or received and resources consulted, borrowed, acquired, or transmitted." See: www.ala.org/alaorg/oif/ethics.html.

11. See these ALA Policies: Access for Children and Young People to Videotapes and Other Nonprint Formats; *Free Access to Libraries for Minors; Freedom to Read* (www.ala.org/alaorg/oif/freeread.html); *Libraries: An American Value*; the newly revised Library Principles for a Networked World; Policy Concerning Confidentiality of Personally Identifiable Information about Library Users; *Policy on Confidentiality of Library Records; Suggested Procedures for Implementing Policy on the Confidentiality of Library Records*.

12. Adopted June 18, 1948; amended February 2, 1961, and January 23, 1980; inclusion of "age" reaffirmed January 23, 1996, by the ALA Council. See: www.ala.org/work/freedom/lbr.html.

13. Existing ALA policy asserts, in part, that: "The government's interest in library use reflects a dangerous and fallacious equation of what a person reads with what that person believes or how that person is likely to behave. Such a presumption can and does threaten the freedom of access to information." Policy Concerning Confidentiality of Personally Identifiable Information about Library User.s

14. See: *Guidelines for the Development and Implementation of Policies, Regulations and Procedures Affecting Access to Library Materials, Services and Facilities*.

Resource D

ALA Resolutions

RESOLUTION ON THE USE OF FILTERING SOFTWARE IN LIBRARIES

WHEREAS, On June 26, 1997, the United States Supreme Court issued a sweeping re-affirmation of core First Amendment principles and held that communications over the Internet deserve the highest level of Constitutional protection; and

WHEREAS, The Court's most fundamental holding is that communications on the Internet deserve the same level of Constitutional protection as books, magazines, newspapers, and speakers on a street corner soapbox. The Court found that the Internet "constitutes a vast platform from which to address and hear from a worldwide audience of millions of readers, viewers, researchers, and buyers," and that "any person with a phone line can become a town crier with a voice that resonates farther than it could from any soapbox"; and

WHEREAS, For libraries, the most critical holding of the Supreme Court is that libraries that make content available on the Internet can continue to do so with the same Constitutional protections that apply to the books on libraries' shelves; and

WHEREAS, The Court's conclusion that "the vast democratic fora of the Internet" merit full constitutional protection will also serve to protect libraries that provide their patrons with access to the Internet; and

WHEREAS, The Court recognized the importance of enabling individuals to receive speech from the entire world and to speak to the entire world. Libraries provide those opportunities to many who would not otherwise have them; and

WHEREAS, The Supreme Court's decision will protect that access; and

WHEREAS, The use in libraries of software filters that block Constitutionally protected speech is inconsistent with the United States Constitution and federal law and may lead to legal exposure for the library and its governing authorities; now, therefore, be it

RESOLVED, That the American Library Association affirms that the use of filtering software by libraries to block access to constitutionally protected speech violates the *Library Bill of Rights*.

Adopted by the ALA Council, July 2, 1997.

RESOLUTION ON OPPOSITION TO FEDERALLY MANDATED INTERNET FILTERING

WHEREAS, The American Library Association has as its cornerstone the First Amendment and free and open access to the information people need and want regardless of the format in which that information appears; and

WHEREAS, Millions of our nation's library users cannot afford computers, require assistive technology to use them, and therefore rely on public access computers in their local libraries for Internet access; and

WHEREAS, Libraries depend on federal funding, such as E-rate discounts, LSTA grants, and ESEA Title III grants to provide Internet access; and

WHEREAS, Librarians are partners with parents and work to help their communities—adults and children—become information literate by teaching them how to access, evaluate, and use information; and

WHEREAS, The ALA strongly believes that educating children to use the Internet wisely provides children their best protection, now and in the future; and

WHEREAS, The ALA strongly encourages local libraries to adopt and implement Internet use policies in the same way they develop other policies, based on the needs of their communities; and

WHEREAS, The ALA does not endorse blocking or filtering Internet content in libraries because there is no proven technology that both blocks out all illegal content and allows access to all constitutionally protected material; and

WHEREAS, The 106th Congress passed the Neighborhood Children's Internet Protection Act, which mandates the adoption of a prescriptive Internet safety policy that undermines local control for recipients of E-rate discounts as part of a major spending bill (H.R. 4577) which was signed by the President on December 21, 2000 (PL 106-554); and

WHEREAS, The 106th Congress passed the Children's Internet Protection Act mandating filtering or blocking for recipients of E-rate discounts, LSTA grants, and ESEA Title III grants as part of a major spending bill (H.R. 4577) which was signed by the President on December 21, 2000 (PL 106-554); now, therefore be it

RESOLVED, That the American Library Association will work with the 107th Congress to encourage lawmakers to repeal the portions of Children's Internet Protection Act and the Neighborhood Children's Internet Protection Act that usurp and undermine local control; and be it further

RESOLVED, That the ALA will continue to work with the Federal Communications Commission, the Institute of Museum and Library Services, and the U.S. Department of Education, to ensure that the values of full and open access for all, are considered as they administer these grants and discounts; and be it further

RESOLVED, That ALA will continue to support and encourage local libraries as they educate children and adults in the safe and effective use of the Internet; and be it further

RESOLVED, That ALA will initiate litigation against these Acts to ensure that the people of America have unfettered access to information; and be it further

RESOLVED, That the ALA transmit this resolution to United States President-elect George W. Bush and Members of Congress.

Adopted by the ALA Council, January 17, 2001.

RESOLUTION ON RADIO FREQUENCY IDENTIFICATION (RFID) TECHNOLOGY AND PRIVACY PRINCIPLES

WHEREAS, Radio Frequency Identification (RFID) is a technology that uses various electronic devices, such as microchip tags, tag readers, computer servers, and software, to automate library transactions; and

WHEREAS, The use of RFID technology promises to improve library operations by increasing the efficiency of library transactions, reducing workplace injuries, and improving services to library users; and

WHEREAS, Many libraries are adopting or in the process of adopting RFID technology to automate library circulation, inventory management, and security control; and

WHEREAS, Consumers, consumer groups, librarians, and library users have raised concerns about the misuse of RFID technology to collect information on library users' reading habits and other activities without their consent or knowledge; and

WHEREAS, Protecting user privacy and confidentiality has long been an integral part of the mission of libraries; and

WHEREAS, The ALA Code of Ethics states, "We protect each library user's right to privacy and confidentiality with respect to information sought or received and resources consulted, borrowed, acquired or transmitted"; and

WHEREAS, Privacy: An Interpretation of the Library Bill of Rights states that "The American Library Association affirms that rights of privacy are necessary for intellectual freedom and are fundamental to the ethics and practice of librarianship," and calls upon librarians "to maintain an environment respectful and protective of the privacy of all users"; and

WHEREAS, The ALA Intellectual Freedom Committee recognizes the importance of developing policies and guidelines for appropriate implementation of RFID technology in light of the profession's commitment to preserving user privacy and its concern for preserving the trust of library users; and

WHEREAS, The ALA Intellectual Freedom Committee and the ALA Office for Information Technology Policy, recognizing the immediate need to draft privacy principles to protect and promote ALA's values, joined with the Book Industry Study Group (BISG) to form a working group dedicated to developing a set of privacy principles to govern the use of RFID technology by all organizations and industries related to the creation, publication, distribution, and retail sale of books and their use in libraries; now, therefore, let it be

RESOLVED, That the American Library Association endorse the "BISG Policy Statement Policy #002: RFID—Radio Frequency Identification Privacy Principles" (PDF) developed by the IFC and the OITP with the BISG and other working groups; and be it further

RESOLVED, That ALA affirm established privacy norms within and across the business, government, educational, and nonprofit spectrum, specifically acknowledging two essential privacy norms:

> Data transferred among trading partners related to customer and/or patron transactions shall be used solely for related business practices and no unauthorized transaction shall be permitted.
> Data related to customer and/or patron transactions shall not compromise standard confidentiality agreements among trading partners or information users; and be it further

RESOLVED, That the ALA adopt the following "RFID Privacy Principles" developed by the IFC and OITP with the BISG RFID working group:

> All businesses, organizations, libraries, educational institutions, and nonprofits that buy, sell, loan, or otherwise make available books and other content to the public utilizing RFID technologies shall:
> Implement and enforce an up-to-date organizational privacy policy that gives notice and full disclosure as to the use, terms of use, and any change in the terms of use for data collected via new technologies and processes, including RFID.
> Ensure that no personal information is recorded on RFID tags which, however, may contain a variety of transactional data.
> Protect data by reasonable security safeguards against interpretation by any unauthorized third party.
> Comply with relevant federal, state, and local laws as well as industry best practices and policies.
> Ensure that the four principles outlined above must be verifiable by an independent audit; and be it further

RESOLVED, That the ALA continue to monitor and to address concerns about the potential misuse of RFID technology to collect information on library users' reading habits and other activities without their consent or knowledge; and be it further

RESOLVED, That the ALA develop implementation guidelines for the use of RFID technologies in libraries.

Adopted by the ALA Council, January 19, 2005.

Resource E

Guidelines for the Development of Policies and Procedures Regarding User Behavior and Library Usage

INTRODUCTION

Libraries are faced with problems of user behavior that must be addressed to ensure the effective delivery of service and full access to facilities. Library governing bodies should approach the regulation of user behavior within the framework of the ALA *Code of Ethics*, the *Library Bill of Rights*, and the law, including local and state statutes, constitutional standards under the First and Fourteenth Amendments, due process, and equal and equitable treatment under the law.

Publicly supported library service is based upon the First Amendment right of free expression. Publicly supported libraries are recognized as limited public forums for access to information. Courts have recognized a First Amendment right to receive information in a public library. Library policies and procedures that could impinge upon such rights are subject to a higher standard of review than may be required in the policies of other public services and facilities.

There is a significant government interest in maintaining a library environment that is conducive to all users' exercise of their constitutionally protected right to receive information. This significant interest authorizes publicly supported libraries to maintain a safe and healthy environment in which library users and staff can be free from harassment, intimidation, and threats to their safety and well-being. Libraries should provide appropriate safeguards against such behavior and enforce policies and procedures addressing that behavior when it occurs.

In order to protect all library users' right of access to library facilities, to ensure the safety of users and staff, and to protect library resources and facilities from damage, the library's governing authority may impose reasonable restrictions on the time, place, or manner of library access.

GUIDELINES

The American Library Association's Intellectual Freedom Committee recommends that publicly supported libraries use the following guidelines, based upon constitutional principles, to develop policies and procedures governing the use of library facilities:

1. Libraries are advised to rely upon existing legislation and law enforcement mechanisms as the primary means of controlling behavior that involves public safety, criminal behavior, or other issues covered by existing local, state, or federal statutes. In many instances, this legal framework may be sufficient to provide the library with the necessary tools to maintain order.
2. If the library's governing body chooses to write its own policies and procedures regarding user behavior or access to library facilities, services, and resources, the policies should cite statutes or ordinances upon which the authority to make those policies is based.
3. Library policies and procedures governing the use of library facilities should be carefully examined to ensure that they embody the principles expressed in the *Library Bill of Rights*.
4. Reasonable and narrowly drawn policies and procedures designed to prohibit interference with use of the facilities and services by others, or to prohibit activities inconsistent with achievement of the library's mission statement and objectives, are acceptable.
5. Such policies and the attendant implementing procedures should be reviewed frequently and updated as needed by the library's legal counsel for compliance with federal and state constitutional requirements, federal and state civil rights legislation, all other applicable federal and state legislation, and applicable case law.
6. Every effort should be made to respond to potentially difficult circumstances of user behavior in a timely, direct, and open manner. Common sense, reason, and sensitivity should be used to resolve issues in a constructive and positive manner without escalation.

7. Libraries should develop an ongoing staff training program based upon their user behavior policy. This program should include training to develop empathy and understanding of the social and economic problems of some library users.

8. Policies and regulations that impose restrictions on library access:

    a. should apply only to those activities that materially interfere with the public's right of access to library facilities, the safety of users and staff, and the protection of library resources and facilities;

    b. should narrowly tailor prohibitions or restrictions so that they are not more restrictive than needed to serve their objectives;

    c. should attempt to balance competing interests and avoid favoring the majority at the expense of individual rights, or allowing individual users' rights to supersede those of the majority of library users;

    d. should be based solely upon actual behavior and not upon arbitrary distinctions between individuals or classes of individuals. Policies should not target specific users or groups of users based upon an assumption or expectation that such users might engage in behaviors that could disrupt library service;

    e. should not restrict access to the library by persons who merely inspire the anger or annoyance of others. Policies based upon appearance or behavior that is merely annoying or that merely generates negative subjective reactions from others, do not meet the necessary standard. Such policies should employ a reasonable, objective standard based on the behavior itself;

    f. must provide a clear description of the behavior that is prohibited and the various enforcement measures in place so that a reasonably intelligent person will have both due process and fair warning; this description must be continuously and clearly communicated in an effective manner to all library users;

    g. to the extent possible, should not leave those affected without adequate alternative means of access to information in the library;

    h. must be enforced evenhandedly, and not in a manner intended to benefit or disfavor any person or group in an arbitrary or capricious manner.

The user behaviors addressed in these Guidelines are the result of a wide variety of individual and societal conditions. Libraries should take advantage of the expertise of local social service agencies, advocacy groups, mental health professionals, law enforcement officials, and other community resources to develop community strategies for addressing the needs of a diverse population.

Adopted by the Intellectual Freedom Committee January 24, 1993; revised November 17, 2000; revised January 19, 2005.

Resource F

Confidentiality Policy and Procedures

POLICY ON CONFIDENTIALITY OF LIBRARY RECORDS

The Council of the American Library Association strongly recommends that the responsible officers of each library, cooperative system, and consortium in the United States:

1. Formally adopt a policy that specifically recognizes its circulation records and other records identifying the names of library users to be confidential. (See also *ALA Code of Ethics*, Article III, "We protect each library user's right to privacy and confidentiality with respect to information sought or received, and resources consulted, borrowed, acquired or transmitted" and *Privacy: An Interpretation of the Library Bill of Rights*.)
2. Advise all librarians and library employees that such records shall not be made available to any agency of state, federal, or local government except pursuant to such process, order, or subpoena as may be authorized under the authority of, and pursuant to, federal, state, or local law relating to civil, criminal, or administrative discovery procedures or legislative investigative power.
3. Resist the issuance of enforcement of any such process, order, or subpoena until such time as a proper showing of good cause has been made in a court of competent jurisdiction.[1]

Adopted January 20, 1971; revised July 4, 1975, July 2, 1986, by the ALA Council.

SUGGESTED PROCEDURES FOR IMPLEMENTING "POLICY ON CONFIDENTIALITY OF LIBRARY RECORDS"

When drafting local policies, libraries should consult with their legal counsel to ensure these policies are based upon and consistent with applicable federal, state, and local law concerning the confidentiality of library records, the disclosure of public records, and the protection of individual privacy. (See Interpretations to the *Library Bill of Rights*, including *Access to Electronic Information, Services, and Networks* and *Privacy*.)

Suggested procedures include the following[2]:

1. The library staff member receiving the request to examine or obtain information relating to circulation or other records identifying the names of library users must immediately refer the person making the request to the responsible officer of the institution, who shall explain the confidentiality policy.
2. The director, upon receipt of such process, order, or subpoena, shall consult with the appropriate legal officer assigned to the institution to determine if such process, order, or subpoena is in good form and if there is a showing of good cause for its issuance.
3. If the process, order, or subpoena is not in proper form or if good cause has not been shown, the library should insist that such defects be cured before any records are released.
4. The legal process requiring the production of circulation or other library records is ordinarily in the form of a subpoena duces tecum (bring your records) requiring the responsible library officer to attend court or to provide testimony at his or her deposition. It also may require him or her to bring along certain designated circulation or other specified records.
5. Staff should be trained and required to report any threats or unauthorized demands (e.g., those not supported by a process, order, or subpoena) concerning circulation and other records to the appropriate officer of the institution.
6. Any problems relating to the privacy of circulation and other records identifying the names of library users that are not provided for above shall be referred to the responsible officer.

Adopted by the ALA Intellectual Freedom Committee, January 9, 1983; revised January 11, 1988; revised March 18, 2005.

NOTES

1. Point 3, above, means that upon receipt of such process, order, or subpoena, the library's officers will consult with their legal counsel to determine if such process, order, or subpoena is in proper form and if there is a showing of good cause for its issuance; if the process, order, or subpoena is not in proper form or if good cause has not been shown, they will insist that such defects be cured.

2. See also "Confidentiality and Coping with Law Enforcement Inquiries: Guidelines for the Library and its Staff," available on the ALA Web site.

Resource G

Freedom Statements

THE FREEDOM TO READ

The freedom to read is essential to our democracy. It is continuously under attack. Private groups and public authorities in various parts of the country are working to remove or limit access to reading materials, to censor content in schools, to label "controversial" views, to distribute lists of "objectionable" books or authors, and to purge libraries. These actions apparently rise from a view that our national tradition of free expression is no longer valid; that censorship and suppression are needed to counter threats to safety or national security as well as to avoid the subversion of politics and the corruption of morals. We, as individuals devoted to reading and as librarians and publishers responsible for disseminating ideas, wish to assert the public interest in the preservation of the freedom to read.

Most attempts at suppression rest on a denial of the fundamental premise of democracy: that the ordinary individual, by exercising critical judgment, will select the good and reject the bad. We trust Americans to recognize propaganda and misinformation, and to make their own decisions about what they read and believe. We do not believe they are prepared to sacrifice their heritage of a free press in order to be "protected" against what others think may be bad for them. We believe they still favor free enterprise in ideas and expression.

These efforts at suppression are related to a larger pattern of pressures being brought against education, the press, art and images, films, broadcast media, and the Internet. The problem is not only one of actual censorship. The shadow of fear cast by these pressures leads, we suspect, to an even larger voluntary curtailment of expression by those who seek to avoid controversy or unwelcome scrutiny by government officials.

Such pressure toward conformity is perhaps natural to a time of accelerated change. And yet suppression is never more dangerous than in such a time of social tension. Freedom has given the United States the elasticity to endure strain. Freedom keeps open the path of novel and creative solutions, and enables change to come by choice. Every silencing of a heresy, every enforcement of an orthodoxy, diminishes the toughness and resilience of our society and leaves it the less able to deal with controversy and difference.

Now as always in our history, reading is among our greatest freedoms. The freedom to read and write is almost the only means for making generally available ideas or manners of expression that can initially command only a small audience. The written word is the natural medium for the new idea and the untried voice from which come the original contributions to social growth. It is essential to the extended discussion that serious thought requires, and to the accumulation of knowledge and ideas into organized collections.

We believe that free communication is essential to the preservation of a free society and a creative culture. We believe that these pressures toward conformity present the danger of limiting the range and variety of inquiry and expression on which our democracy and our culture depend. We believe that every American community must jealously guard the freedom to publish and to circulate, in order to preserve its own freedom to read. We believe that publishers and librarians have a profound responsibility to give validity to that freedom to read by making it possible for the readers to choose freely from a variety of offerings. The freedom to read is guaranteed by the Constitution. Those with faith in free people will stand firm on these constitutional guarantees of essential rights and will exercise the responsibilities that accompany these rights.

We therefore affirm these propositions:

1. *It is in the public interest for publishers and librarians to make available the widest diversity of views and expressions, including those that are unorthodox, unpopular, or considered dangerous by the majority.*

    Creative thought is by definition new, and what is new is different. The bearer of every new thought is a rebel until that idea is refined and tested. Totalitarian systems attempt to maintain themselves in power by the ruthless suppression of any concept that challenges the established orthodoxy. The power of a democratic system to adapt to change is vastly strengthened by the freedom of its citizens to choose widely from among conflicting opinions offered freely to them. To stifle every nonconformist idea at birth would mark the end of the democratic process. Furthermore, only through the constant activity of weighing and selecting can the democratic mind attain the strength demanded by times like these. We need to know not only what we believe but why we believe it.

2. *Publishers, librarians, and booksellers do not need to endorse every idea or presentation they make available. It would conflict with the public interest for them to establish their own political, moral, or aesthetic views as a standard for determining what should be published or circulated.*

    Publishers and librarians serve the educational process by helping to make available knowledge and ideas required for the growth of the mind and the increase of learning. They do not foster education by imposing as mentors the patterns of their own thought. The people should have the freedom to read and consider a broader range of ideas than those that may be held by any single librarian or publisher or government or church. It is wrong that what one can read should be confined to what another thinks proper.

3. *It is contrary to the public interest for publishers or librarians to bar access to writings on the basis of the personal history or political affiliations of the author.*

    No art or literature can flourish if it is to be measured by the political views or private lives of its creators. No society of free people can flourish that draws up lists of writers to whom it will not listen, whatever they may have to say.

4. *There is no place in our society for efforts to coerce the taste of others, to confine adults to the reading matter deemed suitable for adolescents, or to inhibit the efforts of writers to achieve artistic expression.*

    To some, much of modern expression is shocking. But is not much of life itself shocking? We cut off literature at the source if we prevent writers from dealing with the stuff of life. Parents and teachers have a responsibility to prepare the young to meet the diversity of experiences in life to which they will be exposed, as they have a responsibility to help them learn to think critically for themselves. These are affirmative responsibilities, not to be discharged simply by preventing them from reading works for which they are not yet prepared. In these matters values differ, and values cannot be legislated; nor can machinery be devised that will suit the demands of one group without limiting the freedom of others.

5. *It is not in the public interest to force a reader to accept the prejudg-ment of a label characterizing any expression or its author as sub-versive or dangerous.*

   The ideal of labeling presupposes the existence of individuals or groups with wisdom to determine by authority what is good or bad for others. It presupposes that individuals must be directed in making up their minds about the ideas they examine. But Ameri-cans do not need others to do their thinking for them.

6. *It is the responsibility of publishers and librarians, as guardians of the people's freedom to read, to contest encroachments upon that freedom by individuals or groups seeking to impose their own stan-dards or tastes upon the community at large; and by the govern-ment whenever it seeks to reduce or deny public access to public information.*

   It is inevitable in the give and take of the democratic process that the political, the moral, or the aesthetic concepts of an indi-vidual or group will occasionally collide with those of another indi-vidual or group. In a free society individuals are free to determine for themselves what they wish to read, and each group is free to determine what it will recommend to its freely associated mem-bers. But no group has the right to take the law into its own hands and to impose its own concept of politics or morality upon other members of a democratic society. Freedom is no freedom if it is accorded only to the accepted and the inoffensive. Further, demo-cratic societies are more safe, free, and creative when the free flow of public information is not restricted by governmental prerogative or self-censorship.

7. *It is the responsibility of publishers and librarians to give full mean-ing to the freedom to read by providing books that enrich the qual-ity and diversity of thought and expression. By the exercise of this affirmative responsibility, they can demonstrate that the answer to a "bad" book is a good one, the answer to a "bad" idea is a good one.*

   The freedom to read is of little consequence when the reader cannot obtain matter fit for that reader's purpose. What is needed is not only the absence of restraint, but the positive provision of op-portunity for the people to read the best that has been thought and said. Books are the major channel by which the intellectual inherit-ance is handed down, and the principal means of its testing and growth. The defense of the freedom to read requires of all publish-ers and librarians the utmost of their faculties, and deserves of all Americans the fullest of their support.

We state these propositions neither lightly nor as easy generalizations. We here stake out a lofty claim for the value of the written word. We do so because we believe that it is possessed of enormous variety and usefulness, worthy of cherishing and keeping free. We realize that the application of these propositions may mean the dissemination of ideas and manners of expression that are repugnant to many persons. We do not state these propositions in the comfortable belief that what people read is unimportant. We believe rather that what people read is deeply important, that ideas can be dangerous, but that the suppression of ideas is fatal to a democratic society. Freedom itself is a dangerous way of life, but it is ours.

This statement was originally issued in May of 1953 by the Westchester Conference of the American Library Association and the American Book Publishers Council, which in 1970 consolidated with the American Educational Publishers Institute to become the Association of American Publishers.

Adopted June 25, 1953; revised January 28, 1972, January 16, 1991, July 12, 2000, June 30, 2004, by the ALA Council and the AAP Freedom to Read Committee.

A Joint Statement by: American Library Association and Association of American Publishers.

Subsequently endorsed by: American Booksellers Foundation for Free Expression, The Association of American University Presses, Inc., The Children's Book Council, Freedom to Read Foundation, National Association of College Stores, National Coalition Against Censorship, National Council of Teachers of English, The Thomas Jefferson Center for the Protection of Free Expression.

FREEDOM TO VIEW STATEMENT

The FREEDOM TO VIEW, along with the freedom to speak, to hear, and to read, is protected by the First Amendment to the Constitution of the United States. In a free society, there is no place for censorship of any medium of expression. Therefore these principles are affirmed:

- To provide the broadest access to film, video, and other audiovisual materials because they are a means for the communication of ideas. Liberty of circulation is essential to insure the constitutional guarantee of freedom of expression.
- To protect the confidentiality of all individuals and institutions using film, video, and other audiovisual materials.

To provide film, video, and other audiovisual materials which represent a diversity of views and expression. Selection of a work does not constitute or imply agreement with or approval of the content.

To provide a diversity of viewpoints without the constraint of labeling or prejudging film, video, or other audiovisual materials on the basis of the moral, religious, or political beliefs of the producer or film-maker or on the basis of controversial content.

To contest vigorously, by all lawful means, every encroachment upon the public's freedom to view.

This statement was originally drafted by the Freedom to View Committee of the American Film and Video Association (formerly the Educational Film Library Association) and was adopted by the AFVA Board of Directors in February 1979. This statement was updated and approved by the AFVA Board of Directors in 1989. Endorsed January 10, 1990, by the ALA Council.

Resource H

2007 Public Library Service Responses

INTRODUCTION

The Public Library Association, as part of its mission to strengthen public libraries and enhance their role in the communities they serve, developed a planning process for libraries to follow. Over the past two decades that process has been refined and streamlined. The current iteration is outlined in a manual, *The New Planning for Results: A Streamlined Approach*, written by Sandra Nelson. A supplemental document released in 2007 updates the various service responses that many public libraries use to concisely define the primary functions that the community expects their library to fulfill.

Service responses are labels used to succinctly describe or categorize the priority services that a public library will provide. The concept is based on the realization that one size doesn't fit all and that no library can be all things to all people. The idea that developed says that libraries should focus on providing a few services well rather than trying to do everything poorly. These service responses, also sometimes called priorities or roles, have been evolving for more than two decades.

The first set of roles was articulated in *Planning and Role-Setting for Public Libraries*, published in [McClure] 1987. In [Himmel and Wilson] 1997, thirteen service responses were outlined in *Planning for Results: A Public Library Transformation Process*. In 2007, these descriptors were re-named and expanded to provide eighteen service responses. Although these service responses are not intended to offer a comprehensive list of every service provided by any library in the United States, they do describe "the most common clusters of services and programs that libraries provide."[1] No individual service response is better than another and there is no "typical" set of service responses for libraries of a specific size or demographic. It is strongly recommended that these service responses be explored as part of a long-range planning process and that as part of that process policymakers understand the meaning and implications for each service response.

Although Garcia and Nelson provide detailed information about each service response, including suggested target audiences, typical services and programs, potential partners, policy implications, critical resources, and possible evaluation measures in their document, published by the American Library Association, only the brief description is provided here. Library directors and other policy developers should carefully examine the information provided in 2007 *Public Library Service Responses* for those descriptors that match the three or four top priorities for service provision at their library, paying careful attention, of course to policy implications.

THE SERVICE RESPONSES

Be an Informed Citizen: Local, national, and world affairs.
Residents will have the information they need to support and promote democracy; to fulfill their civic responsibilities at the local, state, and national levels; and to fully participate in community decision making.

Build Successful Enterprises: Business and nonprofit support.
Business owners and nonprofit organization directors and their managers will have the resources they need to develop and maintain strong, viable organizations.

Celebrate Diversity: Cultural awareness.
Residents will have programs and services that promote appreciation and understanding of their personal heritage and the heritage of others in the community.

Connect to the Online World: Public Internet access.
Residents will have high-speed access to the digital world with no unnecessary restrictions or fees to ensure that everyone can take advantage of the ever-growing resources and services available through the Internet.

Create Young Readers: Early literacy.
Children from birth to age five will have programs and services designed to ensure that they will enter school ready to learn to read, write, and listen.

Discover Your Roots: Genealogy and local history.
Residents and visitors will have the resources they need to connect the past with the present through their family histories and to understand the history and traditions of the community.

Express Creativity: Create and share content.
Residents will have the services and support they need to express themselves by creating original print, video, audio, or visual content in a real-world or online environment.

Get Facts Fast: Ready reference.
Residents will have someone to answer their questions on a wide array of topics of personal interest.

Know Your Community: Community resources and services.
Residents will have a central source for information about the wide variety of programs, services, and activities provided by community agencies and organizations.

Learn to Read and Write: Adult, teen, and family literacy.
Adults and teens will have the support they need to improve their literacy skills in order to meet their personal goals and fulfill their responsibilities as parents, citizens, and workers.

Make Career Choices: Job and career development.
Adults and teens will have the skills and resources they need to identify career opportunities that suit their individual strengths and interests.

Make Informed Decisions: Health, wealth, and other life choices.
Residents will have the resources they need to identify and analyze risks, benefits, and alternatives before making decisions that affect their lives.

Satisfy Curiosity: Lifelong learning.
Residents will have the resources they need to explore topics of personal interest and continue to learn throughout their lives.

Stimulate Imagination: Reading, viewing, and listening for pleasure.
Residents will have materials and programs that excite their imaginations and provide pleasurable reading, viewing, and listening experiences.

Succeed in School: Homework help.
Students will have the resources they need to succeed in school.

Understand How to Find, Evaluate, and Use Information: Information fluency.
Residents will know when they need information to resolve an issue or answer a question and will have the skills to search for, locate, evaluate, and effectively use information to meet their needs.

Visit a Comfortable Place: Physical and virtual spaces.
Residents will have safe and welcoming physical places to meet and interact with others or to sit quietly and read and will have open and accessible virtual spaces that support networking.

Welcome to the United States: Services for new immigrants.
New immigrants will have information on citizenship, English Language Learning (ELL), employment, public schooling, health and safety, available social services, and any other topics that they need to participate successfully in American life.

NOTE

1.   Garcia, June and Sandra Nelson. *2007 Public Library Service Responses.* Chicago: American Library Association, 2007: p. 2.

Bibliography

Alcorn, Louise. Steal This Wireless Policy Checklist. MaintainIT Project (October 22, 2007). Available: http://maintainitproject.org/node/219.

American Library Association. 1993. *Suggested Procedures for Implementing Policy on Confidentiality of Library Records*. Adopted January 9; revised January 11, 1988; revised March 18, 2005. Chicago: ALA Intellectual Freedom Committee.

American Library Association. 1994. *The Interlibrary Loan Code for the United States*. Chicago: Interlibrary Loan Committee, Reference and User Services Association, revised 2001.

American Library Association. Confidentiality and Coping with Law Enforcement Inquiries: Guidelines for the Library and Its Staff (April 2005). Available: www.ala.org/ala/oif/ifissues/confidentiality.htm.

American Library Association. Homeless Patrons Win in Worcester. *American Libraries* (September 15, 2006). Available: www.ala.org/ala/alonline/currentnews/newsarchive/2006abc/september2006a/worcester.cfm.

American Library Association. 2006. *Intellectual Freedom Manual,* 7th edition. Chicago: American Library Association.

American Library Association. 2006. *RFID in Libraries: Privacy and Confidentiality Guidelines*. Adopted June 27. Chicago: ALA.

Baumbach, Donna J. and Linda L. Miller. 2006. *A Practical Guide to Weeding School Library Collections*. Chicago: American Library Association.

Bertot, John Carlo et al. 2006. *Public Libraries and the Internet 2006*. Tallahassee, FL: Florida State University.

Bielefield, Arlene and Lawrence Cheeseman. 1995. *Library Patrons and the Law*. New York: Neal-Schuman.

Boon, Belinda. 1995. *The CREW Method: Expanded Guidelines for Collection Evaluation and Weeding for Small and Medium-Sized Public Libraries*. Austin, TX: Texas State Library. Available: http://www. tsl.state.tx.us/ld/pubs/crew/crewmethod.pdf.

Checklist for New Employee Orientation. 2000. *Library Personnel News* 13, no. 1–2 (Spring/Summer): 15–16.

Code of Federal Regulations. 2007. Washington, DC: Government Printing Office.

Crawford, Walt. 2005. Policy and Library Technology. *Library Technology Reports* 41, no. 2 (March/April): 4–63.

Crispin, Joanne L. 1993. *The Americans with Disabilities Act: Its Impact on Libraries*. Chicago: American Library Association.

Damast, Alison. 2007. Return of the Dress Code. *Business Week Online*, August 29, p. 15.

Dempsey, Beth. 2005. Responding To Disaster. *Library Journal* 130 (December): 6–8.

Doll, Carol Ann and Pamela Petrick Barron. 2002. *Managing and Analyzing Your Collection: A Practical Guide for Small Libraries and School Media Centers*. Chicago: American Library Association.

Evans, G. Edward. 2004. *Performance Management and Appraisal*. New York: Neal-Schuman.

Findley, Henry et. al. 2005–2006. Dress and Grooming Standards: How Legal Are They? *Journal of Individual Employment Rights*, 12 no. 2: 165–182.

Foos, Donald D. and Nancy C. Pack. 1992. *How Libraries Must Comply with the Americans with Disabilities Act (ADA)*. Phoenix, AZ: Oryx.

Garcia, June and Sandra Nelson. 2007. *2007 Public Library Service Responses*. Chicago: American Library Association.

Gerding, Stephanie. 2006. Fund-Raising Perks of Library Cafés. *Public Libraries* 45, no. 6 (November/December): 40–45.

Giesecke, Joan and Beth McNeil. 2005. *Fundamentals of Library Supervision*. Chicago: American Library Association.

Goodrich, Jeanne and Diane Mayo. 2003. *Staffing for Results*. Chicago: American Library Association.

Goodrich, Jeanne and Paula M. Singer. 2007. *Human Resources for Results*. Chicago: American Library Association.

Goodson, Carol F. 1997. *The Complete Guide to Performance Standards for Library Personnel*. New York: Neal-Schuman.

Guerin, Lisa. 2006. *The Essential Guide to Federal Employment Laws*. Berkeley, CA: Nolo Press.

Hage, Christine Lind. 2003. *Public Library Start-Up Guide*. Chicago: American Library Association.

Hill, Nanci Milone. 2006. Are Collection Agencies the Answer? *Public Libraries* 45 no. 6 (November/December): 18–23

Himmel, Ethel and William James Wilson. 1997. *Planning for Results: A Public Library Transformation Process*. Chicago: American Library Association.

Hoffman, Gretchen McCord. 2002. What Every Librarian Should Know About Copyright Part II: Copyright in Cyberspace. *Texas Library Journal* 78, no. 3(Fall): 15–18.

Hoffman, Gretchen McCord. 2003. What Every Librarian Should Know about Copyright, Part IV: Writing a Copyright Policy. *Texas Library Journal* 79, no. 1 (Spring): 12–15.

Hoffman, Gretchen McCord. 2005. *Copyright in Cyberspace 2*. New York: Neal-Schuman.

Hoffman, Kathy. 2005. Professional Ethics and Librarianship. *Texas Library Journal* 81, no. 3 (Fall): 7–11.

Hopkins, Janet. 2006. Assistive Technology: 10 Things to Know. *Library Media Connection* 25, no. 1 (August/September): 12–14.

Jones, Patrick. 2002. *Running a Successful Library Card Campaign*. New York: Neal-Schuman.

Judge: Dress Code Unconstitutional. 2003. *American Libraries* 34, no. 9 (October): 17.

Kahn, Miriam B. 2002. *Disaster Response and Planning for Libraries*, 2nd edition. Chicago: American Library Association.

Lamothe, Scott. 2006. State Policy Adoption and Content: A Study of Drug Testing in the Workplace Legislation. *SAGE Public Administration Abstracts* 32, no. 4 (January): 25–39.

Manley, Will. 2006. Is Love's Labor a Loss for Libraries? *American Libraries* 37, no. 2 (February): 64.

Mayo, Kathleen and Ruth O'Donnell. 1994. *The ADA Library Kit: Sample ADA–Related Documents to Help You Implement the Law*. Chicago: American Library Association.

McClure, Charles. 1987. *Planning and Role-Setting for Public Libraries.* Chicago: American Library Association.

McCune, Bonnie. 2005. Diversity and Volunteers. *Colorado Libraries* 31, no. 3 (Fall): 43–44.

Million, Angela C. and Kim Fisher. 1986. Library Records: A Review of Confidentiality Laws and Policies. *Journal of Academic Librarianship* 11, no. 6 (January): 346–349.

Milo, Albert. Ten Reasons Why We Buy Spanish Books. Available: www.reforma.org/refogold.htm. Accessed February 21, 2008.

Minow, Mary. Who's In and Who's Out? Library Meeting Room and Exhibit Space Policies. Available: www.librarylaw.com/MeetingRoomHandout.htm. Accessed November 14, 2007.

Minow, Mary and Tomas A. Lipinski. 2003. *The Library's Legal Answer Book*. Chicago: American Library Association.

Model Policy: Responding to Demands for Library Records. 2007. *American Libraries* 38, no. 8 (September): insert 1–4.

Moore, Mary. 2004. *The Successful Library Trustee Handbook*. Chicago: American Library Association.

Moore, Victoria. 2005. Sexual Harassment and the Library Don't Mix. *Library Mosaics* 16, no. 6 (November/December): 18–19.

Nelson, Sandra. 2001. *The New Planning for Results: A Streamlined Approach*. Chicago: American Library Association.

Oder, Norman. 2007. Monroe County Adopts Tough Net Policy. *Library Journal* 132, no. 11 (June 15): 16–17.

Oliver, Kent. 1997. The Spirit of the Law: When ADA Compliance Means Overall Excellence in Service to Patrons with Disabilities. *Public Libraries* 36 (September/October): 294–298.

One Lawyer's Opinion. 1997. *Texas Library Journal* 73, no. 2 (Summer): 71.

Peters, Paula. 2000. Seven Tips for Delivering Performance Feedback. *Supervision* 61, no. 5 (May): 12–14.

Robinson, Charles W. 2005. Anti-Nepotism. *Library Administrator's Digest* 40, no. 2 (February 1): 1.

Rubin, Rhea Joyce. 2001. *Planning for Library Services to People with Disabilities*. Chicago: American Library Association.

Rubin, Richard. 1991. Ethical Issues in Library Personnel Management. *Journal of Library Administration* 14, no. 4 (September): 1–16.

Shanks, Thomas E. and Barry J. Stenger. 2002. *Access, Internet, and Public Libraries: A Report to the Santa Clara County Public Libraries*. Santa Clara, CA: Markkula Center for Applied Ethics. Available: www.scu.edu/ethics/practicing/focusareas/technology/libraryaccess/homepage.html.

Simpson, Carol Mann. 2005. *Copyright for School Libraries: A Practical Guide*. Worthington, OH: Linworth.

Smith, Mark. 2001. *Managing the Internet Controversy*. New York: Neal-Schuman.

State of Michigan: History, Arts and Libraries. Primer on Library Policies (July 2000). Available: www.michigan.gov/hal/0,1607,7-160-17451_18668_18689-54481—,00.html.

Strict Dress Code Blocked by Judge. 2007. *New York Times*, July 4, p. A11.

Stueart, Robert D. and Barbara Moran. 2007. *Library and Information Center Management*. Westport, CT: Libraries Unlimited.

Stueart, Robert D. and Maureen Sullivan. 1991. *Performance Analysis and Appraisal*. New York: Neal-Schuman.

Supreme Court Won't Hear Meeting Room Appeal. *American Libraries* (October 5, 2007). Available: www.ala.org/ala/alonline/currentnews/newsarchive/2007/october2007/meetingroom.cfm.

Symons, Ann. 1997. Kids, Sex and the Internet. *Texas Library Journal* 73, no. 2 (Summer): 69.

Torrans, Lee Ann. 2003. *Law for K-12 Libraries and Librarians*. Westport, CT: Libraries Unlimited.

Torrans, Lee Ann. 2004. *Law and Libraries*. Westport, CT: Libraries Unlimited.

Tryon, Jonathan S. 1994. *The Librarian's Legal Companion*. New York: G.K. Hall.

Turner, Anne M. 1993. *It Comes With the Territory: Handling Problem Situations in Libraries*. Jefferson, NC: McFarland and Company.

Uhler, Scott F. and Rinda Y. Allison. 1997. A 10-Step Program: Reducing the Likelihood of Sexual Harassment and the Possibility of Successful Sexual Harassment Lawsuits. *Illinois Libraries* 79, no. 2 (Spring): 64–65.

Weingand, Darlene E. 1992. *Administration of the Small Public Library*. Chicago: American Library Association.

Weissman, Sara K. Do You Dare? (June 1, 1997). Available: http://members.aol.com/saraweiss/access/index.html.

Woodward, Jeannette. 2007. *What Every Librarian Should Know About Electronic Privacy*. Westport, CT: Libraries Unlimited.

Index

*Page numbers in **bold** indicate model policies.*

About the Authors

Jeanette Larson is a freelance trainer and consultant with more than 30 years experience working with public libraries, serves as an adjunct professor with Texas Woman's University, and is a presenter for the Texas State Library's Small Library Management Training program. She is a certified trainer for the Public Library Association and works with public libraries of all sizes on various aspects of PLA's "For Results" planning process. In 1998 the Texas Library Association named Ms. Larson Librarian of the Year and she received the Siddie Joe Johnson Award for outstanding service to young people in 2002. Ms. Larson is the immediate past-chair of the Public Library Division of the Texas Library Association and has served on numerous committees for the American Library Association and the Texas Library Association. Ms. Larson is also the author of *The CREW Method: Collection Evaluation and Weeding Guidelines for the 21st Century*, the third edition of the popular guide on weeding library collections. She lives in Austin, Texas, with her husband and their two schipperke dogs.

Herman L. Totten, **PhD**, is the Dean of the University of North Texas (UNT) School of Library and Information Sciences (SLIS). He joined the SLIS Faculty in 1977, and became a Regents Professor in SLIS in 1991. He has received numerous awards including the Association for Library and Information Science Education (ALISE) Award for Professional Contribution to Library and Information Science Education, the Alumni Association of the University of Oklahoma School of Library and Information Studies Award of Merit for the Outstanding Alumnus, the American Library Association Black Caucus Award for Outstanding Contribution to the Field of Library and Information Science Education, the ALISE Outstanding Teacher Award, and the Texas Library Association's Lifetime Achievement Award.

He is currently serving on the United States National Commission on Libraries and Information Science, a federal agency charged to advise the President and Congress on information and learning needs of the American people.